Additional Praise for *Endgame*

"There's clearly something important going on in the world economy. Something big. Something powerful and dangerous. But something as yet undefined and uncertain. We are all feeling our way around in the dark, trying to figure out what it is. John Mauldin must have night-vision glasses. He does an excellent job of seeing the obstacles. You should read this book before you knock over a lamp and stumble over the furniture."

—William Bonner, President and CEO of Agora Inc.;
author of *Dice Have No Memory* and *Empire of Debt*

"*Endgame* not only is a highly readable and informative account of the causes of the recent global economic and financial meltdown, but it also provides investors with a concrete investment strategy from which they can benefit while this final act in financial history is being played out."

—Marc Faber, Managing Director, Marc Faber, Ltd.;
Editor, *Gloom Boom & Doom Report*

"I think the book is brilliant. It is well written, crystal clear, and hits the spot. My favorite chapters are the ones on fingers of instability (which I think everyone in finance should read and reread each year lest they forget), and the one on Eastern Europe as both a leading indicator for what's in store and a potential land mine that could yet do for the euro what Credit Anstaldt did for the gold standard. But it's a tough call. Lots of very good stuff in here."

—Dylan Grice, Global Strategy Team, Societe Generale

ENDGAME

ENDGAME

THE END OF
THE DEBT SUPERCYCLE
AND HOW IT
CHANGES EVERYTHING

JOHN MAULDIN
JONATHAN TEPPER

WILEY

John Wiley & Sons, Inc.

Published by John Wiley & Sons, Inc., Hoboken, New Jersey.
Published simultaneously in Canada.

For general information on our other products and services or for technical support, please
contact our Customer Care Department within the United States at (800) 762-2974, outside
the United States at (317) 572-3993 or fax (317) 572-4002.

Wiley also publishes its books in a variety of electronic formats. Some content that appears in
print may not be available in electronic formats. For more information about Wiley
products, visit our web site at www.wiley.com.

Library of Congress Cataloging-in-Publication Data:

Mauldin, John.
    Endgame : the end of the debt supercycle and how it changes everything / John Mauldin
and Jonathan Tepper.
        p. cm.
    Includes index.
    ISBN 978-1-118-00457-9 (hardback); ISBN 978-1-118-05806-0 (ebk.);
    ISBN 978-1-118-05807-7 (ebk.); ISBN 978-1-118-05808-4 (ebk.)
        1. Debt.   2. Debts, Public.   3. Debts, External.   4. Recessions.   5. Business
cycles.   I. Tepper, Jonathan, 1976–   II. Title.
    HG3701.M345 2011
    336.3'4—dc22   2010051231

Printed in the United States of America
10   9   8   7   6   5   4   3   2

This book is dedicated to Peter Bernstein.

Peter Bernstein 1919–2009
Amazing author, devoted husband, loving father
Mentor to generations of investment professionals
A man whose wisdom was always welcome
And who saw The Endgame clearly before everyone

You are missed, my friend, now more than ever
when your wisdom is most sorely needed.

In order to improve your game, you must study the endgame before everything else, for whereas the endings can be studied and mastered by themselves, the middle game and the opening must be studied in relation to the endgame.

Jose Raul Capablanca,
Cuban chess player who was world chess champion from 1921 to 1927
and one of the greatest players of all time

Contents

Preface

It is said that the present is pregnant with the future.

Voltaire

Prediction is very difficult, especially about the future.

Niels Bohr

*E*ndgame is a book about the future of the global economy. When we started writing the book in 2010, we were afraid that by the time it arrived in bookstores many of the things we had predicted or warned about would have already happened. Both of your authors had written extensively about the issues and predicted outcomes we discussed in *Endgame*.

The buildup of debt that caused the financial crisis was still weighing many countries down, and central bankers and governments were responding with unprecedented stimulus. Some countries, such as Greece, were on the verge of defaulting, even though the markets (and European politicians!) were in total denial. We must admit that for us it wasn't rocket science to make the predictions we did, it was simple arithmetic: Greece didn't have enough income to handle its expenses.

As luck would have it, we were able to get *Endgame* out before Greece defaulted and the worst of the European crisis came to pass. For other countries, like Japan, we were able to warn about the extraordinary measures the Bank of Japan would end up taking. We didn't get everything right, but we were able to provide a very useful roadmap for readers. *Endgame* was timely, and we're pleased to see that it still reads well and offers a good look at the future.

Parts of *Endgame* are timeless and are intended to provide a fundamental way of viewing the world. In the first part of the book, we looked at the Debt Supercycle and how a very long period of debt buildup in the US, UK, Japan, and Europe would lead to lower growth and a debt-deflationary dynamic. The events of the past few years have borne out that insight. While developed economies appear to be "in recovery," it is the most anemic recovery of the past 60 years. Welcome to the New Normal.

Each country faces different challenges and paths ahead. For most countries, the choices are stark—between bad options and worse ones. Some sadly face a choice between Disaster A and Disaster B. They merely get to choose which path to take in the lead-up to the destruction of their economies, exactly as we wrote about Greece. The worst-off countries of the developed world are still confronted with staggering debt and ageing populations. They are caught in a tug of war between deflation from too much debt and potential inflation from unconventional central bank monetary policies – quantitative easing (QE), large-scale asset purchase programs (LSAPs), and currency devaluations. Other countries, particularly in emerging markets, have lower debt levels and higher population growth, but they are facing the spillover of loose money policies from their developed neighbors. They must deal with the fickle tides of capital flows from the developed world, as money pours in and out. As a result, they have gone from being darlings of the investment world to pariahs.

We anticipated that we would see the US Federal Reserve, the Bank of Japan, the European Central Bank, and the Bank of England take the world in the direction of extraordinarily loose monetary policies. The events of the past few years have only confirmed our view that central bankers would err on the side of doing too much rather than too little. In the manner of Hollywood blockbusters, we've seen QE1 followed by QE2 and now, seemingly, "QE Infinity."

Endgame was particularly accurate in describing the deflationary dynamics in Europe. The euro is very much like the gold standard; and, as Greece and the rest of the Eurozone periphery have discovered, the burdens of economic adjustment have fallen on the weaker members. We were extremely pessimistic about Europe, but as it turns out, our views now have an almost optimistic ring to them. Who would have guessed that Greek and Spanish unemployment levels would rise above 25% and that almost 60% of Greek and Spanish youths would be unemployed? Reality is almost always more interesting than fiction.

Many of the countries we wrote about have experienced the troubles we foresaw. When we wrote *Endgame*, we warned about Australia's housing bubble; and we are now seeing the Australian dollar fall and the housing market slowly deflate. The chapter on Australia is particularly worth reading in light of that country's weakening domestic economy, the slowdown of exports to China, and the bursting of the housing bubble. The story is still playing itself out.

The chapter on Japan as "a bug in search of a windshield" was perhaps the most farsighted. We did not say anything that other watchful people had not said, but we did emphasize how unsustainable Japan's situation was. Time has only proved us right. The Tohoku earthquake and the Fukushima disaster were the not-so-small final grain of sand that caused the sand pile to collapse. The Bank of Japan (BoJ) has embarked on the largest, most adventurous policy of quantitative easing the world has seen. The BoJ makes the Fed and the Bank of England look like sissies. Japan's ageing population, Godzilla-size government debt, and dismal public finances guarantee that we'll see the yen weaken considerably as the central bank prints money hand over fist to finance government spending.

We did not get everything right, but we did best we could with our cloudy crystal ball. It is a pleasure for us to reread the book after the passage of several years. We must admit, given the volume of writing we have each done, that we can't say the same about everything we have published. So far, *Endgame* has stood the test of time. We hope that you will enjoy it, as well, and find it instructive.

As we were finishing *Endgame*, we already suspected our next book would have to be on currency wars and unconventional monetary policy. We thought we would be able write it at our leisure during 2014 and that it would come out late that year. But then the Japanese launched the first missile in what we think is the beginning of a full-blown currency war that will dominate the latter half of the decade. We started madly writing this summer. Much like *Endgame*, we wrote *Code Red* to provide a roadmap to what will happen now that Japan has gone nuclear and unleashed the boldest, most forceful devaluation the world has seen since the 1970s. We have yet to see the full effects of Japan's monetary policies.

We hope you like *Endgame*. If you do, we would recommend that you also find *Code Red*. We can only hope that *Code Red* reads as well a few years from now as *Endgame* does today.

John Mauldin and Jonathan Tepper
October, 2013

Acknowledgments

We would like to thank our many reviewers and readers. We have had a lot of feedback from reviewers, which has really helped. Martin Barnes of Bank Credit Analyst was particularly vicious, but he really made us do a lot more homework and think through some of our points. Andrew Wynn, Dylan Grice, and Albert Edwards provided very valuable critiques and insight. Lacy Hunt was particularly helpful in his suggestions and criticisms of our deflation and hyperinflation chapters. Simon White at Variant Perception was invaluable in helping draft some of the chapters on the United Kingdom, Eastern Europe, and Australia, and he helped produce most of the charts in the book. Debra Englander and Kelly O'Connor at John Wiley & Sons helped shepherd this book from its original idea to publication. Claus Vistesen and Edward Hugh offered valuable critiques, saw many of the crises before they happened, and have provided valuable insights into demographics.

INTRODUCTION

Endgame

People only accept change in necessity and see necessity only in crisis.
—Jean Monnet

Every child learns about the Great Depression in school, but economists, historians, and commentators have not agreed on what we will
call the turbulent economic period we are currently living in. Some
do call it a depression. Others call it the Great Recession. And some refer to
it as the Great Financial Crisis. The Great Financial Crisis is particularly apt,
because crises force us to make difficult choices. And one thing that
everyone can agree on is that this new era of turbulence will impose difficult choices on governments and voters around the world.

I (John)* am somewhat of an expert on bad choices—not only my
own, but I have had the joys of seven teenage children. As our family
grew, we limited the choices our kids could make, but as they grew into
teenagers, they were given more leeway. Not all of their choices were
good. How many times did Dad say, "What were you thinking?" and
get a mute reply or a mumbled "I don't know."

Yet how else do you teach them that bad choices have bad consequences? You can lecture, you can be a role model, but in the end you

---

*Throughout the book, when the first-person *I* is used, the name in the following parentheses will be
the person speaking. When we use the word *we*, it refers to John and Jonathan.

have to let them make their own choices. And a lot of them make a lot of bad choices. After having raised six, with one more teenage son at home, I have come to the conclusion that you just breathe a sigh of relief if they grow up and have avoided fatal, life-altering choices. I am lucky. So far. Knock on a lot of wood.

I have watched good kids from good families make bad choices, and kids with no seeming chance make good choices. But one thing I have observed: Very few teenagers make the hard choice without some outside encouragement or help in understanding the known consequences, from some source. They nearly always opt for the choice that involves the most fun and/or the least immediate pain and then learn later that they now have to make yet another choice as a consequence of the original one. And thus they grow up. So quickly.

But it's not just teenagers. I am completely capable of making very bad choices as I approach the beginning of my seventh decade of human experiences and observations. In fact, I have made some rather distressing choices over time. Even in areas where I think I have some expertise, I can make appallingly bad choices. Or maybe particularly in those areas, because I have delusions of actually knowing something. In my experience, it takes an expert with a powerful computer to truly foul things up.

Of course, sometimes I get it right. Even I learn, with enough pain. And sometimes I just get lucky. (Although, as my less-than-sainted Dad repeatedly intoned, "The harder I work, the luckier I get.")

Each morning is a new day, but it is a new day affected by all the choices of the previous days and years. My daughter Tiffani and I have literally interviewed in depth more than a hundred millionaires and talked anecdotally with hundreds more over the years. I am struck by how their lives, and those of their families, come down to a few choices: sometimes good choices and sometimes lucky choices; often, difficult ones. But very few were the easy choice.

What Were We Thinking?

As a culture, the current mix of generations, all over much of the developed world, have made some choices—choices that, in hindsight, leave the adult in us asking, "What were we thinking?"

In a way, we acted like teenagers. We made the easy choice, not thinking of the consequences. We never absorbed the lessons of the depression from our grandparents. We quickly forgot the sobering malaise of the 1970s as the bull market of the 1980s and 1990s gave us the illusion of wealth and an easy future. Even the crash of Black Monday seemed a mere bump on the path to success, passing so quickly. And as interest rates came down and money became easier, our propensity to acquire things took over. In Europe, the advent of the euro gave southern Europe the interest rates of the German Bundesbank, and the Germans got a southern European currency in return.

And then something really bad happened. Homes and other assets all over the world started to rise in value, and we learned through new methods of financial engineering that we could borrow against what seemed like their ever-rising value to finance consumption today. Everybody was responding to incentives—the problem was that the incentives were misguided, and the regulators were not doing their job.

We became Wimpie from the Popeye cartoons of our youth: "I will gladly repay you Tuesday for a hamburger today."

Not for us the lay-away programs of our parents, patiently paying something each week or month until the desired object could be taken home.

As a banking system, we made choices. In the United States, we created all sorts of readily available credit and packaged it in convenient, irresistible AAA-rated securities and sold them to a gullible world. We created liar loans, no-money-down loans, and no-documentation loans and expected them to act the same way that mortgages had in the past. What were the rating agencies thinking? Where were the adults supervising the sandbox? (Oh, wait a minute. That's the same group of regulators who now want more power and money.)

It is not as if all this was done in some back alley by seedy-looking characters. This was done on TV and in books and advertisements. I (John) remember the first time I saw an ad telling me to call this number to borrow up to 125 percent of the value of my home and wondering how this could be a good idea.

It turns out it can be a great idea for the salesmen, if they can package those loans into securities and sell them to foreigners, with everyone making large commissions on the way. The choice was to make a lot of money with no downside consequences to you. What teenager could say no?

In the United States, Greenspan kept interest rates low, which aided and abetted the process. The Bush administration started two wars and pushed through a massive health care package, along with no spending control from the Republican Party, thereby running up the fiscal deficits.

The financial industry's regulators allowed credit default swaps to trade without an exchange or supervision. A culture viscerally believed that the McMansions they were buying were an investment and not really debt. Yes, we were adolescents at the party to end all parties. And as our friend Paul McCulley said, the ratings agencies were handing out fake IDs to this underage drinking party.

Not to mention an investment industry that tells its clients that stocks earn 8 percent a year in real return. Even as stocks have gone nowhere for 10 years, we largely believe (or at least hope) that whatever the latest uptrend is will be the beginning of the next bull market.

It was not that there were no warnings. There were many who wrote about the coming train wreck that we are now trying to clean up. But those warnings were ignored.

Derision, scorn, laughter, and dismissal as a nonserious perpetual perma-bear were heaped on these commentators. The good times had lasted so long, how could the trend not be correct? It is human nature to believe the current trend, especially a favorable one that helps us, will continue forever.

And just like a teenager who doesn't think about the consequences of the current fun, we paid no attention. We hadn't experienced the hard lessons of our elders, who learned them in the depths of the depression. This time it was different. We were smarter and wouldn't make those mistakes. Didn't we have the research of Bernanke, the ECB, the BIS, and others, telling us what to avoid?

In millions of different ways, we all partied on. It wasn't exclusively a liberal or a conservative, a rich or a poor, a male or a female addiction. We all (or most of us) borrowed and spent. We did it as individuals, and we did it as cities and states and countries.

In the United States, we ran up unfunded pension deficits at many local and state funds, to the tune of $3 to $4 *trillion* and rising. We have a massive (multiple tens of trillions of dollars) bill coming due for Social Security and Medicare, starting in the next 5 to 7 years, that makes the current fiscal crisis pale in comparison. We now seemingly want to add to this by passing even more spending programs that will only make the hole deeper.

Europe has even larger underfunded social programs and banking systems that are quite suspect and heavily overleveraged with massive loans made to countries that will not be able to pay them back in full. Japan has taken the savings of two generations to amass the largest debt to GDP of any country in history, with little hope of avoiding serious pain as their population ages, needs to stop saving, and will begin selling their bonds to be able to live comfortably in retirement.

Now, we are faced with a continuing crisis and the aftermath of multiple bubbles bursting. We are left with massive government deficits and growing public debts, record unemployment, and consumers who are desperately trying to repair their balance sheets.

We are left with no good choices. For some countries, it is more a case of difficult choices such as reforming the tax system and entitlement programs. These are good things to do, not bad things, but are not easy because of entrenched special interests and political disunity. Some countries (like Greece and its compatriots) must choose between very, very bad and disastrous choices. No matter what they choose, they will have significant economic pain. Merely bad choices would be a luxury. But without making the difficult choices today, many other countries will soon be faced with Greek-like choices.

We have created a situation that is going to cause a lot of pain. It is not a question of pain or no pain; it is just when and how we decide (or are forced) to take it. There are no easy paths, but some bad choices are less bad than others.

At the beginning of this introduction, we quoted Jean Monnet. It bears repeating: *People only accept change in necessity and see necessity only in crisis.*

Each country will face its own moment of necessity. Whether forced by crisis or chosen as the best path, that moment is coming.

Think of the amount of pain that we must accept as in the shape of a wine bottle. Each country has its own wine bottle of pain it must endure. Some bottles are bigger then others. Some are magnum size, and some are jeroboams. You could say Greece has a melchizedek-size bottle of pain (40 times the size of a regular bottle of wine!).

Think of that wine bottle as part of a graph with time along the bottom. You can take the pain all at once, or (using our metaphor) you can take the wine bottle and lay it on its side and spread out the pain over time. But the amount of pain is not reduced. In fact, the longer the hard decisions are put off, the more pain (the bigger the bottle!) a country (or state or city) will have to endure in the end.

But as we will see, taking all the pain at once is no real answer. Such a path, unless it is forced on a country, can quickly morph into a deflationary depression with extremely high unemployment, low tax receipts, and an even worse situation. But as governments all over the world are learning, avoiding making the difficult choices results in a moment when the bond markets simply stop funding your deficits. As we will see in Chapter 6, there is no set point for that loss of confidence. It seemingly happens all at once and is a surprise to the government of the country.

Overcoming Human Nature

Philip G. Zimbardo, Professor Emeritus of Psychology at Stanford University, has studied how we as humans perceive time.[1] It seems that humans live in six psychological time zones: two in the past, two in the present, and two in the future. He divides the past into positive (those who are nostalgic, but also the keepers of family records, etc.) and negative (those who are focused on their regrets).

Likewise, the present is divided into two groups, one hedonistic, who live for the present, which includes babies and others who just simply don't worry about the future and prefer to enjoy the present as much as possible in whatever way they define *enjoy*. Then there are those whose present time orientation is fatalistic. They have little or no control over their lives due to poverty, religion ("my life is fated by God"), or local conditions.

Then there are those who are future oriented. Again, there are two groups, those who, like the ants in the story of the ant and the grasshopper, work today and put off current pleasures and spending, and those who believe life doesn't really start until you are dead.

Studies show that the closer you are to the equator, the more present oriented you are. The more you are in a place where the weather does not change all that much, the more you get a sense of sameness. Interestingly, there are words for *was* and *is* in the Sicilian dialect, but no *will be*. Present oriented indeed!

The purpose of school, Zimbardo notes, is to turn present-oriented little beasts into responsible future-oriented children. The problem in the United States is that a child drops out of school every nine seconds. Everyone is all upset about such a lack of future orientation.

But adult voters show a similar lack of future orientation. We much prefer to vote for benefits that increase our deficits. Even in good times, we do not pay down the debt but accumulate more.

Our friend Dylan Grice of Societe Generale writes:

> Voters don't go for long-term gain when it costs short-term pain. They'll certainly consider the guy who frowns and earnestly tells them that if they don't put down the snacks, go to the gym and work off some of the flab they've been piling on there will be serious consequences *one day,* but they'll only vote for him if he also tells them that they can go ahead and eat cheeseburgers and fries in front of the TV a little bit longer.[2]

One of the reasons Dr. Zimbardo cites for the epidemic of dropouts is the increased use of game devices. It seems the average teenager has played about 10,000 hours of video games and TV (some of it not so wholesome). It is an instant feedback, instant gratification society. And when we send that kid to school, he is in an old-style lecture (*boring!*) with no way to feed back into the system. No dopamine rush from killing yet another zombie or enemy soldier. No thrill of the hunt.

Yet voters all over the world act just like teenagers. We get frustrated when it takes more than a minute for our computers to boot up (thanks, Bill Gates!) or when it takes too long to download a file. And we want our economic and political fixes to be the same: quick and easy. The problem is that the political and economic cycles are not the same. It is difficult for politicians to respond to the longer-term problem when they face voters often.

As we will see, whether you call it the Great Recession or the Great Financial Crisis, what we are in is not a typical business cycle recession. It is a balance sheet recession. It is the end of the debt supercycle that started more than 60 years ago. The recovery time in much of the developed world is going to be measured not in months but in years, perhaps decades for some. It will be a much more volatile economy with more frequent recessions. For some countries, this will be very deflationary; for others, not so much. And for some, the risk of high inflation is very real.

But it will mean that the typical short political cycle will become even more volatile if voters do not understand that there are no easy fixes, no easy choices. There is no magic wand that politicians can wave to make it all disappear and bring back the boom times.

And yet, if we continue to train our politicians and leaders to be short-term thinkers rather than acting as forward-thinking adults, we will end up in a blind canyon where there are dragons of our own making. Think Greece.

Ultimately, that is what *Endgame* is about. In the first half of the book, we look at the basics of economics and recent research to try to understand the situation. Don't get nervous about a little economic study. This book is written (hopefully) so that even a politician can understand the nature of the crisis that is unfolding all around us.

In the second part of the book, we will go around the world, country by country, laying out the problems they face. Admittedly, some are more daunting than others. The real problems, as we will see, are mostly in the developed world. But that means even emerging market countries will feel the pressure as global trade to the developed world (which is two-thirds of the global economy) will suffer. The credit crisis is not yet fixed. We have shifted the crisis from homebuyers to banks and then finally to governments. There is no one else to step in. We are at endgame.

We outline the nature of the problems in each country, hinting at some solutions—but only hint. Each country must conduct its own national conversation as to what is important for it. In the United States, clearly we cannot afford the level of national expenditures at the current tax levels. But increasing taxes has consequences. It is all connected. Do we reduce our levels of Medicare costs, reform Social Security, reduce our defense spending, or increase taxes? Or do we make some combination of other cuts? There are no easy choices. As with teenagers who have put off making the hard choices, when they must be made, it is with great difficulty.

As each country makes its own choices, there will, of course, be significant implications for investments of all types, and we address these at the end of the book. The investments that work in one country and for one set of difficult choices are different than for other countries.

Endgame is not written in stone. The actual outcomes are path dependent. By that, we mean that the paths we choose will determine the outcome. And for those readers who live in countries that make poor choices, or are already faced with nothing but very bad choices, we hope we can offer you a few ideas on how to make good choices in your own personal investment lives. We will show you the signposts that will help you see what choices your country is making and invest accordingly.

And in the end, both of us are optimists. Even if our countries do not make the wise choices, we hope to be able to do so in our own lives and help you do so in yours. Our parents and grandparents survived a century with two major wars, a depression, and more. As we will see, we think that this era of endgame will itself end, and like the reset button on a computer allows you to start over, we believe that what will follow will be a major era of new prosperity, medical marvels, and wonderful new life-changing technology. Opportunities will abound. And now, let's figure out how to make our own wise choices.

PART ONE

THE END OF THE DEBT SUPERCYCLE

My view is that there is an inevitable endgame as a result of all this massive spending of taxpayer money in the West and Japan to bail out bankrupt banking systems, so in my view unfortunately endgame will be a systemic government debt crisis in the western world. It will probably happen in Europe and will climax in the US, and I am expecting on a five year view the collapse of the US Dollar paper standard.

—Chris Wood, CLSA strategist,
former *Economist* correspondent,
and expert on Japan's "Lost Decade"

When we mention endgame, you'll immediately want to know what is ending. What we think is ending for a significant number of countries in the "developed" world is the debt supercycle. The concept of the debt supercycle was originally developed by the Bank Credit Analyst (BCA). It was Hamilton Bolton, the BCA founder, who used the word *supercycle,* and he was referring generally to a lot of things, including money velocity, bank liquidity, and interest rates. Tony Boeckh changed the concept to the simpler "debt supercycle" back in the early 1970s, as he believed the problem was spiraling private-sector debt. The current editor of the BCA, Martin Barnes, has greatly expanded on the concept. (And of course, Irving Fisher talked about the long debt cycle in his famous 1933 article.)*

Essentially, the debt supercycle is the decades-long growth of debt from small and manageable levels, to a point where bond markets rebel and the debt has to be restructured or reduced. A program of austerity must be undertaken to bring the debt back to acceptable levels. While the focus of BCA has primarily been on the debt supercycle in the United States, many of the countries in the developed world are at various stages in their own debt supercycle.

As Bank Credit Analyst wrote back in 2007:

> The history of the U.S. is characterized by a long-run increase in indebtedness, punctuated by occasional financial crises and subsequent policy reflation. The subprime blow-up is the latest installment in this ongoing Debt Supercycle story. During each crisis, there are always fears that conventional reflation will no longer work, implying the economy and markets face a catastrophic debt unwinding. Such fears have always proved unfounded, and the current episode is no exception.
>
> A combination of Fed rate cuts, fiscal easing (aimed at relieving subprime distress), and a lower dollar will eventually trigger another up-leg in the Debt Supercycle, and a new round of leverage and financial excesses. The objects of speculation are likely to be global, particularly emerging markets and resource related assets. The Supercycle will end if foreign investors ever turn their back on U.S. assets, triggering capital flight out of the dollar and robbing U.S. authorities of any room for maneuver. This will not happen any time soon.[1]

---

*Lacy Hunt wrote the following to us: "But the credit for long debt cycle must go to Fisher in his famous 1933 article. Fisher's work was extended by Minsky and Kindleberger. Rogoff was Kindleberger's student. In Bernanke's *Essays in the Great Depression*, Fisher, Minsky, and Kindleberger (as well as some others) are given the credit for the pioneering work debt, which he then trashes as not being useable because it implies irrational behavior. Extension of debt is not bad if the borrower has the ability to repay. Extension of debt turns into a problem when debt is not repayable. That is the essence of Minsky's Ponzi finance."

I (John) was talking with Martin a few months ago, and the topic turned to the culmination of the debt supercycle. Martin said we are nowhere near the end, as the government is stepping in where private debtors are cutting back. We have just shifted the focus of where the debt is coming from. And he is right, in that the debt supercycle in the United States, Great Britain, Japan, and other developed countries (yes, even Greece!) is still very much in play as governments explode their balance sheets. Total debt continues to grow.

As the process shifts from private to public debt, growth in the economic and financial environment will be very different from that we have experienced for so many years. Mohamed El-Erian describes that world as the new normal. As we will see, the road to the new normal is rather bumpy.

Somewhere over the Rainbow

And yet, and yet. While the debt supercycle may not yet have ended, we think we can begin to see a clear case that, like the sandwich-board-wearing cartoon prophet warns, "The End is Nigh!" Greece is the harbinger of fundamental change. Spain and Portugal are pointing to the same outcome, as their cost of debt keeps rising. And Ireland? The Baltics?

There is a limit to how much debt you can pile on. As the work of Reinhart and Rogoff points out in *This Time Is Different* (2009), there is not a fixed limit for debt or some certain percentage of GDP where it all breaks down. Rather, the limit is all about confidence. Everything goes along well, and then "bang!" it doesn't. That "bang" has happened to Greece. Without massive assistance, Greek debt would be unmarketable. Default would be inevitable. (We still think it is!)

The limit is different for every nation. For Russia in the late 1990s, it was a rather minor total debt-to-GDP ratio of around 12 percent. Japan will soon have a debt–to–GDP ratio of 230 percent! The difference? Local savers bought government debt in Japan and did not in Russia.

The end of the debt supercycle does not have to mean calamity for each country, depending on how far down the road they are. Yes, if you are Greece, your choices are between very, very bad and disastrous.

Japan is a bug in search of a windshield. Each country has its own dynamics.

Take the United States. The United States is some way off from the end. We have time to adjust. But let's be under no illusions; we cannot run deficits of 10 percent of GDP forever. At some point, the Fed will either have to monetize the debt, or the bond market will simply demand an ever-higher interest rate. Why can't we go the way of Japan? Because we do not have the level of savings they have traditionally had. But their savings levels are rapidly declining, which says that if they want to continue their deficit spending at 10 percent of GDP, they will have to go into the foreign markets to borrow money at a much higher cost, or their central bank will have to print money. Neither choice is good.

CHAPTER ONE

The Beginning of the End

In retrospect, the temporary breakdown of the financial system seems like a bad dream. There are people in the financial institutions that survived who would like nothing better than to forget it and carry on with business as usual. This was evident in their massive lobbying effort to protect their interests in the Financial Reform Act that just came out of Congress. But the collapse of the financial system as we know it is real, and the crisis is far from over.

Indeed, we have just entered Act II of the drama, when financial markets started losing confidence in the credibility of sovereign debt.
> —George Soros speech at the Institute of International
> Finance in Vienna, June 10, 2010

The bankruptcy of Lehman Brothers in the fall of 2008 drew the curtain on a very long 60-year Act I in the debt supercycle. You could feel in the air the end of a golden period, when ever-increasing quantities of debt could lead to ever more consumption and "wealth." As stock markets crashed globally and the lines of unemployed lengthened, the end of the era was something we could observe in real time.

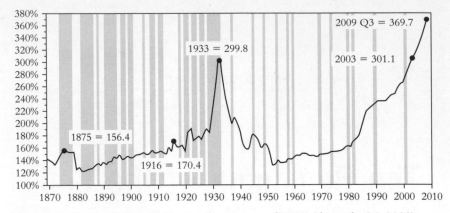

Figure 1.1   Total U.S. Debt as a Percentage of GDP (through Q3 2009)

Source: Hoisington Investment Management, Bureau of Economic Analysis, Federal Reserve, Census Bureau: Historical Statistics of the United States Colonical Times to 1970.

And let's be very clear. That debt did fuel growth, not just in the United States but throughout the developed world. Figure 1.1 shows total U.S. debt as a percentage of GDP. We will return to this chart later, but here you can see the explosion of debt in the United States, both public and private. As we will see, there are any number of countries with similar charts.

Gary Shilling noted, "According to the Federal Reserve, Americans extracted $719 billion in cash from their houses in 2005 after a $633 billion withdrawal in 2004 and $439 billion in 2003. Back in the mid-1990s, it was less than $200 billion per year. This was easily accomplished with the help of accommodative lenders through refinancings and home equity loans. Other homeowners looked on their houses as golden geese that never stop laying, so they simply saved less and borrowed more on credit cards and other means to bridge the gap between their robust spending growth and meager income gains."[1]

That $719 billion in one year is more than the recent stimulus in 2009. That is about 5 percent of GDP that went into all sorts of consumer spending. Clearly, the mortgage equity withdrawal was a large part of the growth after the 2001 recession. Without such "stimulus" the U.S. economy would not have grown nearly as much.

Things always appear more certain and clearer when we look backward. Usually big changes happen imperceptibly, and it is only in retrospect that we recognize them. For example, you can look back at the early 1980s and see the end of stagflation and the beginning of a new bull market in stocks, but at the time it didn't feel like it. In fact, many people even thought we might enter a third recession when Continental Illinois Bank went bankrupt in 1984. Or you can look back at when China joined the World Trade Organization in 2001 and see it as a massive game changer in terms of global trade, but at the time it drew little attention. Do you remember where you were when China joined the WTO on December 11, 2001? Almost no one remembers it, but it has changed our lives.

The end of the debt supercycle is different. We all know we have seen the end of an era, and we have courtside seats to watch endgame unfold. We have seen the end of Act I: the debt supercycle. Now we will get to see how Act II, endgame, plays out.

One of the principal Chinese curses heaped upon an enemy is "May you live in an interesting age." While the outcome of endgame is uncertain, one thing we can count on is that we will indeed live in interesting times.

We face a fundamentally different economic environment than we have lived in for the last 60 years. Throughout this book, we lay out the case that there is a massive reset of the global economy, some of it for the good and some of which will make us very uncomfortable, depending on the country in which you reside. But as individuals and governments come to the end of their ability to borrow massively, growth must come from different sources.

How Did the Debt Supercycle Come About?

Stability leads to instability, and success breeds its own undoing. The trend is your friend until it isn't. Currently, government lending rates are close to zero and are at all time lows. The European Central Bank (ECB) has kept its policy rate at 1 percent, the Fed at 0.25 percent, the Bank of Japan is at 0.10 percent, and the Bank of England is at 0.50 percent. The largest central banks in the world are all afraid of deflation. How times change! If you rewind the clock to 1980, almost all central banks were hiking rates to almost 20 percent because inflation was the biggest fear. The story of how we got from 20 percent interest rates to

0 percent is one of the great ironies of our time. Low rates induced a false sense of confidence. It was possible to take on more and more debt at lower coupons, but the debt then piled so high that people became unable to repay it.

In 1980, most developed countries suffered from high inflation, which was the result of excessively loose monetary and fiscal policies. This had been 15 years in the making. To make matters worse, many workers were trapped in a wage price spiral. Simply put, if prices went up, wages went up automatically as well. If wages went up, then employers raised prices to try to compensate for higher labor costs. Higher prices lead to higher wages, which lead to higher prices. Wash, rinse, and repeat.

After more than a decade of excessive spending and borrowing, combined with a too loose money supply, central banks and governments finally got religion. The United States, the United Kingdom, and many European countries rolled back the unions, breaking the vicious wage price spiral, and central bankers like Paul Volcker showed they were willing to hike rates until it hurt to crush inflation. Inflation fell, and interest rates fell as well. From 1980 to 2010, as Figure 1.2 shows, 10-year yields fell from 16 percent to 3 percent.

When interest rates fall, so does the cost of borrowing. It is easier to make your monthly interest payments. A payment on a 3 percent

Figure 1.2 U.S. 10-Year Bond Yields
Source: Bloomberg, Variant Perception.

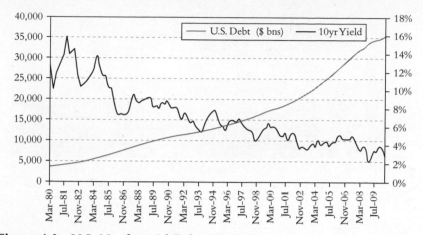

Figure 1.3 U.S. Nonfinancial Debt Outstanding versus U.S. 10-Year Yield
SOURCE: Bloomberg, Variant Perception.

interest rate mortgage is much more manageable than an 8 percent interest mortgage payment, all things being equal. It also means you
can borrow more money and buy a larger house if you choose.

The decline in interest rates and bond yields is almost the mirror
image of rising borrowing, as Figure 1.3 shows. Debt grew much, much
faster than GDP. Total debt rose from a level of 140 percent of GDP to
about 370 percent of GDP today.

Figure 1.4 shows total debt levels for the United States as a percentage of GDP with each component of debt by type: government,
Fannie Mae and Freddie Mac (agencies), bank debt, asset-backed
securities (ABS), household debt, and corporate debt. As you can
see, by far the biggest growth in debt has been in household and
mortgage debt.

Arguably, Figure 1.4 overstates current debt on account of securitization, which allows debt to show up in more than one place. Some
economists argue that ABS, financials, and agencies should not be
included in the debt calculation. Debt issued by a financial or through
securitization is also likely to appear in the nonfinancial data after
financials lend on the money they raised in the debt markets.

Figure 1.5 eliminates such potential double counting and shows that
we are roughly back at 1929 levels. But the ratio spiked in the 1930s
because GDP fell, not because debt rose.

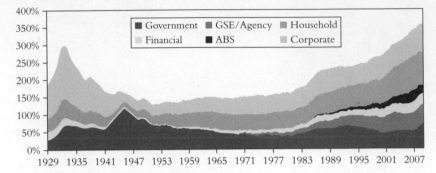

Figure 1.4 U.S. Debt to GDP Back to 1929
SOURCE: Deutsche Bank, Bloomberg, BEA, Federal Reserve.

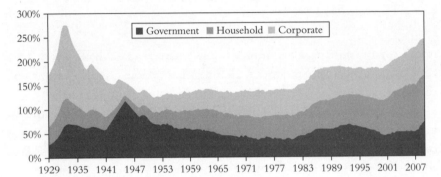

Figure 1.5 U.S. Debt (Excluding Financial, Government-Sponsored Enterprise/ Agency, ABS) to GDP back to 1929
SOURCE: Deutsche Bank, Bloomberg, BEA, Federal Reserve.

Which figure is right? It doesn't really matter. No matter which chart you believe, the total stock of debt is extremely large, and a great deal of it probably will not be paid back in dollars that are close to the value of the dollar in 2011.

And this was not just a phenomenon in the United States. Look at the following charts. It was happening all over the developed world. Take a look at the Figure 1.6, which is a chart of G7 debt. That is one ugly and unsustainable chart. In 1950, the G7 countries were recovering from very large wartime debts. Now we don't have that excuse. Nor do we have the option of doing what they did. They cut military spending, inflated a little in nominal terms, and grew their way out of the problem.

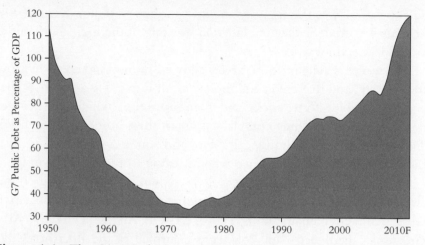

Figure 1.6 The Great Debt Swap (G7 Debt Soars after the Global Financial Crisis)
Source: IMF, Independent Strategy.

Common sense tells you that your debt cannot grow faster than your income forever, and at a certain stage, the huge pile of debt becomes unsustainable. All responsible parents teach their children not to let their debt grow faster than their income. It is only the Fed and Congress that are too foolish to get it.

It wasn't only falling interest rates, though, that built up the pile of debt. Loose monetary policy helped, and deregulation and financial innovation provided a perfect excuse. From the late 1980s onward, monetary policy remained far too loose throughout the entire period. The Fed and other central banks confused low inflation with a successful monetary policy. That is their prime objective. The key, though, was regulatory failure. When the Berlin Wall fell in 1989, and when China and India opened up to world trade, suddenly the global labor pool increased massively. China started producing cheaper and cheaper consumer goods, but they started buying more and more commodities like oil, copper, and lead.

Prices for consumer goods went down while commodity prices went up, sending false signals to central banks. The Fed mainly looks at core inflation, not headline. Consumer goods prices go into core inflation; commodities go into headline inflation. When they saw that core inflation was falling, they thought monetary policy was not too hot, not too cold. Stable core inflation was one of the ingredients of the Goldilocks economy.

However, stable inflation merely allowed money and credit to grow too quickly, and that credit and money went into rising asset prices that became bubbles (first stocks and then housing), which do not get tracked by CPI. No one complained when their home prices inflated. The Fed ignored the housing bubble, and some even denied it. And they were absent without leave when it came to regulatory oversight.

Not only was the Fed excessively lax when it came to inflation but also it provided liquidity as the solution to any crisis. This all started when Alan Greenspan came to the Fed. On August 11, 1987, Alan Greenspan succeeded Paul Volcker as chairman of the Board of Governors of the Federal Reserve. Only two months later, he faced the 1987 stock market crash. Immediately after the crash, Greenspan stated that the Fed "affirmed today its readiness to serve as a source of liquidity to support the economic and financial system." From then on, that was the mantra of the Fed.

Please note that we are not criticizing Greenspan for providing liquidity in 1987. It was an appropriate decision. One of the main tools the Fed has is to provide liquidity. As they say, if all you've got is a hammer, everything looks like a nail. And there are times when the problem is liquidity, and there are times when that is a secondary issue.

After the NASDAQ bubble burst, Greenspan and Bernanke lowered rates to 1 percent and kept them there far too long. The lessons all financial market participants learned was: "Load up on debt and take more risks; the Fed has your back." It was the famous Greenspan put as the Fed stood ready to provide more liquidity when the markets were faltering.

The final blow off the top for the increase in debt was when the Fed kept rates at 1 percent. When the NASDAQ bubble collapsed, the Fed feared that it might be like the bursting of the Japanese bubble in the 1990s and that we might end up with deflation. The solution, in the words of the Fed was: "We draw the general lesson from Japan's experience that when inflation and interest rates have fallen close to zero, and the risk of deflation is high, stimulus, both monetary and fiscal, should go beyond the levels conventionally implied by baseline forecasts of future inflation and economic activity."[2] With that in mind, the Fed kept rates at 1 percent for almost three years and promised it would keep rates low and only raise rates at a "measured pace," which translated into layman's terms was at a snail's pace.

The final ingredient that capped it all off was securitization and the shadow banking system. Almost all bubbles require some form of new financial technology or financial engineering. In the 1920s, installment credit, broker loans, and margin debt helped lead to the debt bubble of the 1920s; in 2008, it was securitization and shadow banking that helped lead to the collapse.

The shadow banking system, a phrase coined by my good friend Paul McCulley at PIMCO, describes the vast financial patchwork of nonbanks that acted like banks. They took deposits, borrowing short, lending long. They took liquid assets and invested them in illiquid assets like mortgages. The beauty of it for the shadow banking system was that they didn't have to hold any capital against their lending. Nice work if you can get it.

The shadow banking system could get away with something like this only with help of the ratings agencies, who should have been the cops but were handing out fake IDs to issuers, as McCulley so memorably put it. The ratings agencies declared that senior short-dated liabilities were just as good as bank deposits. The problem was that, unlike banks, the central bank didn't regulate the shadow banking system and couldn't bail them out without flipping over the chessboard and playing by a different playbook. That is when private debt very quickly became public debt.

Private Deleveraging and Public Leveraging Up

The beginning of the financial crisis and the end of the shadow banking system happened on August 9, 2007, when Bank Paribas (BNP) said that it could not value the mortgage assets in three of its off-balance sheet vehicles and that therefore the liability holders, who thought they could get out at any time, were frozen.[3] When that happened, it kicked off a run on the shadow banking system that finally culminated in the bankruptcy of Lehman Brothers.

Figure 1.7   Growth of U.S. Debt Outstanding
SOURCE: Bloomberg, Variant Perception.

All the assets that had been securitized and sat on the balance sheets of money market funds would eventually make their way back onto the balance sheets of banks. The run wasn't only restricted to the commercial paper market. Foreign central banks started dumping Fannie Mae and Freddie Mac mortgage bonds, forcing the Fed to start buying them unless it wanted to watch a full-scale implosion of the U.S. mortgage market.

Governments tried to stop the effects of the private sector paying back its debt and unleashing a major debt deleveraging cycle by running large fiscal deficits and printing massive amounts of money, causing the balance sheets of central banks and governments to explode. The sovereign sector is hurriedly plugging the gap left by the deleveraging private sector in the wake of the financial crisis. While households and corporations started paying back their debts, governments massively ramped up their borrowing.

Figure 1.7 is one of the most important charts you will see in this book. It is the passing of the baton from the private sector to the public sector. It is the transition from Act I to Act II. The debt supercycle gives way to endgame.

This has pronounced effects on government finances, as the chart for the U.S. fiscal balance going back to 1900 starkly shows. Our deficits are almost literally exploding off the chart, as Figure 1.8 shows.

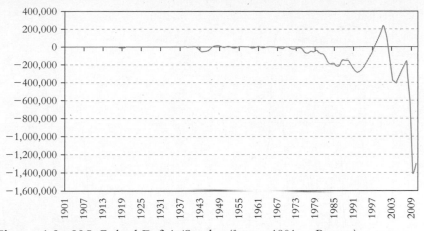

Figure 1.8 U.S. Federal Deficit/Surplus ($ mns, 1901 to Present)
SOURCE: Bloomberg, Variant Perception.

The extremely important point is this: for the most part, **debts have not been extinguished, merely transferred.** Debt is moving from consumer and household balance sheets to the government. While the debt supercycle was about the unsustainable rise of debt in the private sector, endgame is the crisis we will see in the public sector debt. Real endgame is when governments begin to run into the limits of their ability to borrow money at today's low rates. Greece already has. Others will follow.

When *people* have too much debt, they typically default. When *countries* have too much debt, you have one of three options.

1. They can inflate away the debt.
2. They can default on it.
3. They can devalue and hurt any foreigners who are holding the debt. This is really just a variant of inflating it away.

The last point is particularly important. Figure 1.9 shows that stock market collapse of 1929 was followed by banking collapse of 1931. Both episodes were a prelude to the currency crises of the 1930s. Many people say that the United States has never defaulted, but it did leave the gold standard and impose a 30 percent loss on foreigners who were holding U.S. bonds. The debts they held from the United States were repaid in dollars that were worth much less.

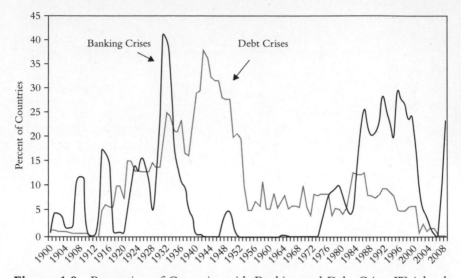

Figure 1.9 Proportion of Countries with Banking and Debt Crises Weighted by Their Share of World Income
SOURCE: Reinhart and Rogoff, "Banking Crises: An Equal Opportunity Menace," www.bresserpereira .org.br/terceiros/cursos/Rogoff.Banking_Crises.pdf, National Bureau of Economic Research.

Needless to say, whenever one country devalues, its neighbors almost always follow right behind. Barry Eichengreen, who is one of the world experts on the 1930s, describes the situation:

> In the 1930s, one country after another pushed down its exchange rate in a desperate effort to export its way out of depression. But each country's depreciation only aggravated the problems of its trading partners, who saw their own depressions deepen. Eventually even countries that valued currency stability were forced to respond in kind.
>
> In the end competitive devaluation benefited no one, it is said, since all countries can't devalue their exchange rates against each another. The only effects were to fan political tensions, heighten exchange rate uncertainty, and upend the global trading system. Financial protectionism if you will.[4]

Clearly, not everyone can win devaluing, but we know that throughout history, that is what happens after banking crises.

As we wrote earlier, the outcomes for various countries around the world are path dependent. By that, we mean that the paths we choose

will determine the outcome. Politicians can choose between bad outcomes and worse ones. Let's hope they can choose wisely.

Large banking crises and deleveraging episodes typically lead to
crises for countries. This has already started. In the past year, we have
seen sovereign debt crises in Latvia, Greece, Hungary, Dubai, Iceland,
and elsewhere. Dubai has little to do with Latvia and is nowhere close to
the others. However, history teaches us that sovereign countries rarely
default alone. Figure 1.10 shows a chart going back to 1800, from
Carmen Reinhart and Ken Rogoff's book *This Time Is Different*. It
shows that sovereign defaults tend to cluster and they tend to happen
suddenly after quiet periods. (Reinhart and Rogoff pretty much wrote
the bible on debt cycles, and we'll be devoting a chapter later to their
impressive work, as well as a special interview with them.)

These clusters match the boom and bust cycles in international
capital flows. The bursting of the global debt bubble guarantees beyond
a doubt that we will have more sovereign crises ahead of us.

Many governments are finding it easy to borrow right now, but
bad habits from the crisis may become entrenched. It is clear that nations
whose public debt is mainly denominated in domestic currency
and whose central bank is not very independent are likely to choose

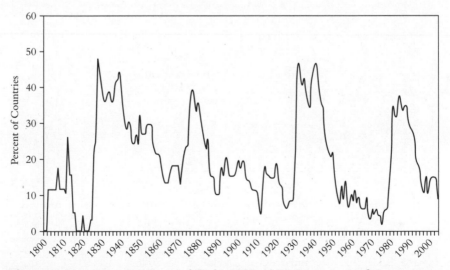

Figure 1.10 Sovereign External Debt 1800–2006, Percentage of Countries in
Default or Restructuring
SOURCE: Reinhart and Rogoff, *This Time Is Different.*

inflation and exchange rate depreciation over default as a way out of fiscal and financial unsustainability. That category could eventually (not this year!) include the United States and, to perhaps an even greater extent, the United Kingdom. (We will deal with competitive devaluations and the problems they present in a few chapters.)

Previously, central banks would do anything rather than monetize debt, but as Bernanke said about the Fed's role in the crisis, "There are no atheists in the foxhole." Going forward, now that the line of monetizing debt has been crossed, it will be easier and easier to do the wrong thing. The Fed and the Bank of England have in fact coordinated their actions with their treasuries, making a mockery of monetary independence. Going forward, they are likely to have a tendency to coordinate their actions again. That is exactly what has happened after previous banking crises.

As Figure 1.11 from Reinhart and Rogoff shows, inflation globally has risen as countries have monetized debts.

We suspect that if the Federal Reserve or the Bank of England were in Caracas, Venezuela, or Bogota, Colombia, instead of in Washington

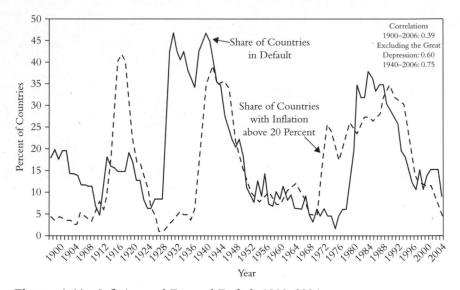

Figure 1.11 Inflation and External Default 1900–2006
Source: Reinhart and Rogoff, "Banking Crises: An Equal Opportunity Menace," www.bresserpereira .org.br/terceiros/cursos/Rogoff.Banking_Crises.pdf, National Bureau of Economic Research.

or London, we would probably have a currency crisis and inflation because of a crisis of confidence. You could say we are lucky that the United States and the United Kingdom have a store of credibility, but it is not unlimited.

Once again, governments and central banks are pursuing a risk management strategy and attempting to put out a global fire. Their responses will put us on a path-dependent outcome toward a bigger blowup.

Consider the following analogy. Global markets and economies are like forest fires. California and Baja California both have very similar forests and vegetation but have very different fire control policies. In California, small fires are put out regularly by firefighters. In Baja California, they are not. Paradoxically, this means that Baja California has many more small fires and almost no major fires, while California has very limited small fires and occasional major, catastrophic fires.

Lesson: Without small fires to clear the brush, enrich the soil, and unlock pine seeds, nature isn't in balance. Avoiding small problems creates greater systemic problems when brush between the trees builds up.

Trying to micromanage the small fires in central banking and fiscal policy leads to growing confidence by risk takers, so you get fewer small fires and paradoxically a greater chance of a major catastrophic fire. Mopping up after financial bubbles with massive liquidity is merely chasing the wind, insofar as monetary and fiscal policies operate with a lag, but intervention is also creating greater systemic instability. The source of that greater instability is likely to be caused by out-of-control fiscal policies. Avoiding the pain of the current downturn will create larger fires in the future with more macroeconomic volatility and greater variability of inflation rates.

The bigger fire is ahead of us, not behind us. It is global endgame. For some countries, the end will mean default, for others inflation, and for yet others devaluation. Each country will be different. In this book, we'll examine how each scenario plays out, and we'll go country by country. Some countries have a fairly ugly future, while others still have a good chance of turning things around. We'll be honest and unflinching, so let's dive right in.

CHAPTER TWO

Why Greece Matters

To trace something unknown back to something known is alleviating, soothing, gratifying and gives moreover a feeling of power. Danger, disquiet, anxiety attend the unknown—the first instinct is to eliminate these distressing states. First principle: any explanation is better than none. . . . The cause-creating drive is thus conditioned and excited by the feeling of fear. . . .

—Friedrich Nietzsche

"Any explanation is better than none." And the simpler, it seems in the investment game, the better. "The markets went up because oil went down," we are told, except when it went down, there was another reason for the movement of the markets. We all intuitively know that things are far more complicated than that. But as Nietzsche noted, dealing with the unknown can be disturbing, so we look for the simple explanation.

"Ah," we tell ourselves, "I know why that happened." With an explanation firmly in hand, we now feel we know something. And the behavioral psychologists note that this state actually releases chemicals in our brains that make us feel good. We become literally addicted to the simple explanation. The fact that what we think we know (the explanation for the unknowable) is irrelevant or even wrong is not important to the chemical release. And thus we look for reasons.

The United States is extremely unlikely to default. At worst, we may experience severe inflation while we adjust our taxing and spending—or deflation if markets are forcing austerity! We have the great benefit that all our borrowings are in our own currency, which we can print. Other countries around the world will not be so fortunate, and as we have recently seen in the case of Greece, many countries will need to be bailed out by the European Union or the International Monetary Fund.

How does an event like a problem in Greece (or elsewhere) affect you, gentle reader? And we mean affect you down where the rubber hits your road. Not some formula or theory about the velocity of money or the effect of taxes on GDP.

Put more broadly, why should you care about countries halfway around the world that might go bust? An American might not care about Greece, but most Europeans didn't care about Thailand before it devalued in 1997 or Russia before it went bust in 1998 or Argentina before it went bust in 2002. Yet each of these small crises had much greater effects elsewhere around the world. Like a stone dropped in a pond, the ripples flow much farther than you can see.

This chapter is somewhat of a departure as it is a letter from me to my kids written when they were trying to understand why Greece had him so worked up in his writings.[1]

What Does Greece Mean to Me, Dad?

Tiffani had been talking with her friends.* A lot of them read this letter, and they were asking, "Okay, I get that Greece is a problem. But what does that mean for me here? I want to understand why you think this is so important."

---

*A little background. I have seven kids, five of whom are adopted. A fairly colorful family, so to speak, ages 16 through 33. Daughter Tiffani runs my business and, except for the youngest boy, they are all out on their own. Four are married or attached. It is not easy to watch them struggle to make ends meet, but Dad is proud. And listening to their stories, and the stories of their friends, helps keep me in the real world.

The same day, a friend told me about a conversation she had with her 17-year-old Cal Tech daughter and her daughter's boyfriend, who is also headed to Cal Tech. These are really smart kids, and they were asking her about some of my recent letters. "We understand what he's saying, but we just don't see what it means." (For what it's worth, the boyfriend wants to grow up to be Mohamed El-Erian of PIMCO. Go figure; I just wanted to be Mickey Mantle.)

Twice in one day is a sign, I am sure, so I will try to see if I can explain. And since all my kids must be wondering the same thing, this is a letter from Dad to see if I can help them understand why things are not going as well as they would like.

Dear Kids,

I know what a struggle it has been for most of you, and now three of you have a kid of your own. Expensive little hobbies, aren't they? I know that you read my letter (well, except for Trey) and wonder what it means to you trying to pay your bills. Let me see if I can make a connection from the world of economics to the world of paying your bills. Sadly, what I am going to say is not going to make you feel any better, but reality is what it is. We'll get through it together.

While life looks pretty good for Dad now, when I graduated from seminary in December of 1974, unemployment was at 8 percent, on its way to 9 percent a few months later. We lived in a small mobile home, which seemed wonderful at the time. I was proud of it. We scrimped and got by. My first job was a dead end, so I left after a few months. I guess I was lucky that no one would hire me, because I had to figure out how to make it on my own. All I really knew was the printing business I had grown up in, so I started brokering printing. Pretty soon I was doing just direct mail, and then designing direct mail. But there was never enough money. We were still in that mobile home six years later.

And prices were going up like crazy. We had inflation. I remember going to a bank in the late 1970s and borrowing money for my business at 18 percent, so I could buy paper for a job I had sold. Forget about borrowing for a new home or car. All I knew was that I was struggling to make ends meet (with a new kid!). There were a lot of nights where I would wake up at two in the morning with panic attacks about whether I could make payroll or pay bills until someone paid me. I didn't understand that what the Fed and the government were doing was causing high inflation and unemployment.

I had a bank line I used to buy paper with. One day the bank abruptly canceled that line and demanded their money, which I didn't have—all I had was a warehouse full of paper and a contract that said I had a year to pay for it. The bank didn't care. I told them they would just have to wait. I swear, they actually called my mother and told her they would ruin me if she didn't pay that $10,000 line. She was scared for me (after all, you had to be able to trust your banker) and paid it without asking me. Turned out the bank finally went bankrupt later in the year. They were just desperate and trying anything they could do to get money, so they wouldn't lose everything. They did anyway.

In short, times were not all that good, but we got through it. And now, 35 years later, it seems like déjà vu all over again. Every time we talk, it seems like someone we know has lost a job.

And so how do the problems in a small country like Greece make a difference to you? There is a connection, but it's different than the old "hip bone is connected to the thigh bone to the knee bone" thing. It is a lot more complicated. Let's go back to a letter I wrote four years ago, talking about fingers of instability. One of the best analogies your Dad has ever written, according to many of his 1 million friends. So read with me a few pages, and then we'll get back to Greece. Let's explore something called complexity theory.

Ubiquity, Complexity Theory, and Sand Piles

We are going to start our explorations with excerpts from a very important book by Mark Buchanan called Ubiquity: Why Catastrophes Happen. *I highly recommend it to those of you who, like me, are trying to understand the complexity of the markets. Not directly about investing, although he touches on it, it is about chaos theory, complexity theory, and critical states. It is written in a manner any layman can understand. There are no equations, just easy-to-grasp, well-written stories and analogies.*

We all had fun as kids going to the beach and playing in the sand. Remember taking your plastic buckets and making sand piles? Slowly pouring the sand into ever-bigger piles, until one side of the pile started an avalanche?

Imagine, Buchanan says, dropping just one grain of sand after another onto a table. A pile soon develops. Eventually, just one grain starts an avalanche. Most of the time it is a small one, but sometimes it gains momentum, and it seems like one whole side of the pile slides down to the bottom.

Well, in 1987 three physicists, named Per Bak, Chao Tang, and Kurt Weisenfeld, began to play the sand pile game in their lab at Brookhaven National

Laboratory in New York. Now, actually piling up one grain of sand at a time is a slow process, so they wrote a computer program to do it. Not as much fun, but a whole lot faster. Not that they really cared about sand piles. They were more interested in what are called nonequilibrium systems.

They learned some interesting things. What is the typical size of an avalanche? After a huge number of tests with millions of grains of sand, they found out that there is no typical number. "Some involved a single grain; others, ten, a hundred or a thousand. Still others were pile-wide cataclysms involving millions that brought nearly the whole mountain down. At any time, literally anything, it seemed, might be just about to occur."

It was indeed completely chaotic in its unpredictability. Now, let's read these next paragraphs slowly. They are important, as they create a mental image that helps me understand the organization of the financial markets and the world economy.

> *To find out why [such unpredictability] should show up in their sand pile game, Bak and colleagues next played a trick with their computer. Imagine peering down on the pile from above, and coloring it in according to its steepness. Where it is relatively flat and stable, color it green; where steep and, in avalanche terms, 'ready to go,' color it red.*
>
> *What do you see? They found that at the outset the pile looked mostly green, but that, as the pile grew, the green became infiltrated with ever more red. With more grains, the scattering of red danger spots grew until a dense skeleton of instability ran through the pile. Here then was a clue to its peculiar behavior: a grain falling on a red spot can, by domino-like action, cause sliding at other nearby red spots. If the red network was sparse, and all trouble spots were well isolated one from the other, then a single grain could have only limited repercussions.*
>
> *"But when the red spots come to riddle the pile, the consequences of the next grain become fiendishly unpredictable. It might trigger only a few tumblings, or it might instead set off a cataclysmic chain reaction involving millions. The sand pile seemed to have configured itself into a hypersensitive and peculiarly unstable condition in which the next falling grain could trigger a response of any size whatsoever.*[2]

Something only a math nerd could love? Scientists refer to this as a critical state. The term critical state *can mean the point at which water would go to ice or steam or the moment that critical mass induces a nuclear reaction. It is the point at which something triggers a change in the basic nature or character of the object or group. Thus (and very casually for all you physicists) we refer to something being in a critical state (or use the term* critical mass) *when there is the opportunity for significant change.*

> *But to physicists, [the critical state] has always been seen as a kind of theoretical freak and sideshow, a devilishly unstable and unusual condition that arises only under the most exceptional circumstances [in highly controlled experiments] .... In the sand pile game, however, a critical state seemed to arise naturally through the mindless sprinkling of grains.*[3]

Then they asked themselves, could this phenomenon show up elsewhere? In the earth's crust, triggering earthquakes; in wholesale changes in an ecosystem or a stock market crash? "Could the special organization of the critical state explain why the world at large seems so susceptible to unpredictable upheavals?" Could it help us understand not just earthquakes, but why cartoons in a third-rate paper in Denmark could cause worldwide riots?

Buchanan concludes in his opening chapter,

> *There are many subtleties and twists in the story ... but the basic message, roughly speaking, is simple: The peculiar and exceptionally unstable organization of the critical state does indeed seem to be ubiquitous in our world. Researchers in the past few years have found its mathematical fingerprints in the workings of all the upheavals I've mentioned so far [earthquakes, eco-disasters, market crashes], as well as in the spreading of epidemics, the flaring of traffic jams, the patterns by which instructions trickle down from managers to workers in the office, and in many other things.*
>
> *At the heart of our story, then, lies the discovery that networks of things of all kinds—atoms, molecules, species, people, and even ideas— have a marked tendency to organize themselves along similar lines. On the basis of this insight, scientists are finally beginning to fathom what lies behind tumultuous events of all sorts, and to see patterns at work where they have never seen them before.*[4]

Now, let's think about this for a moment. Going back to the sand pile game, you find that as you double the number of grains of sand involved in an avalanche, the likelihood of an avalanche is 2.14 times as unlikely. We find something similar in earthquakes. In terms of energy, the data indicate that earthquakes simply become four times less likely each time you double the energy they release. Mathematicians refer to this as a "power law," or a special mathematical pattern that stands out in contrast to the overall complexity of the earthquake process.

Fingers of Instability

So what happens in our game?

> *After the pile evolves into a critical state, many grains rest just on the verge of tumbling, and these grains link up into "fingers of instability" of all possible lengths. While many are short, others slice through the pile from one end to the other. So the chain reaction triggered by a single grain might lead to an avalanche of any size whatsoever, depending on whether that grain fell on a short, intermediate or long finger of instability.[5]*

Now, we come to a crucial point in our discussion of the critical state. Again, read this with the markets in mind:

> *In this simplified setting of the sand pile, the power law also points to something else: the surprising conclusion that even the greatest of events have no special or exceptional causes. After all, every avalanche large or small starts out the same way, when a single grain falls and makes the pile just slightly too steep at one point. What makes one avalanche much larger than another has nothing to do with its original cause, and nothing to do with some special situation in the pile just before it starts. Rather, it has to do with the perpetually unstable organization of the critical state, which makes it always possible for the next grain to trigger an avalanche of any size.[6]*

Now let's couple this idea with a few other concepts. First, one of the world's greatest economists (who sadly was never honored with a Nobel), Hyman Minsky, points out that stability leads to instability. The longer a given condition or trend persists (and the more comfortable we get with it), the more dramatic the correction will be when the trend fails. The problem with long-term macroeconomic stability is that it tends to produce highly unstable financial arrangements. If we believe that tomorrow and next year will be the same as last week and last year, we are more willing to add debt or postpone savings for current consumption. Thus, says Minsky, the longer the period of stability, the higher the potential risk for even greater instability when market participants must change their behavior.

Relating this to our sand pile, the longer that a critical state builds up in an economy or, in other words, the more fingers of instability that are allowed to develop connections to other fingers of instability, the greater the potential for a serious avalanche.

Another way to think about it is the way Didier Sornette, a French geophysicist, has described financial crashes in his wonderful book Why Stock Markets Crash (the math, though, was far beyond me!). He wrote,

> The specific manner by which prices collapsed is not the most important problem: a crash occurs because the market has entered an unstable phase and any small disturbance or process may have triggered the instability. Think of a ruler held up vertically on your finger: this very unstable position will lead eventually to its collapse, as a result of a small (or an absence of adequate) motion of your hand or due to any tiny whiff of air. The collapse is fundamentally due to the unstable position; the instantaneous cause of the collapse is secondary.[7]

When things are unstable, it isn't the last grain of sand that causes the pile to collapse or the slight breeze that causes the ruler on your fingertip to fall. Those are the proximate causes. They're the closest reasons at hand for the collapse. The real reason, though, is the remote cause, the farthest reason. The farthest reason is the underlying instability of the system itself.

A fundamentally unstable system is exactly what we saw in the recent credit crisis. Consumers all through the world's largest economies borrowed money for all sorts of things, because times were good. Home prices would always go up, and the stock market was back to its old trick of making 15 percent a year. And borrowing money was relatively cheap. You could get 2 percent short-term loans on homes, which seemingly rose in value 15 percent a year, so why not buy now and sell a few years down the road?

Greed took over. Those risky loans were sold to investors by the tens and hundreds of billions of dollars all over the world. And as with all debt sand piles, the fault lines started to show up. Maybe it was that one loan in Las Vegas that was the critical piece of sand; we don't know, but the avalanche was triggered.

You probably don't remember this, but Dad was writing about the problems with subprime debt way back in 2005 and 2006. But as the problem actually emerged, respected people like Ben Bernanke (the chairman of the Fed) said that the problem was not all that big and that the fallout would be contained. (I bet he wishes he could have that statement back!)

But it wasn't contained. It caused banks to realize that what they thought was AAA credit was actually a total loss. And as banks looked at what was on their books, they wondered about their fellow banks. How bad were they? Who knew? Since no one did, they stopped lending to each other. Credit simply froze. They stopped taking each other's letters of credit, and that hurt world trade. Because banks were losing money, they stopped lending to smaller businesses. Commercial paper dried up. All those safe off-balance-sheet funds that banks created were now folding (what my friend Paul McCulley first labeled as the shadow banking system). Everyone sold what they could, not what they wanted to, to cover their debts. It was a true panic. Businesses started laying off people, who in turn stopped spending as much.

As you saw from my earlier story about my bank experience, banks may do what look like unreasonable things when they get into trouble. (Speaking of which, my smallish Texas bank, where I have been for almost 20 years, just canceled my very modest, unused credit line last month and told me that letters of credit will not be rewritten without 100 percent cash against them. Not to worry, Dad is actually in the best shape of his life, business-wise, knock on wood. I hadn't talked personally to a banker in years. When I asked the young clerk on the phone, "What's going on?" he said it was just an order from his director. I switched banks last week, as I can now smell a bank in trouble. And I again have a credit line—which I hope not to use.)

But the fact is we need banks. They are like the arteries in our bodies; they keep the blood (money) flowing. And when our arteries get hard, we can be in danger of heart attacks. And it's going to get worse, as banks are going to lose more money on their commercial real estate loans. Commercial real estate is already down some 40 percent around the country.

There are a lot of books that try to pinpoint the cause of our current crisis. And some make for fun reading, like a good mystery novel. You can blame it on the Fed or the bankers or hedge funds or the government or ratings agencies or any number of culprits.

Let me be a little controversial here. The blame game that is now going on is in many ways way too simplistic. The world system survived all sorts of crises over recent decades and bounced back. This bust isn't a garden variety bust.

Why is now so different? We are coming to the end of a 60-year debt supercycle. Not just consumers but banks borrowed (and not just in the United States but all over the developed world) like there was no tomorrow. And because we were so convinced that all this debt was safe, we leveraged up, borrowing at first 3 and then 5 and then 10 and then as much as 30 times the actual money we had. And we convinced the regulators that it was a good thing. The longer things remained stable, the more convinced we became they would remain that way. Figure 2.1 shows how our sand pile ended up. It's not pretty.

I know Dad always says it is never different, but in a sense this time is really different from all the other crises we have gone through since the Great Depression that your Less-Than-Sainted Papa Joe used to talk about. What the very important book by professors Reinhart and Rogoff shows is that every debt crisis always ends this way, with the debt having to be paid down or written off or defaulted on. That part is never different. One way or another, we reduce the debt. And that is a painful process. It means that the economy grows much slower, if at all, during the process.

And while the government is trying to make up the difference for consumers who are trying to (or being forced to) reduce their debt, even governments have limits, as the Greeks are finding out.

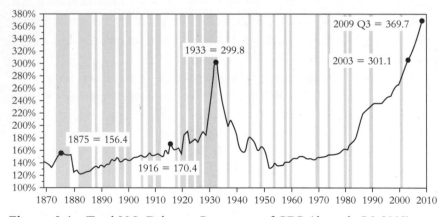

Figure 2.1   Total U.S. Debt as a Percentage of GDP (through Q3 2009)
SOURCE: Hoisington Investment Management, Bureau of Economic Analysis, Federal Reserve, Census Bureau: Historical Statistics of the United States Colonical Times to 1970.

If it were not for the fact that we are coming to the closing innings of the debt supercycle, we would already be in a robust recovery. But we are not. And sadly, we have a long way to go with this deleveraging process. It will take years.

You can't borrow your way out of a debt crisis, whether you are a family or a nation. And as too many families are finding out today, if you lose your job, you can lose your home. What were once very creditworthy people are now filing for bankruptcy and walking away from homes, as all those subprime loans going bad put homes back onto the market, which caused prices to fall on all homes, which caused an entire home-construction industry to collapse, which hurt all sorts of ancillary businesses, which caused more people to lose their jobs and give up their homes, and on and on. The connections in the housing part of the sand pile were long and deep.

It's all connected. We built a very unstable sand pile, it came crashing down, and now we have to dig out from the problem. And the problem was too much debt. It will take years, as banks write off home loans and commercial real estate and more, and we get down to a more reasonable level of debt as a country and as a world.

And here's where I have to deliver the bad news. It seems we did not learn the lessons of this crisis very well. First, we have not fixed the problems that made the crisis so severe. The 2,300-page bill that recently passed for financial reform has more unintended consequences on each page of the bill that will not help get America back on track. (By contrast, the original Social Security bill was 28 pages in length and the original regulatory reform bill call Glass-Steagall was 35 pages back in 1934.) European banks still remain highly leveraged.

Why is Greece important? Because so much of their debt is on the books of European banks. Hundreds of billions of dollars worth. And just a few years ago, this seemed like a good thing. The rating agencies (yes, the same guys who said those subprime bonds were AAA!) made Greek debt AAA, and banks could use massive leverage (almost 40 times in some European banks), buy these bonds, and make good money in the process. (Don't ask Dad why people still trust rating agencies. Some things just can't be explained.)

Except, now that Greek debt is risky. Today, there is some kind of bailout for Greece. But that is just a Band-Aid on a very serious wound. The crisis will not go away. It will come back, unless the Greeks willingly go into their own Great Depression by slashing their spending and raising taxes to a level that no one in the United States could even contemplate. What is being demanded of them is really bad for them, but they did it to themselves.

But those European banks? When that debt goes bad, and it will, they will react to each other just like they did in 2008. Trust will evaporate. Will taxpayers shoulder the burden? Maybe, maybe not. For now, for a few years, it looks like they will. But that won't go on forever. It will be a huge crisis. There are other countries in Europe, like Spain and Portugal, that are almost as bad as Greece. And while Greece and Greek debt makes the European Central Bank act as if Greece is too big to let fail, Spain is too big to save. Great Britain is not too far behind.

The European economy is as large as that of the United States. We feel it when they go into recessions, for many of our largest companies make a lot of money in Europe. A crisis will also make the euro go down, which reduces corporate profits and makes it harder for us to sell our products into Europe, not to mention compete with European companies for global trade. And that means we all buy less from China, which means they will buy fewer of our bonds, and on and on go the connections. And it will all make it much harder to start new companies, which are the source of real growth in jobs.

And then in January 2011 we may have the largest tax increase in U.S. history, with not just federal but state and local taxes going up. (We write this book in November 2010 and do not know what Congress will do.) Even if the Bush tax cuts are all extended, the combined tax increases and reduced spending at state and local levels are just as large an issue.

The research shows that tax increases may have as much as a negative three-times effect on GDP, or the growth of the economy. (There is other research that suggests it is only a multiplier of one. And of course, one can argue that Romer's research does not apply to taxes on the rich.) As we will see later in this book, I think it is likely that the level of tax increases, when combined with the increase in state and local taxes (or the reductions in spending), could be enough to throw us back into recession, even without problems coming from Europe. (And no, Melissa, that is not some Republican research conspiracy. The basic research was done by Christina Romer, who was Obama's chairperson of the Joint Council of Economic Advisors.)*

And sadly, that means even higher unemployment. It means sales at the bar where you work, Melissa, will fall further as more of your friends lose jobs. And commissions at the electronics store where you work, Chad, will be even lower

---

*And as we will see in the next chapter, even if we avoid a repeat recession in 2011, following a credit crisis and in an era of deleveraging, recessions are more frequent, so it is just a matter of time.

than the miserable level they're at now. And Henry, it means the hours you work at UPS will be even more difficult to come by. You are smart to be looking for more part-time work. Abbi and Amanda? People may eat out a little less, and your fellow workers will all want more hours. And Trey? Greece has little to do with the fact that you do not do your homework on time.

And this next time, we won't be able to fight the recession with even greater debt and lower interest rates, as we did this last time. Rates are as low as they can go, and at some point, if we do not get our government fiscal house in order, the bond market will show that it does not like the massive borrowing the United States is engaged in. It is worried about the possibility of "Greece R Us."

Bond markets require confidence above all else. If Greece defaults, then how far away is Spain or Japan? What makes the United States so different, if we do not control our debt? As Reinhart and Rogoff show, when confidence goes, the end is very near. It always comes faster than anyone expects, and it always seems to be unexpected.

The global financial system is all connected. Tiny Greece can make a difference in places far removed from Europe, just like our subprime debt created a crisis all over the world. The world financial system allowed too much risk to be taken and then spread that risk far and wide through fancy new financial engineering and securitizations. Many investors and pension funds thought that by buying a lot of different types of securities, they were diversifying their risk, when in fact the same connected risk was in almost everything.

Investments that were normally not correlated started to show a high degree of correlation during the onset of the recent crisis, just when we needed that diversification of risk to help. And there is no reason to think it will be all that much different in the next crisis period. Investing is not easy.

The next crisis will probably not come from Greece but from some other corner of the world. But Greece is important because it tells us that we have to be very careful and not ignore a problem just because it is not in our back yard. We are all connected through the fingers of instability.

The good news? We will get through this. We pulled through some rough times as a nation in the 1970s. No one, in 2020, is going to want to go back to the good old days of 2010, as the amazing innovations in medicine and other technologies will have made life so much better. You guys are going to live a very long time (and I hope I get a few extra years to enjoy those grandkids as well!). In 1975, we did not know where the new jobs would come from. It was fairly bleak. But the jobs did come, as they will once again.

The even better news? You guys are young, still babies, really. Hell, I didn't have a good year income-wise until I was in my mid-30s, and that was an accident (I literally won a cellular telephone lottery). And it has not always been smooth since then, as you know. But we get through bad stuff. That is what we do as a family and as the larger family of our nation and world.

So, what's the final message? Do what you are doing. Work hard, save, watch your spending, and think about whether your job is the right one if we have another recession. Pay attention to how profitable the company you work for is, and make yourself their most important worker. And know that things will get better. The 2020s are going to be one very cool time, as we shrug off the ending of the debt supercycle and hit the reset button. And remember, Dad is proud of you and loves you very much.

CHAPTER THREE

Let's Look at the Rules

The more constraints one imposes, the more one frees one's self. And the arbitrariness of the constraint serves only to obtain precision of execution.
—Igor Stravinsky

There are rules in sports. Three strikes and you're out. You have to make ten yards in four downs to get another first down. You can't touch the soccer ball with your hands. Rules are a great annoyance to the beginner, but to the experienced player, they make for a beautiful game.

Baseball is a confusing game for most non-Americans. There are so many rules and subtleties. I confess to not understanding the rules in soccer, although I am getting better. And forget about understanding hockey.

There are rules in economics, but many are not as well-known. And breaking these rules has consequences for individuals, companies, and countries. Sadly, there is no independent referee who can blow a whistle and stop the game, assess a penalty, and make you obey the rules. There is, however, a market that can decide not to buy your currency or your bonds if you don't play by the rules.

We are going to look at some of the more important rules in this chapter. But, gentle reader, don't panic. These rules are fairly easy to understand if we take out the academic jargon often associated with them. And if you get it, then it is *much* easier to understand the consequences of what happens when a nation violates the rules, both from a policy perspective and from a personal investing point of view.

Also sadly, there is not necessarily an immediate penalty for a violation. As we saw in the last chapter, a country can rock along for a very long time before that ***Bang!*** comes along and the flag finally gets thrown. But in the fullness of time, if a country does not correct its misbehavior, the end will be full of weeping and wailing and gnashing of teeth. And a *lot* of finger pointing—it is always the other side's fault.

Note that the rules are the same for everyone and every country. These are basically accounting rules known as identity equations. They are like $E = MC^2$ or $F = MA$ (force is equal to mass times acceleration). They are just true. If they are not, then a thousand years of accounting is wrong. You may not like what they say or not like the consequences, but you have to deal with the real world, take it or leave it.

For instance, in 1976, as a *very* young entrepreneur (no one would hire me, so I had to work for myself), I had launched my first business, and my best friend did my taxes. I thought I had sent the IRS more than enough to cover me. Then he came to me with a tax bill that was more money than I had ever seen in one place. I guess the concept that I had to pay the employer's side of Social Security had escaped my attention in my quest to simply survive, along with all sorts of alternative minimum taxes and other things I had never heard of. Reality can be a real bitch.

The importance of knowing the rules was forcefully driven home. And the rules we will now look at are every bit as important as knowing those tax laws. Even if you don't know about them, they exist and will eventually come to haunt you (whether you're an individual, a company, or a nation) if you ignore them.

The Federal Reserve and central banks in general are currently attempting a major and highly experimental operation on the economic body, without benefit of anesthesia. They are testing the theories of four dead white guys: Irving Fisher (representing the classical economists), John Keynes (the Keynesian school), Ludwig von Mises (the Austrian school), and Milton Friedman (the monetarist school). For the most part, the central bankers are Keynesian, with a dollop of monetarist thrown in here and there. They have every intention of using their liquidity tool to try to prevent deflation, spur the economy and encourage us to borrow and spend more. We'll talk about how likely that is to work later.

Six Impossible Things

Alice laughed. "There's no use trying," she said, "one can't believe impossible things."

"I daresay you haven't had much practice," said the Queen. "When I was your age, I always did it for half-an-hour a day. Why, sometimes I've believed as many as six impossible things before breakfast."

—From *Through the Looking Glass,* by Lewis Carroll

Economists and policy makers seem to want to believe impossible things in regard to the debt crisis currently percolating throughout the world. And believing in them, they are adopting policies that could well lead to tragedy.

Let's look at the basic equation that summarizes a nation's gross domestic product:

GDP = C + I + G + Net Exports (that is, exports minus imports)

Which is to say, the gross domestic product of a country is equal to its total consumption (personal and business) plus investments plus government spending plus net exports. Again, this equation is known as an identity equation: It is true for all countries and times. And it is rather simple in concept but has profound implications.

Let's examine some of those implications. First, what happens if the C drops? That means that, absent something happening elsewhere in the equation, GDP is going to drop. That circumstance is typically called a recession.

Keynesian economists argue that the correct policy response is to boost the G through fiscal stimulus, allowing consumers and businesses time to adjust and recover, and to gradually remove that stimulus as the economy returns to its normal growth trajectory. And as an added measure, it helps if the central bank will become more accommodative, with lower interest rates and an easy-money policy to give further stimulus to business and consumers. In most places and in most times in recent (as in 60) years, these policies have worked to help bring an economy through a recession.

There are, however, those who argue that such a policy also keeps in place the imbalances that cause the problems (such as ever-increasing growth in consumer borrowing and housing bubbles), and we'll return to that argument later in the book, but for now let's acknowledge that a boost in G provides a temporary boost in GDP. Elsewhere, we will show that the boost is indeed temporary, but few will argue that it does not make a short-term difference. We believe that the recent stimulus in the United States, as an example, did in fact have a temporary effect and kept the United States out of what might have been a depression, but not without its own costs. That debt must be repaid.*

Again, the idea is to try to offset the effects of a retrenching consumer and business sector and give the overall economy time to recover. The United States began to withdraw from the stimulus in the summer of 2010. And sure enough, the economy is slowing down. Only time will tell whether the economy is strong enough to return to a sustainable growth trajectory.

The hope is that with the stimulus you can give a jump-start to consumer final demand. In macroeconomics, **aggregate demand** is the total demand for final goods and services in the economy at a given time and price level. It is the amount of goods and services in the economy that will be purchased at all possible price levels. This is the demand for the gross domestic product (GDP) of a country when inventory levels are static.

Remember that for most developed economies consumer spending is the biggest part of the economy. In a recession, typically one or more parts of the economy, such as consumer spending and investment, retreat; therefore, the objective of stimulus is to get demand back on

---

*Some people like my friend Martin Barnes from BCA say government debt is never really repaid—it is in effect a giant Ponzi scheme. The way to avoid a crisis is to prevent the Ponzi scheme from spiraling out of control.

track. For economic theories that see final demand as the driving force behind growth, recessions are simply a problem of a lack of some part of our equation like consumer spending and/or investment. Get those back in gear, and the economy moves forward.

Now, in fairness to Keynes, he also asserted that governments should run surpluses in good times, something that most countries have not seemed to be able to do. In our view, one of the main faults of the Bush administration, in conjunction with a profligate Republican Congress, was that they squandered the surpluses that we now need. We will deal with Vice President Cheney's assertion that "deficits don't matter" in due course.

Before we go into the other, more profound implications of our equation, let's visit a few other topics that will give us needed insight into understanding the dynamics of our current economic quandary.

Delta Force

There are two, *and only two,* ways that you can grow your economy. You can either increase your (working-age) population or increase your productivity. That's it. There is no magic fairy dust you can sprinkle on an economy to make it grow. To increase GDP, you actually have to produce something. That's why it's called gross domestic *product.*

The Greek letter delta (Δ) is the symbol for change. So if you want to change your GDP you write that as:

$$\Delta GDP = \Delta Population + \Delta Productivity$$

That is, the change in GDP is equal to the change in population plus the change in productivity. Therefore—and I'm oversimplifying a bit here—a recession is basically a decrease in production (as normally, populations don't decrease).

There is one clear implication: If you want your economy to grow, you *must* have an economic environment that is friendly to increasing productivity.

While government can invest in industries in ways that are productive, empirical evidence and the preponderance of academic studies suggest that private companies are better at increasing productivity and producing long-term job growth.

Going to the United States for a second, studies show that business start-ups have produced nearly all the net new jobs over the last 20 years. Let's look at this analysis by Vivek Wadhwa.

> The Kauffman Foundation has done extensive research on job creation. Kauffman Senior Fellow Tim Kane analyzed a new data set from the U.S. government, called Business Dynamics Statistics, which provides details about the age and employment of businesses started in the U.S. since 1977. What this showed was that startups aren't just an important contributor to job growth: they're the only thing. [Figure 3.1] shows that most net jobs in the US were created by startups. Without startups, there would be no net job growth in the U.S. economy. From 1977 to 2005, existing companies were net job destroyers, losing 1 million net jobs per year. In contrast, new businesses in their first year added an average of 3 million jobs annually as [Figure 3.1] shows.

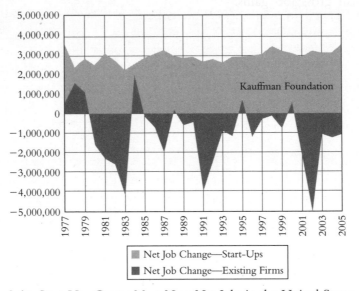

Figure 3.1   Start-Ups Create Most New Net Jobs in the United States

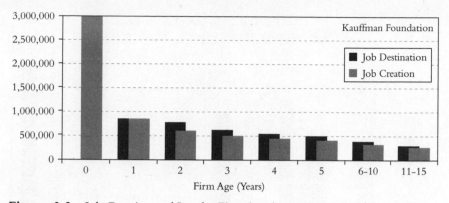

When analyzed by company age, the data are even more startling. Gross job creation at startups averaged more than 3 million jobs per year during 1992–2005, four times as high as any other yearly age group. [See Figure 3.2.] Existing firms in all year groups have gross job losses that are larger than gross job gains.

Half of the startups go out of business within five years; but overall they are still the ones that lead the charge in employment creation. Kauffman Foundation analyzed the average employment of all firms as they age from year zero (birth) to year five. When a given cohort of startups reaches age five, its employment level is 80 percent of what it was when it began. In 2000, for example, startups created 3,099,639 jobs. By 2005, the surviving firms had a total employment of 2,412,410, or about 78 percent of the number of jobs that existed when these firms were born.

So we can't count on the Intels or Microsofts to create employment: we need the entrepreneurs.[1]

This concept is borne out and enhanced by another study by the National Bureau of Economic Research, "Who Creates Jobs? Small vs. Large vs. Young?" by John C. Haltiwanger, Ron S. Jarmin, and Javier Miranda.[2]

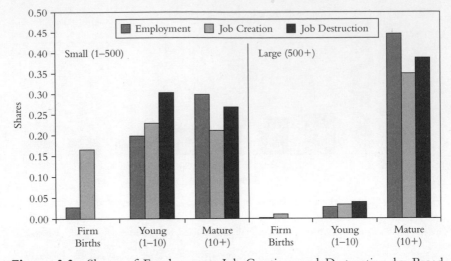

Figure 3.3 Shares of Employment, Job Creation, and Destruction by Broad Firm Size and Age Classes (annual average rates 1992–2005)

SOURCE: National Bureau of Economic Research, "Who Creates Jobs? Small vs. Large vs. Young?" by John C. Haltiwanger, Ron S. Jarmin, and Javier Miranda.

While there are certainly large firms that are adding jobs (Google, Apple, etc.), on *average* large firms (500-plus workers) are net destroyers of jobs. Figure 3.3 makes clear that it is start-ups that add the jobs that drive employment. We commend the study to you.

Run through the data from around the world. Where have the vast majority of long-term net new jobs come from, even in China? The private sector. And what is the mother's milk of the private sector? Money. Investments. Angel investors. Private banking. Private offerings. Public offerings. Loans. Personal savings. Money from friends and family. Borrowing against houses. Credit cards. And anything else that provides capital to business.*

---

*We are reminded of the improbable story of Fred Smith, the founder of FedEx, who early in the history of the company could not make payroll. So he flew to Las Vegas and wagered what little cash they had, and incredibly made enough ($27,000) to keep the company alive. Not exactly orthodox investment banking procedure, but it is illustrative of the crazy, gung-ho nature of some entrepreneurs. Between 50 and 80 percent of all business start-ups in the United States do not exist after five years, depending on your source for the data. We guess Fred figured he could get better odds in Vegas. Starting a business is fraught with peril. Getting the cash is one of the larger problems.

Want to increase productivity and jobs? The best way, it seems, is to encourage private business, especially start-ups.

Now let's go back to our first equation. You remember,

$$GDP = C + I + G + Net\ Exports$$

We will spare you the mathematical rigmarole, but if you play with this equation some, you come up with the following:

$$Savings = Investments$$

That is, the savings of consumers and business equal that which is available to business investment, which in turn helps to grow the economy. But there is a rather large *but*.

Those savings are also what finances government debt. Unless a central bank elects to print money, government debt must be financed by the private sector. That means, if the fiscal deficit is too large, it will crowd out private investment. But as we have seen, private investment is what fuels productivity growth, so if you don't have enough savings to satisfy private investment needs, you are choking off productivity growth and the creation of new jobs.

Japan is an instructive example. The government debt-to-GDP ratio has risen from 51 percent in 1990 to over 220 percent by the end of 2011, absorbing almost all of the rather enormous savings of the Japanese public. And what have they gotten for their largesse? Nominal GDP is where it was 17 years ago, and there have been no net new jobs for two decades. Think about that for a moment. In 1990, many pundits were proclaiming that Japan would overcome the United States in the near future. Now they have suffered two lost decades and are on their way to a third as government debt has absorbed whatever capital would have been available to private investment. (See our analysis of Japan further on.)

If you are a country facing a population decline (like Japan), to keep your GDP growing, you have to increase your productivity even more. That is why we have so much to say about demographics later in the book. Population growth (or the lack thereof) is very important. Russia is facing a very serious problem over the next 20 years that will require either a significant increase in productivity or large immigration to stave off a collapsing economy. Russia's population has declined by almost 7 million in the last 19 years, to 142 million. United Nations estimates are that it may shrink by about a third in the next 40 years. But that's a story for another book.*

Back to Vice President Cheney's famous assertion that "deficits don't matter." In one narrow sense, he is right. Let's play a thought game.

Suppose we start a business where the income grows by $100,000 a year every year. Assuming 5 percent interest rates, we could borrow $1 million every year and never really encounter a problem, as our income would be growing at twice the rate of debt service. We are running a deficit as a business (spending more than we make), but the deficit doesn't matter, since our profits and productivity increase more than the debt service. In 10 years, we owe $10 million, but we are making $1 million and could actually pay down the debt in less than 10 years if we stopped borrowing so much money.

For that business, deficits don't matter.

But what if interest rates rose to 10 percent and our profits dropped in half? Then, Houston, we have a big problem. Now our profits don't cover the interest payments. In fact, we have to borrow money just to make the interest payments. As long as friendly bankers cooperate, we can survive. And because we were so profitable for so long, they might just keep lending, assuming that things will get back to normal.

But at some point we need to start showing a profit, or they will stop making those loans and suggest we sell assets or even take them from us.

In that case, deficits matter a whole lot.

It is the same for countries. Governments cannot run deficits in excess of the growth in GDP without eventual consequences. As we will see in the chapter covering the research of Rogoff and Reinhart, things go along well until **Bang!** bond investors lose confidence in the ability of a government to pay its debt, even if that debt is denominated

---

*We are not against a healthy government sector. But when government becomes too big or absorbs too great a share of private savings, it chokes off productivity and growth. And that hurts job creation. That is especially true when a government runs large fiscal deficits.

in a currency the government can print! Bond investors become concerned that the currency will lose its value faster than the interest on the bond will grow. Then interest rates rise, making it even harder for the country to pay back its debt.

We all know about Greece, but let's look at the United States. Our fiscal deficit for 2010 is projected to be about 9 percent of nominal GDP (now roughly $14.3 trillion), down from 12 to 13 percent a short while ago. The Congressional Budget Office currently projects that the deficit will still be $1 trillion in 10 years. The Heritage Foundation thinks a more realistic estimate is closer to $2 trillion in just nine years as Figure 3.4 shows. Regardless of the eventual outcome, both numbers are very troubling.

Dr. Woody Brock has written a very important paper on why a country cannot grow government debt well above nominal GDP without causing severe disruptions to the overall economic system.[3]

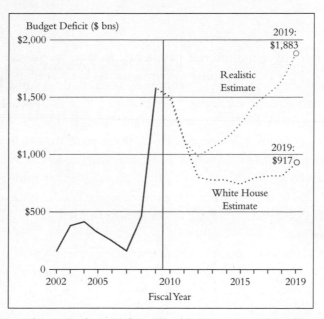

Figure 3.4 Obama Budget Deficit Would Bring Annual Budget Deficits to $2 Trillion

SOURCE: Heritage Foundation. Calculations based on data from the Congressional Budget Office and the U.S. Office of Management and Budget.

Table 3.1 Federal Debt Growth Scenario

		Debt Growing @ 8% and GDP @				
		−1%	1%	2%	3%	4%
2010	Debt (trillions)	$12	$12	$12	$12	$12
	GDP (trillions)	$14	$14	$14	$14	$14
	Debt ÷ GDP	0.9	0.9	0.9	0.9	0.9
2015	Debt (trillions)	$18	$18	$18	$18	$18
	GDP (trillions)	$13	$15	$15	$16	$17
	Debt ÷ GDP	1.3	1.2	1.1	1.1	1.0
2025	Debt (trillions)	$38	$38	$38	$38	$38
	GDP (trillions)	$12	$16	$19	$22	$25
	Debt ÷ GDP	3.2	2.3	2.0	1.7	1.5
2035	Debt (trillions)	$82	$82	$82	$82	$82
	GDP (trillions)	$11	$18	$23	$29	$37
	Debt ÷ GDP	7.5	4.6	3.6	2.8	2.2
2045	Debt (trillions)	$177	$177	$177	$177	$177
	GDP (trillions)	$10	$20	$28	$39	$55
	Debt ÷ GDP	18.0	8.9	6.3	4.5	3.2

SOURCE: Woody Brock.

We are going to reproduce just one table from that piece in Table 3.1. Note that this was Brock's worst-case assumption, adding 8 percent of GDP to the debt each year, and not the 9 to 12 percent we are experiencing today. The Congressional Budget Office long-range projections are growing worse with each estimate, and that assumes a very rosy 3 percent or more growth in the economy for each of the next five years. Under Brock's scenario, the national debt would rise to $18 trillion by 2015, or well over 100 percent of GDP. Take some time to study the tables, but note that we are going to focus on 2015 and not the outlier years.

Brock makes the assumption that U.S. debt will grow about $1.5 trillion a year. That means that by 2015, even assuming an average of 2 percent growth of the economy, the debt-to-GDP ratio would be 110 percent (or 1.1 in Brock's table).

And in just another 10 years, by 2025, if the deficit were not brought under control, debt-to-GDP would climb to 200 percent. Note that the Heritage Foundation suggests that, under current budgetary law, the deficit will grow by more than the $1.5 trillion a year that Brock projects, in the not too distant future.

The point here is not to predict some future catastrophe but to point out what can happen very quickly if deficits are not brought under control.

It is our contention that long before we ever get to that point (say 2020), the bond market will revolt, interest rates will rise, and the results will be very unpleasant. And that's for the United States. As we will see later in the book, without some serious intervention, that unpleasant ending could happen to a host of countries in the developed world.

Killing the Goose

Governments can increase their debt as long as the increase is less than the growth in nominal GDP. It may not be a wise choice to do so, but it does not kill the goose. That is why Cheney argued that deficits don't matter. The deficit he was commenting on was less than the growth in nominal GDP. We assume that he never thought we (in the United States) would see deficits of 12 percent (worse in some countries). But he should have.

Deficits matter because in good times it is helpful to run surpluses and pay down the debt so that there is room for a policy response in bad times. Running deficits all the time limits their use when you may need them most, as many countries are finding out. There are limits to what even the largest and most powerful nations can borrow. Those limits may seem a long way off, but they are there. And as we will see, there is no magic number that says the end is near. There is no way to determine when the crisis comes.

As the highly acclaimed work of Professors Rogoff and Reinhart (to which we later devote a whole chapter) shows:

> Highly indebted governments, banks, or corporations can seem to be merrily rolling along for an extended period, when **bang!**— confidence collapses, lenders disappear, and a crisis hits. (This is going to be a constant theme throughout the book. It is critical to understand the precarious nature of the bond markets!)[4]

Voters around the world are increasingly worried that governments are not only taxing the goose that lays the golden eggs but also risking the very life of the goose. And unchecked deficits do in fact risk the economic life of a country. You can get away with them for a while, but at some point you have to deal with them or risk becoming Greece. Or Argentina.

Let's look at another serious implication, again using the United States as our example.

A $1.5 trillion yearly increase in the national debt means that someone has to invest that much in Treasury bonds. Let's look at where the $1.5 trillion might come from. Let's assume that all of our trade deficit comes back to the United States and is invested in U.S. government bonds. That could be as much as $500 billion, although over time that number has been falling. That still leaves $1 trillion that needs to be found to be invested in U.S. government debt (forget about the financing needs for business and consumer loans and mortgages).

A trillion dollars is roughly 7 percent of total U.S. GDP. That is a staggering amount of money to find each and every year. And again, that assumes that foreigners continue to put 100 percent of their fresh reserves into dollar-denominated assets. That is not a safe assumption, given the recent news stories about how governments are thinking about creating an alternative to the dollar as a reserve currency. (And if we were watching the United States run $1.5 trillion deficits, with no realistic plans to cut back, we would be having private talks, too.)

There are only three sources for the needed funds: an increase in taxes, increased savings put into government bonds, or the Fed monetizing the debt, or some combination of all three.

Leaving aside the monetization of debt (for a later chapter on inflation), using taxes or savings to handle a large fiscal deficit reduces the amount of money available to private investment and therefore curtails the creation of new businesses and limits much-needed increases in productivity. That is the goose we will kill if we don't deal with our deficit.

But It's More Than the Deficit

We talked earlier about how increasing government debt crowds out the necessary savings for private investment, which is the real factor in

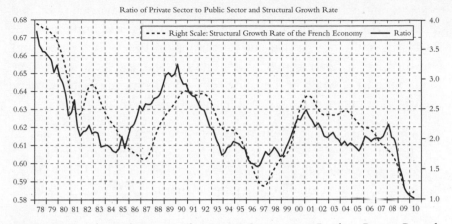

Figure 3.5 The Bad News Is That Bigger Government Leads to Lower Growth
SOURCE: GaveKal Research.

increasing productivity. But there is another part of that equation: the percentage of government spending in relationship to the overall economy. Let's look at some recent analysis by Charles Gave of GaveKal Research.

It seems that bigger government leads to slower growth. Figure 3.5 demonstrates the current situation in France, but the general principle holds across countries. It shows the ratio of the private sector to the public sector and relates it to growth. The correlation is high.

That is not to say that the best environment for growth is a 0 percent government. There is clearly a role for government, but there is a cost to the government sector that takes money away from the productive private sector. Not all private investment is productive, however—for example, housing in the 2000s!

Gave next shows us the ratio of the public sector to the private sector when compared with unemployment (again in France). While there are clearly some periods when there are clear divergences (and those would be even clearer in a U.S. chart), there is clear correlation over time.

And that makes sense with our argument that it is the private sector that increases productivity. Government transfer payments do not. You need a vibrant private sector and small businesses to really see growth in jobs.

At some point, government spending becomes an anchor on the economy. In an environment where assets (stocks and housing) have shrunk over the last decade and consumers in the United States and elsewhere are increasing their savings and reducing debt as retirement looms for a large swath of the aging baby boom generation, the current policies of stimulus make less and less sense. As Gave argues:

> This is the law of unintended consequences at work: if an individual receives US$100 from the government, and at the same time the value of his portfolio/house falls by US$500, what is the individual likely to do? Spend the US$100 or save it to compensate for the capital loss he has just had to endure and perhaps reduce his consumption even further?
>
> The only way that one can expect Keynesian policies to break the "paradox of thrift" is to make the bet that people are foolish, and that **they will disregard the deterioration in their balance sheets and simply look at the improvements in their income statements**.
>
> This seems unlikely. Worse yet, even if individuals are foolish enough to disregard their balance sheets, banks surely won't; policies that push asset prices lower are bound to lead to further contractions in bank lending. This is why "stimulating consumption" in the middle of a balance sheet recession (as Japan has tried to do for two decades) is worse than useless, **it is detrimental to a recovery**.
>
> With fragile balance sheets the main issue in most markets today, the last thing OECD governments should want to do is to boost income statement at the expense of balance sheets. This probably explains why, the more the US administration talks about a second stimulus bill, the weaker US retail sales, US housing and the US$ are likely to be. It probably also helps explain why US retail investor confidence today stands at a record low.[5]

This is the fundamental mistake that so many analysts and economists make about today's economic landscape. They assume that the recent recession and aftermath are like all past recessions since World

War II. A little Keynesian stimulus, and the consumer and business sectors get back on track. But it is a very different environment. It is the end of the debt supercycle. It is Mohamed El-Erian's new normal.

As we will see in a few chapters, the periods following credit and financial crises are substantially different, play out over years (if not decades), and are structural in nature and not merely cyclical recessions. And the policies needed by the government are different than in other cyclical recessions. We will go into those later in the book, as it differs from country to country. Business as normal is not the medicine we need, but it is what many countries are going to attempt.

Not Everyone Can Run a Surplus

The desire of every country is to somehow grow its way out of the current mess. And indeed that is the time-honored way for a country to heal itself. But let's look at yet another equation to show why that might not be possible this time. It is yet another case of people wanting to believe six impossible things before breakfast.

Let's divide a country's economy into three sections: private, government, and exports. If you play with the variables a little, you find that you get the following equation. Keep in mind this is an accounting identity, not a theory. If it is wrong, then five centuries of double-entry bookkeeping must also be wrong.

Domestic Private Sector Financial Balance + Governmental Fiscal Balance

− Current Account Balance (or Trade Deficit/Surplus) = 0

By domestic private sector financial balance, we mean the net balance of businesses and consumers. Are they borrowing money or paying down debt? Government fiscal balance is the same: Is the government borrowing or paying down debt? And the current account balance is the trade deficit or surplus.

The implications are simple. The three items have to add up to zero. That means you cannot have both surpluses in the private and government sectors and run a trade deficit. You have to have a trade surplus.

Let's make this simple. Let's say that the private sector runs a $100 surplus (they pay down debt), as does the government. Now, we subtract the trade balance. To make the equation come to zero, it means that there must be a $200 trade surplus.

$100 (private debt reduction) + $100 (government debt reduction)

— $200 (trade surplus) = 0

But what if the country wanted to run a $100 trade deficit? Then that means that either private or public debt would have to increase by $100. The numbers have to add up to zero. One way for that to happen would be:

$50 (private debt reduction) + (−$150)(government deficit)

— (−$100)(trade deficit) = 0

(Remember that we are adding a negative number and subtracting a negative number.)

Bottom line: It is the change in these things that matters, so you have a trade deficit but it must fall if you want to have more private investments. You can run a trade deficit, reduce government debt. and reduce private debt, but not all three at the same time. Choose two. Choose carefully. It is the relative changes in these three items that matter over time.

We are going to quote from a paper done by Rob Parenteau, the editor of *The Richebacher Letter,* to help us understand why this simple equation is so important. Rob was writing about the problems in Europe, but the principles are the same everywhere.

The question of fiscal sustainability looms large at the moment— not just in the peripheral nations of the eurozone, but also in the UK, the US, and Japan. More restrictive fiscal paths are being proposed in order to avoid rapidly rising government debt to GDP ratios, and the financing challenges they may entail, including the possibility of default for nations without sovereign currencies.

However, most of the analysis and negotiation regarding the appropriate fiscal trajectory from here is occurring in something of a vacuum. The financial balance approach reveals that this way of proceeding may introduce new instabilities. Intended changes to the financial balance of one sector can only be accomplished if the remaining sectors also adjust in a complementary fashion. Pursuing fiscal sustainability along currently proposed lines is likely to increase the odds of destabilizing the private sectors in the eurozone and elsewhere—unless an offsetting increase in current account balances can be accomplished in tandem.

. . . The underlying principle flows from the financial balance approach: the domestic private sector and the government sector cannot both deleverage at the same time unless a trade surplus can be achieved and sustained. Yet the whole world cannot run a trade surplus. More specific to the current predicament, we remain hard pressed to identify which nations or regions of the remainder of the world are prepared to become consistently larger net importers of Europe's tradable products. Countries currently running large trade surpluses view these as hard won and well deserved gains. They are unlikely to give up global market shares without a fight, especially since they are running export led growth strategies. Then again, it is also said that necessity is the mother of all invention (and desperation, its father?), so perhaps current account deficit nations will find the product innovations or the labor productivity gains that can lead to growing the market for their tradable products. In the meantime, for the sake of the citizens in the peripheral eurozone nations now facing fiscal retrenchment, pray there is life on Mars that exclusively consumes olives, red wine, and Guinness beer.[6]

This has profound implications for those countries struggling to deal with large government deficits, large trade deficits, and a desire on the part of individuals and businesses to reduce their debt while wanting the government to curtail its spending. Something in that quest has to give.

The time-honored (and preferred) way a country digs itself out from a debt or financial crisis is for a country to grow its way out of the problem. And that is what Martin Wolf, the highly regarded columnist for the *Financial Times* in London, suggests that Great Britain should do.

Wolf argues (rather cogently) that the answer is to increase exports and for a further weakening of the pound. Quoting:

> Weak sterling, far from being the problem, is a big part of the solution. But it will not be enough. Attention must also be paid to nurturing a more dynamic manufacturing sector. With the decline in energy production under way, this is now surely inescapable.[7]

When Martin Wolf writes, he reflects what the cognoscenti of Britain are thinking. The pound is already down by 25 percent against the dollar as we write. We think it could go down even further. John has long been on public record that the pound could reach parity with the dollar (when the pound was much stronger) and before the Fed decided to go down the path of Quantitative Easing 2 (QE2), which is essentially a potential devaluation of the dollar.

How can Britain accomplish this? The Bank of England will have to print more money to help the current deficit crisis even as the government institutes austerity measures. We see that hand waving in the back. The question is, "Wouldn't that be inflationary?"

Of course it would. That's the plan. A little inflation, along with decreasing deficits, will result in a weaker currency and therefore (hopefully) more exports. In this way, England will grow its way out of the crisis. Of course, inflation means one can buy less with the domestic currency, especially from foreign markets. Those on fixed incomes get hurt, and maybe even savagely hurt, depending on the level of inflation, but the hope is that it will be mild inflation spread out over time, which is better for people (and governments) who are indebted.

Here is their dilemma. To reduce the government's fiscal deficit, either private business must increase their deficits, the trade balance has to shift, or some combination. It is lucky for the United Kingdom that it can, in fact, allow the pound to drift lower by monetizing some of their debt—lucky in the sense that they can at least find a path out of their morass. Of course, that means that pound-denominated assets might drop by another third against the dollar. It means that the buying power of British citizens for foreign goods is crushed. British citizens on pensions in foreign countries could see their locally denominated incomes drop by half from their peak (well, not against the euro, which is also in free fall).

What's the alternative? Keep running those massive deficits until ever-increasing borrowing costs blow a hole in your economy, reducing your currency valuation anyway. Remember that if you reduce government spending, in the short run, it will act as a drag on the economy, so you are guaranteeing slower growth in the short run. As I have been pointing out for a long time, countries around the world are down to no good choices.

Britain's economic path could include a much slower economy (maybe another recession), much lower buying power for the pound, and lower real incomes for its workers, yet they have a path that they can get back on track in a few years. Because they have control of their currency and their debt, which is mostly in their own currency, they can devalue their way to a solution.

Pity the Greeks

Some of my fondest memories were made in Greece. I like the country and the people. But they have made some bad choices and now must deal with the consequences.

We all know that Greek government deficits are somewhere around 14 percent. But their trade deficit is running north of 10 percent. (By comparison, the U.S. trade deficit is now about 4 percent.)

Going back to the equation, if Greece wants to reduce its fiscal deficit by 11 percent over the next three years, then either private debt must increase or the trade deficit must drop sharply. Those are the accounting rules.

But here's the problem. Greece cannot devalue its currency. It is (for now) stuck with the euro. So how can they make their products more competitive? How do they grow their way out of their problems? How do they become more productive relative to the rest of Europe and the world?

Barring some new productivity boost in olive oil and produce production, there is no easy way. Since the beginning of the euro in 1999, Germany has become some 30 percent more productive than Greece. Very roughly, that means it costs 30 percent more to produce the same amount of goods in Greece than in Germany. That is why Greece imports $64 billion of goods and exports only $21 billion.

What needs to happen for Greece to become more competitive? Labor costs must fall by a lot, and not by just 10 or 15 percent. But if labor costs drop (deflation), then that means that taxes also drop. The government takes in less, and GDP drops. The perverse situation is that the debt-to-GDP ratio gets worse, even as they enact their austerity measures.

In short, Greek lifestyles are on the line. They are going to fall. They have no choice. They are going to willingly have to put themselves into a severe recession or, more realistically, a depression.

Just as British incomes relative to their competitors will fall, Greek labor costs must fall as well. But the problem for Greeks is that the costs they bear are still in euros. It becomes a most vicious spiral. The more cuts they make, the less income there is to tax, which means less government revenue, which means more cuts, and so on.

And the solution is to borrow more money they cannot at the end of the day hope to pay. All that is happening is that the day of reckoning is delayed in the hope for some miracle.

What are their choices? They can simply default on the debt. Stop making any payments. That means they cannot borrow any more money for a minimum of a few years (Argentina seemed to be able to come back fairly quickly after default), but it would go a long way toward balancing the government budget. Government employees would need to take large pay cuts, and there would be other large cuts in services. It would be a depression, but you work your way out of it. You are still in the euro and need to figure out how to become more competitive.

Or you could take the austerity, downsize your labor costs, and borrow more money, which means even larger debt service in a few years. Private citizens can go into more debt. (Remember, we have to have our balance!) This is also a depression.

Finally, you could leave the euro, which implies a devaluation. This is a very ugly scenario, as contracts are in euros. The legal bills would go on forever.

There are no good choices for the Greeks. No easy way. And then you wonder why people worry about contagion to Portugal and Spain?

We see that hand asking another question: Since the euro is falling, won't that make Greece more competitive? The answer is yes and no. Yes, relative to the dollar and a lot of emerging market currencies but not to the rest of the European countries, which are their main trading partners. A falling euro just makes economic export power Germany and the other northern countries even more competitive.

Europe as a whole has a small trade surplus. But the bulk of it comes from a few countries. For Greece to reduce its trade deficit is a very large lifestyle change.

Germany is basically saying you should be like us. And everyone wants to be. Just not everyone can.

Every country cannot run a trade surplus. Someone has to buy. But the prescription that politicians want is for fiscal austerity and trade surpluses, at least for European countries. That is the import of Martin Wolf's editorial we quoted previously. He is as wired in as you get in Britain. And in a few short sentences, he laid out the formula that Britain will pursue. Devalue and put your goods and services on sale. Figure out how to get to that surplus.

Germany has been thriving because much of Europe has been buying its goods. If the rest of Europe is forced by circumstances to buy less, that will not be good for Germany. It's all connected.

Yet politicians want to believe that somehow we all can run surpluses, at least in their country. We can balance the budgets. We can reduce our private debts. We all want to believe in that mythical Lake Woebegone, where all the kids are above average. Sadly, it just isn't possible for everyone to have a happy ending.

Before we leave this part of the chapter, here are a few thoughts about the situation in the United States. The mood in the country, if not in Washington (at least before the elections last November), is that the deficit needs to be brought down. Consumers are clearly increasing savings and cutting back on debt. But those accounts must balance. If we want to reduce the deficits *and* reduce our personal debt, we must then find a way to reduce the trade deficit, which is running about $500 billion a year as we write, or about $1 trillion less than the deficit.

First off, saving more, as we think likely, will mean less spending and thus fewer imports over time. But if the United States is going to really attempt to balance the budget over time, reduce our personal leverage, and save more, then we have to address the glaring need to import $300 billion in oil (give or take, depending on the price of oil).

This can only partially be done by offshore drilling. The real key is to reduce the need for oil. Nuclear power, renewables, and a shift to electric cars will be most helpful. Let us suggest something a little more radical. When the price of oil approached $4 a few years ago, Americans changed their driving and car-buying habits.

Perhaps we need to see the price of oil rise. What if we increased the price of oil with an increase in gas taxes by 2 or 3 cents a gallon each and every month until the demand for oil dropped to the point where we did not need foreign oil? If we had European gas mileage standards, that would be the case now.

And take that 2 or 3 cents and dedicate it to fixing our infrastructure, which is badly in need of repair. In fact, the U.S. Infrastructure Report Card (www.infrastructurereportcard.org) grades the United States on a variety of factors (and the link has a very informative short video). Done by the American Society of Civil Engineers, the 2009 grades include:

Aviation (D)	Hazardous Waste (D)	Roads (D−)
Bridges (C)	Inland Waterways (D−)	Schools (D)
Dams (D)	Levees (D−)	Solid Waste (C+)
Drinking Water (D−)	Public Parks and Recreation (C−)	Transit (D)
Energy (D+)	Rail (C−)	Wastewater (D−)

Overall, America's infrastructure GPA was graded a D. To get to an A requires a five-year infrastructure investment of $2.2 trillion.

That infrastructure has to be paid for, and we need to buy less oil. We know price makes a difference, and the majority of that 2 or 3 cents needs to stay in the United States, where it was taxed, and forbidden to be used on anything other than infrastructure. (And while we are at it, why not build 50 nuclear plants now? We'll get into this and more when we get to the chapter on the way back for the United States.)

The Competitive Currency Devaluation Raceway

Greg Weldon described the competitive currency devaluations in Asia in the middle of the last decade as similar to that of a NASCAR race. Each country tried to get in the draft of the other countries, keeping their currency and selling power more or less in line as they tried to market their products to the United States and Europe. This is a form of mercantilism, where countries encourage exports and, by reducing the value of their currencies, discourage imports. It also helps explain the massive current account surpluses building up in emerging market countries, especially in Asia.

There is the real potential for this race to become far more competitive. Indeed, Martin Wolf's few sentences are the equivalent of the NASCAR announcer saying, "Gentlemen, start your engines."

We touched on Britain. But there are structural weaknesses in the euro as well (again, discussed in later chapters). In the early part of the last decade, when the euro was at $0.88, John wrote that the euro would rise to $1.50 (seemingly unattainable at the time) and then fall back to parity with the dollar by the middle of this decade. He was an optimist, as the euro went to $1.60 but is now retracing that rise.

The title for the chapter on Japan is "A Bug in Search of a Windshield." While the currency of the Land of the Rising Sun is very strong as we write, there are real structural reasons, as well as political ones, that lead us to predict that the yen will begin to weaken. At first, it will be gradual. But without real reform in government expenditures, the yen could weaken substantially. A fall of 50 percent or more against the dollar by the middle of this decade (if not sooner) is quite thinkable.

The euro at parity. The pound at parity. The value of the yen cut in half. What is the response of emerging market countries around the world? Do they sit by and allow their currencies to rise and make it more difficult to compete with Europe and Japan? The Swiss are clearly not happy with the rise of the Swiss franc. The Scandinavian countries? The rest of Asia?

And now the Fed is embarking on QE2 under the guise of fighting deflation and a possible slowing of the economy into recession, but one of the outcomes will be a lower dollar as we put our own car into the competitive devaluation raceway. And as long as the Fed is printing, all bets are off as to who will win the race to the bottom.

And what of China? Europe is an extremely important market to them. Do they sit by and let their currency rise (a lot!) against the euro and hurt their exports? But if they react, then that makes the United States unhappy and starts another competitive devaluation throughout Asia.

What does the United States do? Its senators are mad enough about the valuation of the Chinese yuan. Do Schumer, Graham, and colleagues start talking about tariffs on European goods? On Japanese goods?

The United States and the world went into a deep recession in the early 1930s, but it took the protectionist Smoot-Hawley Act to stretch it out into a prolonged recession. It was a beggar-thy-neighbor policy that swept the world. It was disastrous and sowed the seeds for World War II. There was an unintended consequence on every page of that bill.

In a few years, the world will be at a significant risk of protectionist policies damaging world trade. Let us hope that cool heads will be at the forefront and avoid the policies that so clearly would hurt all.

Final Thoughts . . .

This chapter has been a kind of introduction to the macroeconomic forces that are at play in the world in which we find ourselves. While much of the developed world has no good choices, we (each country on its own) still must decide on a path forward. We can choose between bad choices and what will be disastrous choices. We can make the best of what we have created and move on. If we make the correct choices to solve the structural problems, we can emerge with a brighter future for ourselves and our children. If we choose to avoid the problems, we will hit the wall in spectacular and dramatic fashion.

As Ollie said to Stan (Laurel and Hardy), "Here's another nice mess you've gotten me into!" A nice mess indeed!

And now, let's spend the next few chapters examining some of the problems we face.

CHAPTER FOUR

The Burden of Lower Growth and More Frequent Recessions

My best guess is that we'll have a continued recovery, but it won't feel terrific. Even though technically we'll be in recovery and the economy will be growing, unemployment will still be high for a while and that means that a lot of people will be under financial stress.
—Benjamin Bernanke, Chairman of the Federal Reserve
in a Q&A at the Woodrow Wilson International
Center for Scholars

W e're optimists by nature. The natural order of the world is growth. Trees tend to grow, and economies do, too. Real economic growth solves most problems and is the best antidote to high deficits, but the problems that we have now won't be solved by growth. They're simply too big. Unless we have another Industrial Revolution or another profound technological revolution like electrification in the 1920s or the IT revolution in the 1990s, we will not be able to grow enough to pull ourselves out of the debt hole we're in.

After the dot-com bust in 2000, the phrase "the muddle through economy" (a term coined by John) best described the U.S. economic situation. The economy would indeed be growing, but the growth would be below the long-term trend (which in the United States is about 3.3 percent) for the rest of the decade. (Indeed, growth for the decade was an anemic 1.9 percent annualized, the weakest decade since the Great Depression. Muddle through, indeed.)

The muddle through economy would be more susceptible to recession. It would be an economy that would move forward burdened with the heavy baggage of old problems while facing the strong headwinds of new challenges. The description of the world was accurate then, and it is even more accurate now.

In March 2009, when almost everyone was predicting the apocalypse, it was hard to see how things could improve. The GDP turned around, industrial production has shot up, retail sales have bounced back, and the stock market rebounded strongly. Everything has turned up. However, GDP growth is slowing in the United States as we write in November 2010. Compared with previous recoveries, growth does not look that great, and people don't feel the recovery. This is unlikely to change.

The muddle through economy is the product of a few major structural breaks in the world's economies that have important implications for growth, jobs, and when we might see a recession again. The U.S. and most developed economies are currently facing many major headwinds that will mean that going forward, we'll have slower economic growth, more recessions, and higher unemployment. All of these are hugely important for endgame since they vastly complicate policy making.

Lower growth will make our fiscal choices that much scarier. Importantly, these big changes also mean that governments, pension funds, and even private savers are probably making unreasonably rosy assumptions about how quickly the economy and asset prices will be able to increase in the future. As endgame unfolds, the reality of these big changes will set in.

Three Structural Changes

Investors are good at absorbing short-term information, but they are much less successful at absorbing bigger structural trends and understanding when secular breaks have occurred. Perhaps investors are like the proverbial frogs in the frying pan and do not notice long, slow changes around them.

There are three large structural changes that have happened slowly over time that we expect to continue going forward. The U.S. economy will have:

1. Higher volatility
2. Lower trend growth
3. Higher structural levels of unemployment (The United States here is a proxy for many developed countries with similar problems, so much of this chapter applies elsewhere.)

1. *Higher Volatility*

Before the crash of October 2008, the world was living in "the great moderation," a phrase coined by Harvard economist James Stock to describe the change in economic variables in the mid-1980s, such as GDP, industrial production, monthly payroll employment, and the unemployment rate, which all began to show a decline in volatility. As Figures 4.1 and 4.2 from the Federal Reserve Bank of Dallas show, the early 1980s in fact constituted a structural break in macroeconomic volatility.

The GDP became a lot less volatile.

As did employment.

The great moderation was seductive, and government officials, hedge fund managers, bankers, and even journalists believed "this time is different." Journalists like Gerard Baker of the *Times of London* wrote in January 2007:

> Welcome to "the Great Moderation": Historians will marvel at the stability of our era.
>
> Economists are debating the causes of the Great Moderation enthusiastically and, unusually, they are in broad agreement.

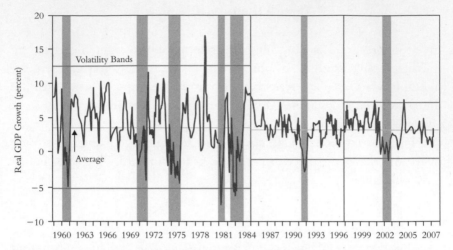

Figure 4.1 GDP Growth Volatility Dropped Off Sharply in the 1980s

NOTE: Shaded areas denote recessions.

SOURCE: Federal Reserve Bank of Dallas, Bureau of Economic Analysis, National Bureau of Economic Research.

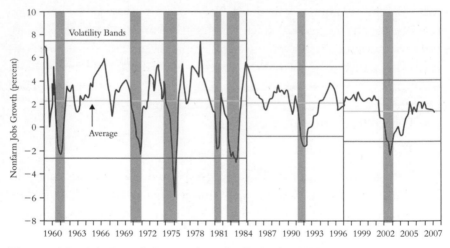

Figure 4.2 Job Growth Dropped Markedly in the 1990s

NOTE: Shaded areas denote recessions.

SOURCE: Federal Reserve Bank of Dallas, Bureau of Labor Statistics, National Bureau of Economic Research.

Good policy has played a part: central banks have got much better at timing interest rate moves to smooth out the curves of economic progress. But the really important reason tells us much more about the best way to manage economies.

It is the liberation of markets and the opening-up of choice that lie at the root of the transformation. The deregulation of financial markets over the Anglo-Saxon world in the 1980s had a damping effect on the fluctuations of the business cycle.... The economies that took the most aggressive measures to free their markets reaped the biggest rewards.[1]

In retrospect, this line of thinking looks hopelessly optimistic, even deluded. We do not write this to pick on Gerard Baker, but rather to point out that low volatility breeds complacency and increased risk taking. The greater predictability in economic and financial performance led hedge funds to hold less capital and to be less concerned with the liquidity of their positions.

Those heady days are now over, and we have now entered "the great immoderation." One can confidently say that 2008 represents a structural break, moving back toward a period of greater volatility. Robert F. Engle, a finance professor at New York University who was the Nobel laureate in economics in 2003, has shown that periods of greatest volatility are predictable. Market sessions with particularly good or bad returns don't occur randomly but tend to be clustered together. The market's behavior illustrates this clustering. Volatility follows the credit cycle like night follows day, and periods following credit booms are marked by high volatility, for example, 2000–2003 and 2007–2008.

The period of low volatility of GDP, industrial production, and initial unemployment claims is now over. For a period of more than 20 years, excluding the brief 2001–2002 recession, volatility of real economic data was extremely low, as Figure 4.3 shows.

Going forward, higher economic volatility, combined with a secular downtrend in economic growth, will create more frequent recessions. This is likely to lead to more market volatility as well.

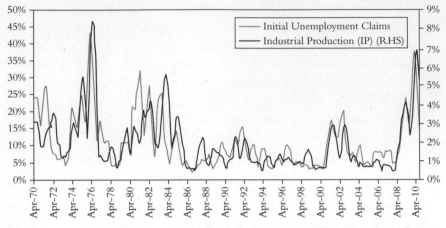

Figure 4.3 Year-over-Year Volatility of the Business Cycle, Industrial Production, and Claims
SOURCE: Bloomberg, Variant Perception.

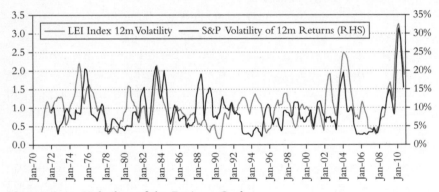

Figure 4.4 Volatility of the Business Cycle
SOURCE: Bloomberg, Variant Perception.

You can measure economic volatility in a variety of ways. Our preferred way is on a forward-looking basis. We have seen the highest volatility in the last 40 years across leading indicators, as Figure 4.4 shows. These typically lead the economic cycle. This only means one thing, higher volatility going forward.

For far too long, volatility was low and bred investor complacency. Going forward, we can expect a lot more economic and market volatility. We have had a strong cyclical upturn, but we will continue to face major structural headwinds. This means more frequent recessions and resultant higher volatility.

If we look at Japan following the Nikkei bust in 1989, we can see that volatility increased. Note that before the peak in the Nikkei, volatility had been largely subdued, with periodic movements corresponding to increases in the level of the market. As Figure 4.5 shows, following the crash, stock market volatility increased markedly, and volatility to the downside became far more prevalent.

Equity volatility follows the credit cycle. If you push commercial and industrial (C&I) loans forward two years, it predicts increases in the Market Volatility Index (VIX) almost down to the month. We should expect heightened episodes of volatility for the next two years at a minimum. (See Figure 4.6.)

Fixed-income volatility also follows the credit cycle with a three-year lag. Figure 4.7 shows how the Fed Funds rate lags Merrill Lynch's MOVE Index, which is a measure of fixed-income volatility, by three years.

Another very good reason to believe we'll continue to have high volatility even after we recover from the hangover of the credit binge is that the world is now much more integrated. This is a paradox and may

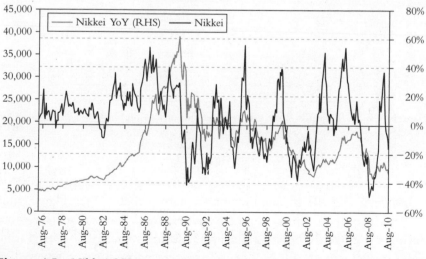

Figure 4.5   Nikkei 225
SOURCE: Bloomberg, Variant Perception.

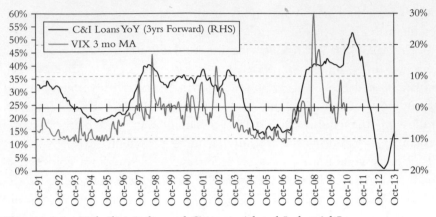

Figure 4.6 Volatility Index and Commercial and Industrial Loans
SOURCE: Bloomberg, Variant Perception.

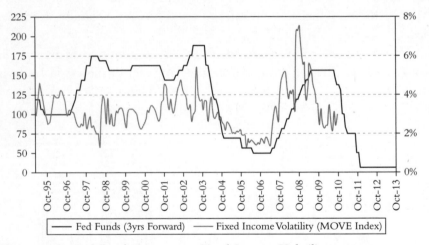

Figure 4.7 Fed Funds Rate versus Fixed-Income Volatility
SOURCE: Bloomberg, Variant Perception.

seem hard to believe, but increased globalization actually makes the world more volatile through extended supply chains! (See Figure 4.8.)

Production in Japan, Germany, Korea, and Taiwan fell far more during the 2007–2009 recession than U.S. production fell even during the Great Depression. Not only was the downturn steeper than during the Great Depression but also the bounce back was even bigger.

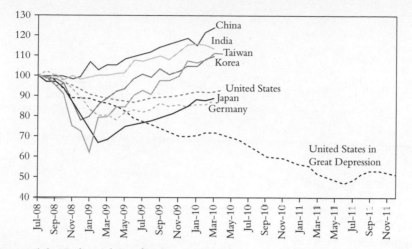

Figure 4.8 Industrial Production in Key Economies (2008 = 100) and U.S. Great Depression (1929 = 100)

SOURCE: ECRI, www.businesscycle.com/news/press/1870/.

This is truly staggering. If you believed in globalization, supply chain management, and deregulation, you would have thought they would lead to greater moderation, but the opposite happened. This was due to the credit freeze that particularly hit export-oriented economies because trade credit temporarily dried up. It was not about globalization per se.

Why has the world economy been so volatile? One of the main reasons is exports. If you look at exports as a percentage of GDP since the end of the Cold War, you'll see that in almost all countries around the world, exports have rapidly risen in the last 20 years. In Asia, they have doubled, in India they have tripled, and in the United States they have increased by 50 percent. This makes us all more inter-connected, and it means that supply chains become longer and longer.

Longer supply chains have enormous macroeconomic implications. As the Economic Cycle Research Institute points out, we're now experiencing the bullwhip effect, "where relatively mild fluctuations in end demand are dramatically amplified up the supply chain, just as a flick of the wrist sends the tip of a bullwhip flying in a great arc."[2]

The bullwhip effect makes greater export dependence very dangerous to supplier countries, which only contributes to cyclical volatility. This is easily seen in Figure 4.9. That is why Asian countries had

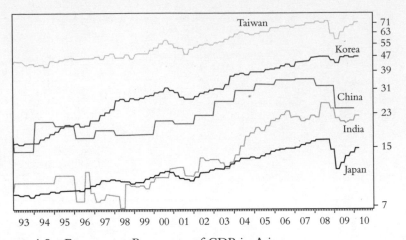

Figure 4.9   Exports as a Percentage of GDP in Asia
SOURCE: ECRI, www.businesscycle.com/news/press/1870/.

some of the largest downturns and steepest upturns in the Great Recession and the following recovery.

2. Lower Trend Growth

We are also seeing a secular decline over the last four cycles in trend growth across GDP, personal income, industrial production, and employment. You can see that in Figure 4.10.

Another view of declining trend growth is the decline in nominal GDP. Figure 4.11 shows that the 12-quarter rolling average has been on a steady decline for the last two decades.

A combination of lower trend growth and higher volatility means more frequent recessions. Put another way, the closer trend growth is to zero and the higher volatility is, the more likely U.S. growth is to frequently dip below zero. Figure 4.12 shows a stylized view of recessions, but as trend growth dips, the economy will fall below zero percent growth more often.

Higher volatility has very important implications for equity and bond investors across asset classes. Indeed, the last three economic expansions were almost 10 years, but in previous decades, they averaged four or five years. From now on, we are apt to see recessions every three to five years.

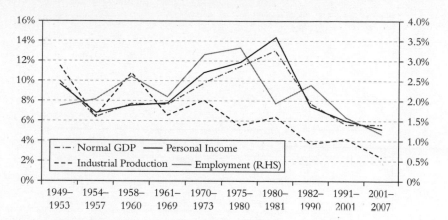

Figure 4.10   Annual Growth of Indicators through Expansions
SOURCE: Bloomberg, Variant Perception.

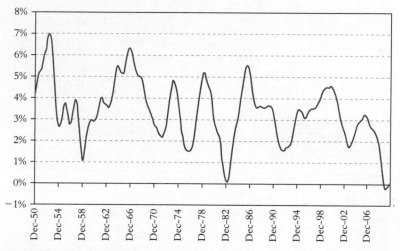

Figure 4.11   Twelve-Quarter Average of U.S. Nominal GDP, Year-over-Year
SOURCE: Bloomberg, Variant Perception.

3. Higher Levels of Structural Unemployment

There is a growing disparity in unemployment rates between the well-educated and the poorly educated, between the haves and have-nots. This is a structural shift that began before the recession and has grown only stronger during the recession. The disparity in the unemployment situation is far more dramatic if you look at the breakdown of

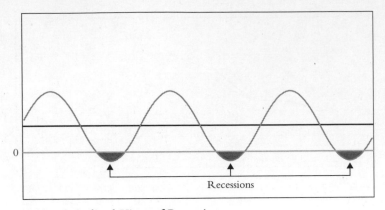

Figure 4.12   A Stylized View of Recessions
SOURCE: ECRI, www.businesscycle.com/news/press/1870/.

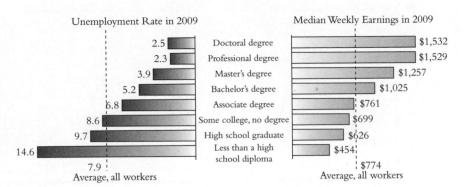

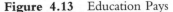

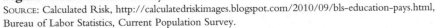

Figure 4.13   Education Pays
SOURCE: Calculated Risk, http://calculatedriskimages.blogspot.com/2010/09/bls-education-pays.html,
Bureau of Labor Statistics, Current Population Survey.

unemployment rates by educational attainment. Indeed, you can see
that unemployment rates and average hourly wages correlate very well
by income level. (See Figure 4.13.)

The clear problem in the United States is this: If the highly skilled
have 2.5 percent unemployment, how do you reduce that? You can't.
That is probably the natural frictional rate of unemployment, that is,
people naturally moving between jobs or geographies. Faster economic
growth or more money supply won't bring down a 2.5 percent
unemployment rate.

The question then is why the unskilled unemployment rate is so high. In part, the answer is emergency benefits. In the depths of the recession in March 2009, 3.9 million people were hired and 4.7 million were fired. That gives us a loss of 800,000 jobs in one month, but notice that *3.9 million people were hired!* So the economy produces jobs. The issue is at what price does labor clear. In a globalized economy, wages are falling for the unskilled as they compete with cheaper labor from abroad in China, India, Indonesia, and beyond. No politician wants to admit low-end wages are too high. So policy makers have relied on debt and income transfers to mask this. This is why monetary policy has been too loose for too long. If all you have is a hammer, everything looks like a nail.

Looking at unemployment by length of time unemployed also shows growing divergences, as Figure 4.14 shows.

There are clear trends developing. Those who have attained a higher level of education are not suffering to nearly the same extent as those on the lower end of the educational scale. Indeed, conditions for certain higher skilled workers could be described as tight.

Furthermore, those who find themselves out of work are on average out of work longer. The average time of unemployment has sharply increased from less than 20 weeks only two years ago, to more than 30 weeks now—a 50 percent increase. Those unemployed for shorter lengths of time now make up much less of the total than they used to.

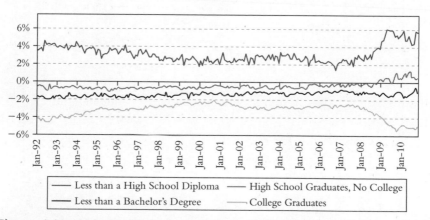

Figure 4.14 U.S. Unemployment Rate by Educational Level above/below Overall Employment Rate
SOURCE: Bloomberg, Variant Perception.

The majority of unemployed workers are instead primarily those in a chronic state of joblessness. Such people find it ever harder to get back into employment as their skills become rusty.

This phenomenon is not confined to the United States. A similar pattern is developing in the United Kingdom, as Figure 4.15 shows.

There are two main types of unemployment: structural and cyclical. In this downturn, we have seen fewer hours worked and lower pay; these are cyclical. More ominously, though, has been the structural decline in the civilian participation rate. There has been an extreme rise in the number of long-term unemployed, who now make up almost 3.5 percent of the labor force. Because the U.S. economy needs to shift from consumption, real estate, and finance toward manufacturing, many of the unemployed will not return to their old jobs. Indeed, the unemployment rate for those permanently laid off reached an all-time high of 5.5 percent in the month of September.

The structural problems with unemployment are also reflected in the very large gap between the official unemployment rate and the actual rate of people out of work, as Figure 4.17 shows.

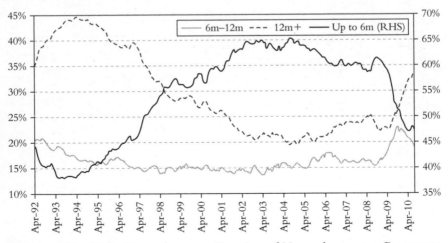

Figure 4.15 U.K. Unemployment: Duration of Unemployment as Percentage of Total Unemployed
SOURCE: Bloomberg, Variant Perception.

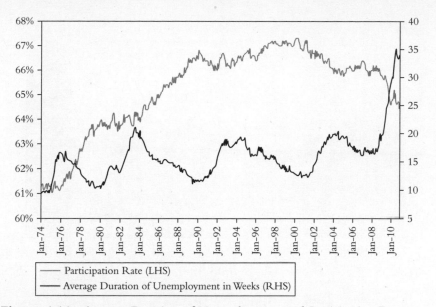

Figure 4.16   Average Duration of Unemployment and Participation Rate
SOURCE: Bloomberg, Variant Perception.

Lower Growth, Fewer Jobs, Bigger Deficits, Lower Returns

What do we get when we put the three structural breaks together? Higher volatility and lower trend growth produce more frequent recessions. More frequent recessions and stubbornly high unemployment rates mean that the recovery will not be long-lasting enough to put everyone back to work who would like to work. This in large part explains why high unemployment currently is so problematic.

For unskilled workers, this means the news is not great. If you can stick with a job, do. The longer you are unemployed, the less likely you are to find another job. As Bernanke has pointed out, the longer you are outside the workforce, the rustier your skills get and the less likely you are to be employed.

The muddle through economy has important implications for investors. Investors will have to adjust to this new reality. Reducing leverage is one way. Another is to reduce the average holding period of

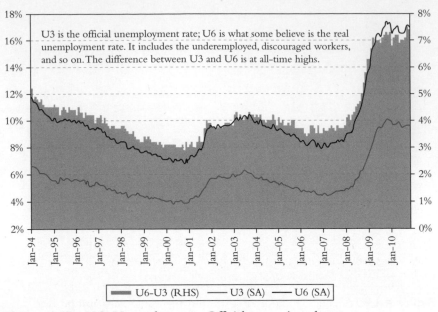

Figure 4.17 U.S. Unemployment: Official versus Actual
Source: Bloomberg, Variant Perception.

investments. Investors have to become nimbler. This in itself may add to market volatility.

For longer-term investors, this change of paradigm means that achieving consistent solid returns becomes even more difficult. Investors with a shorter-term, more tactical outlook may find these new, more volatile conditions a source of great opportunities.

What do more frequent recessions and higher structural unemployment mean for politicians and central bankers? Sadly, it probably means that we'll see more frequent stimulus measures to fight recessions, as well as more unconventional monetary measures on the part of the Fed. This means oceans more of red ink and the potential for the Fed to monetize government debt—that is, print money—unless we change the way Congress operates.

Lower growth rates only complicate an already difficult fiscal situation. According to the Committee on the Fiscal Future of the United States, "Over the long term, three major programs—Medicare, Medicaid, and Social Security—account for the projected faster growth in federal spending relative to revenues. No reasonably foreseeable rate of economic growth would overcome this structural deficit. Thus, any efforts to rein in future deficits must entail either large increases in taxes to support these programs or major restraints on their growth—or some combination of the two."[3] That is a very polite way of saying that anyone who is counting on receiving the same safety net and social programs that our parents are receiving at the current tax levels is terribly deluded. In part, entitlement programs are too generous given their financing, but lower growth will only make the situation that much worse.

If growth and employment were to come back, our problems would be much smaller. More employees would mean more payroll taxes, and more taxes would mean lower government debt and a natural deleveraging through growth. Unfortunately, we don't have any easy solutions. Any way you look at it, we will not be able to find an easy way out of our problems.

CHAPTER FIVE

This Time Is Different

Our immersion in the details of crises that have arisen over the past eight centuries and in data on them has led us to conclude that the most commonly repeated and most expensive investment advice ever given in the boom just before a financial crisis stems from the perception that "this time is different." That advice, that the old rules of valuation no longer apply, is usually followed up with vigor. Financial professionals and, all too often, government leaders explain that we are doing things better than before, we are smarter, and we have learned from past mistakes. Each time, society convinces itself that the current boom, unlike the many booms that preceded catastrophic collapses in the past, is built on sound fundamentals, structural reforms, technological innovation, and good policy.
— Carmen M. Reinhart and Kenneth Rogoff,
This Time Is Different

Capitalism without failure is like religion without sin.
— Charles Kindleberger, *Manias, Panics and Crashes*

When does a potential crisis become an actual crisis, and how and why does it happen? Why did almost everyone believe there were no problems in the U.S. (or Japanese or European or British) economies in 2006? Yet now we are mired in a very difficult situation. "The subprime problem will be contained," said Fed

Chairman Bernanke, just months before the implosion and significant Fed intervention.

This chapter will attempt to distill the data assembled and the wisdom contained in a very important book by Professors Carmen Reinhart (of the University of Maryland) and Ken Rogoff (of Harvard University), which has catalogued more than 250 financial crises in 66 countries over 800 years and then analyzed them for differences and similarities.[1] The database the authors have assembled is a first. What it does is allow us to see what has actually happened in a crisis rather than making assumptions (which assume away the real world—a favorite pastime of economists) or using theories that don't seem to work out in the real world.

Rogoff was at the International Monetary Fund as the chief economist and director of research, and he persuaded Reinhart to join him as deputy director. It was the beginning of a collaboration in the exploration of the history of debt and crises that has given us so much new material. It is difficult to overstate the importance of this book, as heretofore we dealt with anecdotal evidence about crises. Their assembled data is a treasure trove of knowledge. The authors have conveniently organized the book so that one can read the first and the last five chapters, purposefully allowing people to get the main points without drilling into the mountain of details they provide. We strongly suggest you get the book and read it! Our summary in no way does justice to the sweep and scope of the book.

This is also a *very* sobering book. It does not augur well as for the ability of the developed world to blithely exit from our woes. *This Time Is Different* gives evidence to one of the main points of this book: that we have a lot of pain to experience because of the bad choices we have made. This pain will be felt throughout the entire developed world to varying degrees, and the emerging world will suffer, too, as we go through it. It is not a matter of pain or no pain. There is no way to avoid it. It is simply a matter of when and over how long a period we deal with the pain.

In fact, Reinhart and Rogoff's research suggests that the longer we try to put off the pain, the worse the total pain will be. We have simply overleveraged ourselves, and the deleveraging process will not be fun, whether on a personal or sovereign level.

We are going to look at several quotes from the book, as well as an extensive interview they graciously granted. We have also taken the great liberty of mixing paragraphs from various chapters that we feel are important. Please note that all the emphasis is our editorial license. Let's start by looking at part of their conclusion, which we think eloquently sums up the problems we face:

> The lesson of history, then, is that even as institutions and policy makers improve, there will always be a temptation to stretch the limits. **Just as an individual can go bankrupt no matter how rich she starts out, a financial system can collapse under the pressure of greed, politics, and profits no matter how well regulated it seems to be.** Technology has changed, the height of humans has changed, and fashions have changed.
>
> Yet the ability of governments and investors to delude themselves, giving rise to periodic bouts of euphoria that usually end in tears, seems to have remained a constant. No careful reader of Friedman and Schwartz will be surprised by this lesson about the ability of governments to mismanage financial markets, a key theme of their analysis.
>
> As for financial markets, we have come full circle to the concept of financial fragility in economies with massive indebtedness. All too often, periods of heavy borrowing can take place in a bubble and last for a surprisingly long time. **But highly leveraged economies, particularly those in which continual rollover of short-term debt is sustained only by confidence in relatively illiquid underlying assets, seldom survive forever, particularly if leverage continues to grow unchecked.**
>
> This time may seem different, but all too often a deeper look shows it is not. Encouragingly, history does point to warning signs that policy makers can look at to assess risk—if only they do not become too drunk with their credit bubble–fueled success and say, as their predecessors have for centuries, "This time is different."

Sadly, the lesson is not a happy one. There are no good endings once you start down a deleveraging path. As I have been writing for several years, much of the entire developed world is now faced with choosing from among several bad choices, some being worse than others. *This Time Is Different* offers up some ideas as to which are the worst choices.

A Crisis of Confidence

There seems to be no magic point at which a crisis develops. Things go along, and then the bond market loses confidence, seemingly in a short period. It is that ephemeral quality of confidence that is crucial to the operation of a bond market and the lack thereof that so quickly erodes any semblance of its normal functioning. Without confidence, the ability to roll over debt or borrow new debt at affordable rates collapses, as does the liquidity in the financial markets and the economy. It is a sad story that has been repeated over and over again over the centuries. We think we have progressed, but as previous chapters have demonstrated, we can no more repeal the basic laws of economics than we can repeal the law of gravity.

Let's jump to an interview John did with the authors:

KENNETH ROGOFF: One of the epiphanies that I had sort of in the process of doing the book and Carmen may well have had this epiphany a decade before me, but it was that a lot of the academic writing on debt and the research on debt is about, "Gosh it's tough. We're giving this debt to our children and we should really care about our children and our grandchildren and if we run big debts that's not a good thing." There was a Nobel Prize given a couple of decades ago to James Buchannan basically for his writings about learning about debt and how to think about it. But you know the fact is that when you run these big debts, the problem is not with your children or your grandchildren, it's in your lifetime. If you get to really high debt levels, you don't make it. The market eventually gets concerned. They get concerned about whether your grandchildren or your children are going to pay, and suddenly interest rates go up and you run into problems. But you are absolutely right, this is something in our lifetime, not necessarily a debt crisis, but we have to deal with it. It's not something we can just put off completely to our children.

CARMEN REINHART: Let me just add to that. I think one of the reasons to be concerned right now about debt issues is that it cuts across both the public sector and the private sector. The last time that the U.S. and some of the major advanced economies had debt levels that encroach on where we are now was around World War II. And around World War II, the private sector was lean and mean; they had worked down their debts during the depression and during the war. But now everyone is indebted.

JOHN MAULDIN: Yes, and what is happening, it seems, is that the government is trying to step in and take up the slack as the private sector reduces its leverage, and so overall leverage in the economy is not being reduced; it's actually growing. And with your work—and this was one of the things that kind of struck me—it's the combined debt. It's not just government debt or private debt, it's that combined debt that gets to a point where something has to give. Leverage has to go down, it has to be defaulted on, you've got to—we don't want to use the word *austerity* too much, but you've got to start paying it down. You've reached an end point.

KENNETH ROGOFF: It's particularly external debt that you owe to foreigners that is particularly an issue. Where the private debt so often, especially for emerging markets, but it could well happen in Europe today, where a lot of the private debt ends up getting assumed by the government and you say, but the government doesn't guarantee private debts; well, no, they don't. We didn't guarantee all the financial debt either before it happened, yet we do see that. I remember when I was first working on the 1980s Latin Debt Crisis and piecing together the data there on what was happening to public debt and what was happening to private debt, and I said, gosh the private debt is just shrinking and shrinking, isn't that interesting. Then I found out that it was being "guaranteed" by the public sector, who were in fact assuming the debts to make it easier to default on.

Now back to the book:

If there is one common theme to the vast range of crises we consider in this book, it is that excessive debt accumulation, whether it be by the government, banks, corporations, or consumers, often poses greater systemic risks than it seems during a boom. **Infusions of cash can make a government look like it is providing greater growth to its economy than it really is.** Private-sector borrowing binges can inflate housing and stock prices far beyond their long-run sustainable levels and make banks seem more stable and profitable than they really are. Such large-scale debt buildups pose risks because they make an economy vulnerable to crises of **confidence,** particularly when debt is short term and needs to be constantly refinanced. Debt-fueled booms all too often provide false affirmation of a government's policies, a financial institution's ability to make outsize profits, or a country's standard of living. Most of these booms end badly. Of course, debt instruments are crucial to all economies, ancient and modern, but balancing the risk and opportunities of debt is always a challenge, a challenge that policy makers, investors, and ordinary citizens must never forget.

And this is key. Read it twice (at least!):

Perhaps more than anything else, failure to recognize the precariousness and fickleness of **confidence**—especially in cases in which large short-term debts need to be rolled over continuously—is the key factor that gives rise to the this-time-is-different syndrome. **Highly indebted governments, banks, or corporations can seem to be merrily rolling along for an extended period, when bang!—confidence collapses, lenders disappear, and a crisis hits.**

Economic theory tells us that it is precisely the fickle nature of confidence, including its dependence on the public's expectation of future events, which makes it so difficult to predict the timing of debt crises. High debt levels lead, in many mathematical economics models, to "multiple equilibria" in which the debt level might be sustained—or might not be. Economists do not have a terribly good idea of what kinds of events shift confidence and of how to concretely assess confidence vulnerability. What one does see, again and again, in the history of financial crises is that when an accident is waiting to happen, it eventually does. When countries become too deeply indebted, they are headed for trouble. When debt-fueled asset price explosions seem too good to be true, they probably are. But the exact timing can be very difficult to guess, and a crisis that seems imminent can sometimes take years to ignite.

How confident was the world in October 2006? John was writing that there would be a recession, a subprime crisis, and a credit crisis in our future. He was on Larry Kudlow's show with Nouriel Roubini, and Larry and John Rutledge were giving him a hard time about his so-called doom and gloom. "If there is going to be a recession, you should get out of the stock market" was John's call. He was a tad early, as the market proceeded to go up another 20 percent over the next eight months. And then the crash came.

But that's the point. There is no way to determine when the crisis comes.

As Reinhart and Rogoff wrote:

> Highly indebted governments, banks, or corporations can seem to be merrily rolling along for an extended period, when **bang!**—confidence collapses, lenders disappear, and a crisis hits.

Bang is the right word. It is the nature of human beings to assume that the current trend will work out, that things can't really be that bad. The trend is your friend until it ends. Look at the bond markets only a year and then just a few months before World War I. There was no sign of an impending war. Everyone knew that cooler heads would prevail.

We can look back now and see where we made mistakes in the current crisis. We actually believed that this time was different, that we had better financial instruments, smarter regulators, and were so, well, modern. Times were different. We knew how to deal with leverage. Borrowing against your home was a good thing. Housing values would always go up. And so on.

Now, there are bullish voices telling us that things are headed back to normal. Mainstream forecasts for GDP growth this year (2010) are quite robust, north of 4 percent for the year, based on evidence from past recoveries. However, the underlying fundamentals of a banking crisis are far different from those of a typical business-cycle recession, as Reinhart and Rogoff's work so clearly reveals. It typically takes years to work off excess leverage in a banking crisis, with unemployment often rising for four years running.[*]

It's the Deleveraging, Stupid!

The reason this recession is different is that it is a deleveraging recession. We borrowed too much (all over the developed world) and now have to repair our balance sheets as the assets (housing, bonds, securities, etc.) we bought have fallen in value. A new and very interesting (if somewhat long) study by the McKinsey Global Institute (MGI) found that periods of overleveraging are often followed by six to seven years of slow growth as the deleveraging process plays out. No quick fixes.

Figure 5.1 shows the phases of deleveraging.

Let's look at some of their main conclusions (and they have a solid 10-page executive summary, worth reading.) This analysis adds new details to the picture of how leverage grew around the world before the crisis and how the process of reducing it could unfold.

- Leverage levels are still very high in some sectors of several countries—and this is a global problem, not just a U.S. one.
- To assess the sustainability of leverage, one must take a granular view using multiple sector-specific metrics. The analysis has identified 10 sectors within five economies that have a high likelihood of deleveraging.
- Empirically, a long period of deleveraging nearly always follows a major financial crisis.
- Deleveraging episodes are painful, lasting six to seven years on average and reducing the ratio of debt to GDP by 25 percent. Typically, GDP contracts during the first several years and then recovers.

---

[*]Reinhart and Rogoff's work assesses only federal debt. If you add in state and local debt, which must be paid for by the same tax base, it is actually worse than the federal numbers indicate.

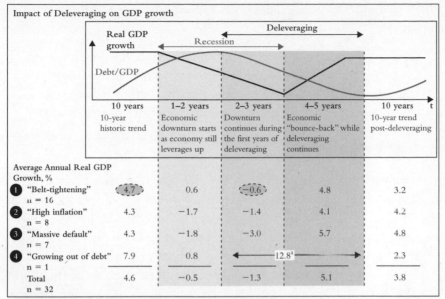

Impact of Deleveraging on GDP growth

Average Annual Real GDP Growth, %	10 years 10-year historic trend	1–2 years Economic downturn starts as economy still leverages up	2–3 years Downturn continues during the first years of deleveraging	4–5 years Economic "bounce-back" while deleveraging continues	10 years 10-year trend post-deleveraging
❶ "Belt-tightening" n = 16	4.7	0.6	−0.6	4.8	3.2
❷ "High inflation" n = 8	4.3	−1.7	−1.4	4.1	4.2
❸ "Massive default" n = 7	4.3	−1.8	−3.0	5.7	4.8
❹ "Growing out of debt" n = 1	7.9	0.8	12.8[a]		2.3
Total n = 32	4.6	−0.5	−1.3	5.1	3.8

[a] Deleveraging driven by off-trend growth is not linked to a recession.

Figure 5.1 Real GDP Growth Is Significantly Slower in the First Two to Three Years of Deleveraging

SOURCE: International Monetary Fund, McKinsey Global Institute analysis.

- If history is a guide, many years of debt reduction are expected in specific sectors of some of the world's largest economies, and this process will exert a significant drag on GDP growth.
- Coping with pockets of deleveraging is also a challenge for business executives. The process portends a prolonged period in which credit is less available and costlier, altering the viability of some business models and changing the attractiveness of different types of investments. In historic episodes, private investment was often quite low for the duration of deleveraging. Today, the household sectors of several countries have a high likelihood of deleveraging. If this happens, consumption growth is likely to be slower than the pre-crisis trend, and spending patterns will shift. Consumer-facing businesses have already seen a shift in spending toward value-oriented goods and away from luxury goods, and this new pattern may persist while households repair their balance sheets. Business leaders will need flexibility to respond to such shifts.[2]

The Lex column in the *Financial Times* observed, concerning the report:

> It may be economically and politically sensible for governments to spend money on making life more palatable at the height of the crisis. But the longer countries go on before paying down their debt, the more painful and drawn-out the process is likely to be. Unless, of course, government bond investors revolt and expedite the whole shebang.[3]

And that is the crux of the matter. We have to raise more than $1 trillion annually in the United States from domestic sources for as far as the Budget Office makes its projections. Great Britain has the GDP-equivalent task. So does much of Europe. Japan is simply off the radar. Japan, as John has noted, is a bug in search of a windshield.

Sometime in the coming few years, the bond markets of the world will be tested. Normally, a deleveraging cycle would be deflationary, and lower interest rates would be the outcome. But in the face of such large deficits, with no home-grown source to meet them? That worked for Japan for 20 years, as their domestic markets bought their debt. But that process is coming to an end.

James Carville once famously remarked that when he died, he wanted to come back as the bond market, because that is where the real power is. And we think we will find out all too soon what the bond vigilantes have to say.

The point is that complacency almost always ends suddenly. You just don't slide gradually into a crisis, over years. It *happens!* All of a sudden, there is a trigger event, and it is August 2008. And the evidence in the book is that things go along fine until there is that crisis of confidence. There is no way to know when it will happen. There is no magic debt level, no magic drop in currencies, no percentage level of fiscal deficits, no single point where we can say, "This is it." It is different in different crises.

One point we found fascinating. When it comes to the various types of crises the authors identify, there is very little difference between developed and emerging-market countries, especially as to the fallout. It seems that the developed world has no corner on special wisdom that would allow crises to be avoided or allow quicker recovery. In fact, because of their overconfidence—because they actually feel they have superior systems—developed countries can dig deeper holes for themselves than emerging markets.

Oh, and the Fed should have seen this crisis coming. The authors point to some very clear precursors to debt crises.

> As we will show, the outsized U.S. borrowing from abroad that occurred prior to the crisis (manifested in a sequence of gaping current account and trade balance deficits) was hardly the only warning signal. **In fact, the U.S. economy, at the epicenter of the crisis, showed many other signs of being on the brink of a deep financial crisis. Other measures such as asset price inflation, most notably in the real estate sector, rising household leverage, and the slowing output—standard leading indicators of financial crises—all revealed worrisome symptoms. Indeed, from a purely quantitative perspective, the run-up to the U.S. financial crisis showed all the signs of an accident waiting to happen.**

Of course, the United States was hardly alone in showing classic warning signs of a financial crisis, with Great Britain, Spain, and Ireland, among other countries, experiencing many of the same symptoms.

> On the one hand, the Federal Reserve's logic for ignoring housing prices was grounded in the perfectly sensible proposition that the private sector can judge equilibrium housing prices (or equity prices) at least as well as any government bureaucrat. On the other hand, it might have paid more attention to the fact that the rise in asset prices was being fueled by a relentless increase in the ratio of household debt to GDP, against a backdrop of record lows in the personal saving rate. This ratio, which had been roughly stable at close to 80 percent of personal income until 1993, had risen to 120 percent in 2003 and to nearly 130 percent by mid-2006. Empirical work by Bordo and Jeanne and the Bank for International Settlements suggested

that when housing booms are accompanied by sharp rises in debt, the risk of a crisis is significantly elevated. Although this work was not necessarily definitive, it certainly raised questions about the Federal Reserve's policy of benign neglect.

The U.S. conceit that its financial and regulatory system could withstand massive capital inflows on a sustained basis without any problems arguably laid the foundations for the global financial crisis of the late 2000s. The thinking that "this time is different"—because this time the U.S. had a superior system—once again proved false. **Outsized financial market returns were in fact greatly exaggerated by capital inflows, just as would be the case in emerging markets.** What could in retrospect be recognized as huge regulatory mistakes, including the deregulation of the subprime mortgage market and the 2004 decision of the Securities and Exchange Commission to allow investment banks to triple their leverage ratios (that is, the ratio measuring the amount of risk to capital), appeared benign at the time. Capital inflows pushed up borrowing and asset prices while reducing spreads on all sorts of risky assets, leading the International Monetary Fund to conclude in April 2007, in its twice-annual World Economic Outlook, that risks to the global economy had become extremely low and that, for the moment, there were no great worries. **When the international agency charged with being the global watchdog declares that there are no risks, there is no surer sign that this time is different.**

By that, Reinhart and Rogoff mean that the attitude of the market in general and central bankers in particular was that "this time is different," and so we did not need to worry about the warning signs. The entire point of the book is that it is never different. We just somehow believe we are in a special situation.

We have focused on macroeconomic issues, but many problems were hidden in the "plumbing" of the financial markets, as has become painfully evident since the beginning of the crisis. Some of these problems might have taken years to address. Above all, the huge run-up in housing prices—over 100 percent nationally over five years—should have been an alarm, especially fueled as it was by rising leverage. At the beginning of 2008, the total value of mortgages in the United States was approximately 90 percent of GDP. Policy makers should have decided several years prior to the crisis to deliberately take some steam out of the system. **Unfortunately, efforts to maintain growth and prevent significant sharp stock market declines had the effect of taking the safety valve off the pressure cooker**.

Remember the illustration we used in Chapter 1 about the difference between small fires in Baja California and large destructive fires in California proper? Trying to prevent small crises only leads to bigger ones if the system is not allowed to operate freely.

The signals approach (or most alternative methods) will not pinpoint the exact date on which a bubble will burst or provide an obvious indication of the severity of the looming crisis. What this systematic exercise can deliver is valuable information as to whether an economy is showing one or more of the classic symptoms that emerge before a severe financial illness develops. The most significant hurdle in establishing an effective and credible early warning system, however, is not the design of a systematic framework that is capable of producing relatively reliable signals of distress from the various indicators in a timely manner. **The greatest barrier to success is the well-entrenched tendency of policy makers and market participants to treat the signals as irrelevant archaic residuals of an outdated framework, assuming that old rules of valuation no longer apply.** If the past we have studied in this book is any guide, these signals will be dismissed more often than not. That is why we also need to think about improving institutions.

. . . Second, policy makers must recognize that banking crises tend to be protracted affairs. Some crisis episodes (such as those of Japan in 1992 and Spain in 1977) were stretched out even longer by the authorities by a lengthy period of denial.

The evidence was there. So why did the Fed miss it?

A pointed critique is leveled at the Fed and Greenspan, and at Bernanke in particular, by Andrew Smithers in his powerful book (now updated) *Wall Street Revalued: Imperfect Markets and Inept Central Bankers*. The foreword is by one of our favorite analysts, Jeremy Grantham. This ties nicely into the themes explored by Reinhart and Rogoff.

The book is a withering critique of the efficient market hypothesis (EMH), among other economic theories. Smithers argues that because the tenets of EMH are so ingrained, Greenspan and Bernanke could not recognize the bubble, because they believed in the efficiency of markets. "Dismissing financial crisis on the grounds that bubbles and busts cannot take place because that would imply irrationality is to ignore a condition for the sake of theory." Which they did.

As Grantham wrote in the foreword:

> My own favorite illustration of their views was Bernanke's comment in late 2006 at the height of a 3-sigma (100-year) event in a US housing market that had no prior housing bubbles: "The US housing market merely reflects a strong US economy." He was surrounded by statisticians and yet could not see the data. . . . His profound faith in market efficiency, and therefore a world where bubbles could not exist, made it impossible for him to see what was in front of his own eyes.[4]

Reinhart and Rogoff show time and time again that bubbles always end in tears. Markets and investors are, in fact, irrational. What kind of Fed governor would it have taken to suggest that housing was in a bubble and we were going to have to take steps to slow it down— raising rates, analyzing securitization and ratings? It would have taken one tough hombre. In fact, we had Greenspan, who encouraged the unchecked expansion of the securitized derivatives market. And a Congress that would not allow proper supervision of Fannie and Freddie (which is going to cost U.S. taxpayers on the order of $400 billion). The list is long.

Some Parting Words from Rogoff and Reinhart

And in the coming crisis? Who will step forward and channel their inner Paul Volcker, forcing the economy back from the precipice?

Let's finish this chapter with a few paragraphs from the end of the interview John did with Rogoff and Reinhart:

JOHN MAULDIN: Well let's bring that back now to the U.S. and our situation. We're not without some choices, but our choices to me seem to be either take the Japanese direction and end up where Japan does in something unsustainable or to begin to gradually, but significantly, reducing the debt. We're not going to take the Austrian solution and just shut it all down and throw ourselves into a depression. But somehow or another, we've got to show some fiscal discipline so that the bond market will behave. Is that your assessment as well? Or do you see a different path for us?

CARMEN REINHART: I don't think we have as much time as Japan. We are borrowing from the rest of the world, and our saving rates are pretty low despite the anemic uptake we've had, which seems huge from a recent standpoint, but it's anemic by historic standards. So we don't have as much time as Japan does.

JOHN MAULDIN: Really? [As in I was both shocked and scared!]

CARMEN REINHART: I think that if you look at the more aggregated debt picture in the United States, there are outside— I was listening to some analysts who are fluent in an area that I am not, which is state finances. And we of course all know about California, but what was alarming about their presentation was that they had tiered up the various states that had debt problems of different degrees. What I'm getting at is the debt situation in the United States, on the whole, doesn't offer you I think the length of time that many politicians think we have because of the reasons I just enumerated.

KENNETH ROGOFF: I would say that virtually every country in the world is grappling right now with how fast we get out of our fiscal stimulus and how much do we worry about this longer term problem of debt. And I fear that altogether too many countries will wait too long, which doesn't mean you end up getting forced to default, it just means the choices get more painful. Something we just find as a recurrent theme, is you're just rolling along, borrowing money and it seems okay, and that's what a lot of people say and wham, you hit some limit. No one knows where it is, what it is, but we know you hit it. Carmen and I do have numbers of what are really high debts and what aren't. And the U.S. will hit that [limit] and there are people who say it is not a problem and everyone loves us, greatest country in the world, where else will the Chinese invest? And you *want* to hear a great "this time it's different" theme that's a new one.

John, you started out this conversation on how we got started in this research and this was one of the things in our 2003 paper that is now built into the early chapter or two of the book that just got us really excited was this realization of how not only theoretically but quantitatively you see it, that countries have the threshold that they hit that we've found ways to try and crudely measure, where the interest rates you're charged just explode.

It was an epiphany for us because it helped us understand in a really clear way, why it was that the IMF program that we were involved with, and watching and commenting on, so many of them seemed to run awry. We would be presented with this calculation with, "Oh well, their debt is 50 percent, and we're going to let them go slow and run it up to 55 percent before we start getting it down." But you know if they are running into trouble at 50 percent, and you let it go up to 55 percent, the interest rate could just explode on you as the markets just don't have confidence. And then in our more recent works that we just finished, this paper, "Growth in a Time of Debt," we found that there was a parallel effect for advanced countries where they hit these growth limits at 90 and 100 percent.

And just again and again, this theme that there is a ceiling out there, and absolutely what Carmen said was right. We do know something about it, there is a big standard error around it, but if you don't owe any money, you don't have to worry if the market loses confidence and what kind of debtor you are going to be. And if you owe a ton of money, especially if you borrowed a lot short term, you've got a lot to worry about, and in our more recent work we were able to sort of demonstrate that somewhat more indirectly, but nevertheless feel that we really saw evidence of that. Not only for emerging markets, but for advanced countries like the United States.

CARMEN REINHART: Let me make a remark that sort of highlights my wet rag personality. One of the emphases in our analysis is that you do have these long cycles of indebtedness. Both the buildup and the unwinding show a lot of persistence; it's not quick. During the buildup phase, this is when we are all geniuses. We are all geniuses because usually asset prices are going up and growth is buoyant. I think without even calling on extreme scenarios, I think if you look not just at the United States, but the global situation, apart from some emerging markets, which in the past few years have delivered. There is a lot of public and private debt so that on the public side, you can't expect continued stimulus because they actually have debt problems that are actually pushing them in the other direction. And on the private side, if you look at the historical statistics in the United States on the last piece that Ken and I did, we plot those statistics since 1916 for the United States. And we haven't been as levered, not withstanding whatever deleveraging we have seen in the very recent past; we are still highly, highly leveraged as a **nation.** And the same can be said for most other advanced economies. So what am I getting at to your question, John, is that I think we are in for a period of subpar growth. And in a period of subpar growth, I think that it is not something that you are going to have the same kind of investment environment that we had in the run-ups to the IT bubble and in the run-ups to the subprime crisis. I think it's going to be a different, more sobering environment.

JOHN MAULDIN: It's what I call a muddle through economy. It makes it very, very difficult for us to say we're going to grow our way out of this problem. But Carmen, what you seem to be saying—and maybe Ken as well—is unless we really do something much quicker. Quite frankly when you said we don't have as much time as the Japanese, that was very disconcerting to me. What you are suggesting is that interest rates could take a run up in a deflationary environment that we are in right now, which seems almost is a contradiction.

KENNETH ROGOFF: I just want to say something a little calmer, but not necessarily calm, but reinforcing what Carmen said. Slow growth is here, that's just [comes] with this debt, no matter what way you turn. Greece is extreme, but they've got to tighten their belt and whatever they figure out how to get help, doing it gradually or whether they do it quickly, they've got to tighten their belt and it's going to mean slower growth. It's going to mean raising taxes, etc. Same thing in many, many countries in the world, it's a matter of figuring out the timing. Some countries won't tighten their belts soon enough, won't figure out how to do it. They will actually go to the IMF first and then after failures with the IMF, eventually some of them will even default. But with the slow growth, whatever way you turn, you tighten your belt. Barring certainly a great, unbelievable period of technology growth or a friend from outer space helping us out, we do face slow growth, as Carmen said. I don't know if that means you want to jump on it faster, hyperfast, but it certainly is something to be aware of in planning for everyone.

CHAPTER SIX

The Future of Public Debt

An Unsustainable Path

*Those who are most commonly creditors of a nation are, generally
speaking, enlightened men; and there are signal examples to warrant a
conclusion that when a candid and fair appeal is made to them, they will
understand their true interest too well to refuse their concurrence in such
modifications of their claims, as any real necessity may demand.*
     —Alexander Hamilton, *Report on Public Credit,*
            January 9, 1790

O ur argument in *Endgame* is that while the debt supercycle is still
growing on the back of increasing government debt, there is an
end to that process, and we are fast approaching it. It is a world
where not only will expanding government spending have to be
brought under control but also it will actually have to be reduced.

In this chapter, we will look at a crucial report, "The Future of
Public Debt: Prospects and Implications," by Stephen G. Cecchetti,
M. S. Mohanty, and Fabrizio Zampolli, published by the Bank of
International Settlements (BIS).[1] The BIS is often thought of as the

central banker to central banks. It does not have much formal power, but it is highly influential and has an esteemed track record; after all, it was one of the few international bodies that consistently warned about the dangers of excessive leverage and extremes in credit growth. Although the BIS is quite conservative by its nature, the material covered in this paper is startling to those who read what are normally very academic and dense journals. Specifically, it looks at fiscal policy in a number of countries and, when combined with the implications of age-related spending (public pensions and health care), determines where levels of debt in terms of GDP are going.

Throughout this chapter, we are going to quote extensively from the paper, as we let the authors' words speak for themselves. We'll also add some of our own color and explanation as needed. (Please note that all emphasis in bold is our editorial license and that we have chosen to retain the original paper's British spelling of certain words.)

After we look at the BIS paper, we will also look at the issues it raises and the implications for public debt. If public debt is unsustainable and the burden on government budgets is too great, what does this mean for government bonds? The inescapable conclusion is that government bonds currently are a Ponzi scheme. Governments lack the ability to reduce debt levels meaningfully, given current commitments. Because of this, we are likely to see "financial oppression," whereby governments will use a variety of means to force investors to buy government bonds even as governments actively work to erode their real value. It doesn't make for pretty reading, but let's jump right in.

A Bit of Background

But before we start, let's explain a few of the terms the BIS will use. They can sound complicated, but they're not that hard to understand. There is a big difference between the cyclical versus structural deficit. The total deficit is the structural plus cyclical.

Governments tax and spend every year, but in the good years, they collect more in taxes than in the bad years. In the good years, they typically spend less than in the bad years. That is because spending on unemployment insurance, for example, is something the government does to soften the effects of a downturn. At the lowest point in the business cycle, there is a high level of unemployment. This means that tax revenues are low and spending is high. On the other hand, at the peak of the cycle, unemployment is low, and businesses are making money, so everyone pays more in taxes. The additional borrowing required at the low point of the cycle is the *cyclical deficit*.

The *structural deficit* is the deficit that remains across the business cycle, because the general level of government spending exceeds the level of taxes that are collected. This shortfall is present regardless of whether there is a recession.

Now let's throw out another term. The primary balance of government spending is related to the structural and cyclical deficits. The *primary balance* is when total government expenditures, except for interest payments on the debt, equal total government revenues. The crucial wrinkle here is interest payments. If your interest rate is going up faster than the economy is growing, your total debt level will increase.

The best way to think about governments is to compare them to a household with a mortgage. A big mortgage is easier to pay down with lower monthly mortgage payments. If your mortgage payments are going up faster than your income, your debt level will only grow. For countries, it is the same. The point of no return for countries is when interest rates are rising faster than their growth rates. At that stage, there is no hope of stabilizing the deficit. This is the situation many countries in the developed world now find themselves in.

Drastic Measures

Our projections of public debt ratios lead us to conclude that the path pursued by fiscal authorities in a number of industrial countries is unsustainable. Drastic measures are necessary to check the rapid growth of current and future liabilities of governments and reduce their adverse consequences for long-term growth and monetary stability.

Drastic measures is not language you typically see in an economic paper from the Bank for International Settlements. But the picture painted in a very concise and well-written report by the BIS for 12 countries they cover is one for which the words *drastic measures* are well warranted.

The authors start by dealing with the growth in fiscal (government) deficits and the growth in debt. The United States has exploded from a fiscal deficit of 2.8 percent to 10.4 percent today, with only a small 1.3 percent reduction for 2011 projected. Debt will explode (the correct word!) from 62 percent of GDP to an estimated 100 percent of GDP by the end of 2011 or soon thereafter. The authors don't mince words. They write at the beginning of their work:

> The politics of public debt vary by country. In some, seared by unpleasant experience, there is a culture of frugality. In others, however, profligate official spending is commonplace. In recent years, consolidation has been successful on a number of occasions. But fiscal restraint tends to deliver stable debt; rarely does it produce substantial reductions. And, most critically, swings from deficits to surpluses have tended to come along with either falling nominal interest rates, rising real growth, or both. Today, interest rates are exceptionally low and the growth outlook for advanced economies is modest at best. **This leads us to conclude that the question is when markets will start putting pressure on governments, not if**.
>
> When, in the absence of fiscal actions, will investors start demanding a much higher compensation for the risk of holding the increasingly large amounts of public debt that authorities are going to issue to finance their extravagant ways? In some countries, unstable debt dynamics, in which higher debt levels lead to higher interest rates, which then lead to even higher debt levels, are already clearly on the horizon.
>
> It follows that the fiscal problems currently faced by industrial countries need to be tackled relatively soon and resolutely. **Failure to do so will raise the chance of an unexpected and abrupt rise in government bond yields at medium and long maturities, which would put the nascent economic recovery at risk. It will also complicate the task of central banks in controlling inflation in the**

immediate future and might ultimately threaten the credibility of present monetary policy arrangements.

While fiscal problems need to be tackled soon, how to do that without seriously jeopardizing the incipient economic recovery is the current key challenge for fiscal authorities.

Remember that Rogoff and Reinhart show that when the ratio of debt to GDP rises above 90 percent, there seems to be a reduction of about 1 percent in GDP. The authors of this paper, and others, suggest that this might come from the cost of the public debt crowding out productive private investment.

Think about that for a moment. We are on an almost certain path to a debt level of 100 percent of GDP in just a few years, especially if you include state and local debt. If trend growth has been a yearly rise of 3.5 percent in GDP, then we are reducing that growth to 2.5 percent at best. And 2.5 percent trend GDP growth will *not* get us back to full employment. We are locking in high unemployment for a very long time, and just when some 1 million people will soon be falling off the extended unemployment compensation rolls.

Government transfer payments of some type now make up more than 20 percent of all household income. That is set up to fall rather significantly over the year ahead unless unemployment payments are extended beyond the current 99 weeks. There seems to be little desire in Congress for such a measure. That will be a significant headwind to consumer spending.

Government debt-to-GDP for Britain will double from 47 percent in 2007 to 94 percent in 2011 and rise 10 percent a year unless serious fiscal measures are taken. Greece's level will swell from 104 percent to 130 percent, so the United States and Britain are working hard to catch up to Greece, a dubious race indeed. Spain is set to rise from 42 percent to 74 percent and *only* 5 percent a year thereafter, but their economy is in recession, so GDP is shrinking and unemployment is 20 percent. Portugal? In the next two years, 71 percent to 97 percent, and there is almost no way Portugal can grow its way out of its problems. These increases assume that we accept the data provided in government projections. Recent history argues that these projections may prove conservative.

Japan will end 2011 with a debt ratio of 204 percent and growing by 9 percent a year. They are taking almost all the savings of the country into government bonds, crowding out productive private capital. Reinhart and Rogoff, with whom you should by now be familiar, note that three years after a typical banking crisis, the absolute level of public debt is 86 percent higher, but in many cases of severe crisis, the debt could grow by as much as 300 percent. Ireland has more than tripled its debt in just five years.

The BIS paper continues:

> We doubt that the current crisis will be typical in its impact on deficits and debt. **The reason is that, in many countries, employment and growth are unlikely to return to their pre-crisis levels in the foreseeable future.** As a result, unemployment and other benefits will need to be paid for several years, and high levels of public investment might also have to be maintained.
>
> The permanent loss of potential output caused by the crisis also means that government revenues may have to be permanently lower in many countries. Between 2007 and 2009, the ratio of government revenue to GDP fell by 2–4 percentage points in Ireland, Spain, the United States, and the United Kingdom. It is difficult to know how much of this will be reversed as the recovery progresses. **Experience tells us that the longer households and firms are unemployed and underemployed, as well as the longer they are cut off from credit markets, the bigger the shadow economy becomes.**

Clearly, we are looking at a watershed event in public spending in the United States, United Kingdom, and Europe. Because of the Great Financial Crisis, the usual benefit of a sharp rebound in cyclical tax receipts will not happen. It will take much longer to achieve any economic growth that could fill the public coffers.

Now, let's skip a few sections and jump to the heart of their debt projections.

The Future Public Debt Trajectory

There was some discussion whether we should summarize the following section or use the actual quotation. We opted to use the quotation, as the language from the normally conservative BIS is most graphic. We want the reader to understand their concerns in a direct manner. This is in many ways the heart of the crisis that is leading the developed countries to endgame. It is startling to compare this with the seeming complacency of so many of our leading political figures all over the world.

> We now turn to a set of 30-year projections for the path of the debt/GDP ratio in a dozen major industrial economies (Austria, France, Germany, Greece, Ireland, Italy, Japan, the Netherlands, Portugal, Spain, the United Kingdom, and the United States). We choose a 30-year horizon with a view to capturing the large unfunded liabilities stemming from future age-related expenditure without making overly strong assumptions about the future path of fiscal policy (which is unlikely to be constant). In our baseline case, we assume that government total revenue and non-age-related primary spending remain a constant percentage of GDP at the 2011 level as projected by the OECD. Using the CBO and European Commission projections for age-related spending, we then proceed to generate a path for total primary government spending and the primary balance over the next 30 years. Throughout the projection period, the real interest rate that determines the cost of funding is assumed to remain constant at its 1998–2007 average, and potential real GDP growth is set to the OECD-estimated post-crisis rate.

Here, we feel a need to distinguish here for the reader the difference between real GDP and nominal GDP. *Nominal GDP* is the numeric vale of GDP, say, $103. If inflation is 3 percent, then real GDP would be $100. Often governments try to create inflation to flatter growth. This leads to higher prices and salaries, but they are not real; they are merely inflationary. That is why economists always look at real GDP, not nominal GDP. Reality is slightly more complicated, but that is the general idea. That makes these estimates quite conservative, as growth-rate estimates by the OECD are well on the optimistic side. If they used less optimistic projections and factored in the current euro crisis (it is our bet that when you read this in 2011, there will still be a euro crisis, and that it may be worse) and potential recessions in the coming decades (there are always recessions that never get factored into these types of projections), the numbers would be far worse. Now, back to the paper.

Debt Projections

As noted previously, this text is important to the overall intent.

From this exercise, we are able to come to a number of conclusions. **First, in our baseline scenario, conventionally computed deficits will rise precipitously.** Unless the stance of fiscal policy changes, or age-related spending is cut, **by 2020 the primary deficit/GDP ratio will rise to 13% in Ireland; 8–10% in Japan, Spain, the United Kingdom and the United States;** [Wow! Note that they are not assuming that these issues magically go away in the United States as the current administration does using assumptions about future laws that are not realistic.] and 3–7% in Austria, Germany, Greece, the Netherlands and Portugal. Only in Italy do these policy settings keep the primary deficits relatively well contained—a consequence of the fact that the country entered the crisis with a nearly balanced budget and did not implement any real stimulus over the past several years.

But the main point of this exercise is the impact that this will have on debt. The results [in Figure 6.1] show that, in the baseline scenario, debt/GDP ratios rise rapidly in the next decade, **exceeding 300% of GDP in Japan; 200% in the United Kingdom; and 150% in Belgium, France, Ireland, Greece, Italy and the United States.** And, as is clear from the slope of the line, without a change in policy, the path is unstable. This is confirmed by the projected interest rate paths, again in our

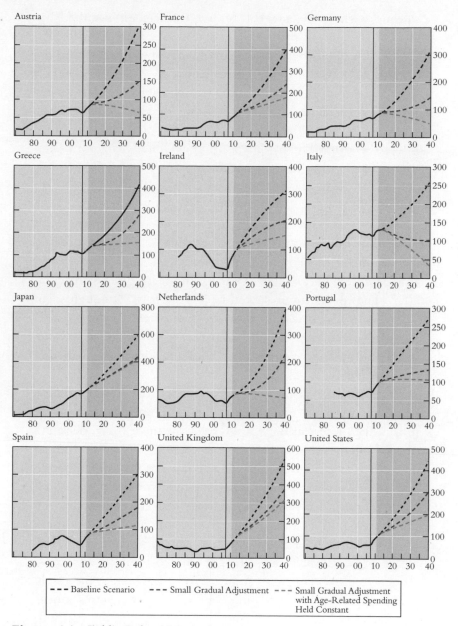

Figure 6.1 Public Debt/GDP Projections

SOURCE: Bank for International Settlements.

baseline scenario. [Figure 6.1] shows the fraction absorbed by interest payments in each of these countries. **From around 5% today, these numbers rise to over 10% in all cases, and as high as 27% in the United Kingdom**.

Seeing that the status quo is untenable, countries are embarking on fiscal consolidation plans. In the United States, the aim is to bring the total federal budget deficit down from 11% to 4% of GDP by 2015. In the United Kingdom, the consolidation plan envisages reducing budget deficits by 1.3 percentage points of GDP each year from 2010 to 2013 (see e.g. OECD (2009a)).

To examine the long-run implications of a gradual fiscal adjustment similar to the ones being proposed, we project the debt ratio assuming that the primary balance improves by 1 percentage point of GDP in each year for five years starting in 2012. The results are presented in [Figure 6.1]. Although such an adjustment path would slow the rate of debt accumulation compared with our baseline scenario, it would leave several major industrial economies with substantial debt ratios in the next decade.

This suggests that consolidations along the lines currently being discussed will not be sufficient to ensure that debt levels remain within reasonable bounds over the next several decades.

An alternative to traditional spending cuts and revenue increases is to change the promises that are as yet unmet. Here, that means embarking on the politically treacherous task of cutting future age-related liabilities. With this possibility in mind, we construct a third scenario that combines gradual fiscal improvement with a freezing of age-related spending-to-GDP at the projected level for 2011. [Figure 6.1] shows the consequences of this draconian policy. Given its severity, the result is no surprise: what was a rising debt/GDP ratio reverses course and starts heading down in Austria, Germany and the Netherlands. In several others, the policy yields a significant slowdown in debt accumulation. **Interestingly, in France, Ireland, the United Kingdom and the United States, even this policy is not sufficient to bring rising debt under control.**

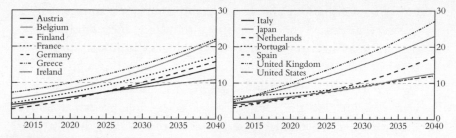

Figure 6.2   Projected Interest Payments as a Percentage of GDP
SOURCE: Bank for International Settlements, OECD, authors' projections.

And yet, many countries, including the United States, will have to contemplate something along these lines. We simply cannot fund entitlement growth at expected levels. Note that in the United States, even by draconian cost-cutting estimates, debt-to-GDP still grows to 200 percent in 30 years. That shows you just how out of whack our entitlement programs are, and we have no prospect of reform in sight. It also means that if we—the United States—decide as a matter of national policy that we do indeed want these entitlements, it will most likely mean a substantial value added tax, as we will need vast sums to cover the costs, but with that will lead to even slower growth.

Long before interest costs rise even to 10 percent of GDP in the early 2020s, the bond market will have rebelled. (See Figure 6.2.) This is a chart of things that cannot be. Therefore, we should be asking ourselves what is endgame if the fiscal deficits are not brought under control. Quoting again from the BIS paper:

> All of this leads us to ask: what level of primary balance would be required to bring the debt/GDP ratio in each country back to its pre-crisis, 2007 level? Granted that countries which started with low levels of debt may never need to come back to this point, the question is an interesting one nevertheless. [Table 6.1] presents the average primary surplus target required to bring debt ratios down to their 2007 levels over horizons of 5, 10 and 20 years. An aggressive adjustment path to achieve this objective within five years would mean generating an average annual primary surplus of 8–12% of GDP in the United States, Japan,

the United Kingdom and Ireland, and 5–7% in a number of other countries. A preference for smoothing the adjustment over a longer horizon (say, 20 years) reduces the annual surplus target at the cost of leaving governments exposed to high debt ratios in the short to medium term.

Can you imagine the United States being able to run a budget surplus of even 2.4 percent of GDP? More than $350 billion a year? That would be a swing in the budget of almost 12 percent of GDP.

Now, we come to the section where they talk about the risks associated with the fiscal deficits. And by the way, we should note that 25 of 27 European countries are running deficits in excess of 3 percent of GDP. Ireland has a deficit of 14.3 percent. Portugal is at almost 10 percent. Greece is at almost 14 percent.

Look at the Figure 6.3 showing fiscal deficits. Notice that France is over 8 percent. The Eurozone as a whole is over 6 percent. Wow. We'll look at the implications of this later.

The first risk is, of course, higher interest rates brought about by what the BIS authors term *increased risk premia*. In essence, investors want

Table 6.1   Average Primary Balance Required to Stabilize the Public Debt/GDP Ratio at 2007 Level (as percentage of GDP)[1]

	Over 5 years	Over 10 years	Over 20 years	Memo: Primary balance in 2011 (forecast)
Austria	5.1	3.0	2.0	−2.9
France	7.3	4.3	2.8	−5.1
Germany	5.5	3.5	2.4	−2.0
Greece	5.4	2.8	1.5	−5.3
Ireland	11.8	5.4	2.2	−9.2
Italy	5.1	3.4	2.5	0.0
Japan	10.1	6.4	4.5	−8.0
Netherlands	6.7	3.7	2.3	−3.4
Portugal	5.7	3.1	1.8	−4.4
Spain	6.1	2.9	1.3	−6.6
United Kingdom	10.6	5.8	3.5	−9.0
United States	8.1	4.3	2.4	−7.1

SOURCE: Bank for International Settlements, OECD, authors' calculations.

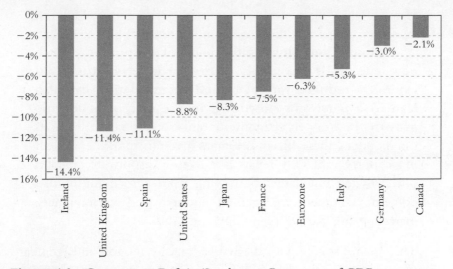

Figure 6.3   Government Deficits/Surpluses as Percentage of GDP
Source: Bloomberg, Variant Perception.

to get paid more for their increased risk. Interest on Greek debt for five-year bonds was 15 percent in May 2010. Now it is artificially propped up, but 10-year bonds are still yielding 10 percent. There is no way for the Greeks to grow their way out of the problem if interest rates are at 10 percent to 15 percent, up almost fourfold in less than a year. Rates are rising for other European peripheral countries as well. Ireland and Spain have seen their bonds rise whenever the European Central Bank hasn't stepped in to help out.

> [The second risk] associated with high levels of public debt comes from potentially lower long-term growth. A higher level of public debt implies that a larger share of society's resources is permanently being spent servicing the debt. This means that a government intent on maintaining a given level of public services and transfers must raise taxes as debt increases. Taxes distort resource allocation, and can lead to lower levels of growth. Given the level of taxes in some countries, one has to wonder if further increases will actually raise revenue.
>
> The distortionary impact of taxes is normally further compounded by the crowding-out of productive private capital. In a closed economy, a higher level of public debt will eventually

absorb a larger share of national wealth, pushing up real interest rates and causing an offsetting fall in the stock of private capital. **This not only lowers the level of output but, since new capital is invariably more productive than old capital, a reduced rate of capital accumulation can also lead to a persistent slowdown in the rate of economic growth.** In an open economy, international financial markets can moderate these effects so long as investors remain confident in a country's ability to repay. But, even when private capital is not crowded out, larger borrowing from abroad means that domestic income is reduced by interest paid to foreigners, increasing the gap between GDP and GNP.

This squares solidly with the work done by Rogoff and Reinhart, showing that when the debt of a country reaches about 100 percent of GDP, there is a reduction in potential GDP growth of about 1 percent. As we wrote earlier, government debt and spending do not increase productivity. That takes private investment. And if government debt crowds out private investment, then there is lower growth, which is what the Rogoff and Reinhart study clearly shows.

And finally, the BIS authors note the risk that a government cannot run deficits in times of crisis to offset the effects of the crisis, if they already are running large deficits and have a large debt. In effect, fiscal policy is hamstrung.

The Challenge for Central Banks

Interestingly, the authors worry that one of the real problems central banks may face is that inflation expectations may become unanchored in the absence of a willingness on the part of the government to show fiscal constraint. Without some evidence of that willingness, monetary policy could lose any ability of being effective.

In other words, no matter how much the people at the Fed might like to help in a crisis, they may not be able to do anything effective if the U.S. government does not deal with its deficits. Again, from the BIS paper:

A second mechanism by which public debt can lead to inflation focuses on the political and economic pressures that a monetary policymaker may face to inflate away the real value of debt. The payoff to doing this rises the bigger the debt, the longer its average maturity, the larger the fraction denominated in domestic currency, and the bigger the fraction held by foreigners. Moreover, the incentives to tolerate temporarily high inflation rise if the tax and transfer system is mainly based on nominal cash flows and if policymakers see a social benefit to helping households and firms to reduce their leverage in real terms. **It is, however, worth emphasizing that the costs of creating an unexpected inflation would almost surely be very high in the form of permanently high future real interest rates (and any other distortions caused by persistently higher inflation).**

In John's recent discussion with Richard Fisher, president of the Dallas Fed, he made it clear that the current leadership of the Fed knows it cannot excessively print money. So who is the BIS looking at when they talk about the temptation to inflate?

The Bank of England comes to mind, where inflation has surprised to the upside for the past two years (either the Bank of England is really bad at forecasting inflation, or they may not be too uncomfortable with it). Also Japan. And a number of smaller European central banks. Countries that would not mind their currencies falling, especially if the euro continues to slide. As the BIS notes, the temptation is going to be large. But there is no free lunch. Such things can spiral out of control and either end in tears or in someone like a Paul Volcker wrenching the economy into serious recession. We think the final sentence of the paragraph just quoted serves as a warning that such a policy dooms a country to even worse nightmares.

Now we come to the conclusion of the paper (again, all emphasis is ours):

Our examination of the future of public debt leads us to several important conclusions. First, fiscal problems confronting industrial economies are bigger than suggested by official debt figures that show the implications of the financial crisis and recession for fiscal balances. **As frightening as it is to consider public debt increasing to more than 100% of GDP, an even greater danger arises from a rapidly ageing population. The related unfunded liabilities are large and growing, and should be a central part of today's long-term fiscal planning.**

It is essential that governments not be lulled into complacency by the ease with which they have financed their deficits thus far. In the aftermath of the financial crisis, the path of future output is likely to be permanently below where we thought it would be just several years ago. As a result, government revenues will be lower and expenditures higher, making consolidation even more difficult. **But, unless action is taken to place fiscal policy on a sustainable footing, these costs could easily rise sharply and suddenly.**

Second, large public debts have significant financial and real consequences. The recent sharp rise in risk premia on long-term bonds issued by several industrial countries suggests that **markets no longer consider sovereign debt low-risk**. The limited evidence we have suggests default risk premia move up with debt levels and down with the revenue share of GDP as well as the availability of private saving. **Countries with a relatively weak fiscal system and a high degree of dependence on foreign investors to finance their deficits generally face larger spreads on their debts.** This market differentiation is a positive feature of the financial system, but it could force governments with weak fiscal systems to return to fiscal rectitude sooner than they might like or hope.

Third, we note the risk that persistently high levels of public debt will drive down capital accumulation, productivity growth and long-term potential growth. Although we do not provide direct evidence of this, a recent study suggests that there may be non-linear effects of public debt on growth, with adverse output effects tending to rise as the debt/GDP ratio approaches the 100% limit (Reinhart and Rogoff (2009b)).

Finally, looming long-term fiscal imbalances pose significant risk to the prospects for future monetary stability. We describe two channels through which unstable debt dynamics could lead to higher inflation: direct debt monetization, and the temptation to reduce the real value of government debt through higher inflation. Given the current institutional setting of monetary policy, both risks are clearly limited, at least for now.

How to tackle these fiscal dangers without seriously jeopardizing the incipient recovery is the key challenge facing policymakers today. **Although we do not offer advice on how to go about this, we believe that any fiscal consolidation plan should include credible measures to reduce future unfunded liabilities**. Announcements of changes in these programs would allow authorities to wait until the recovery from the crisis is assured before reducing discretionary spending and improving the short-term fiscal position. An important aspect of measures to tackle future liabilities is that any potential adverse impact on today's saving behavior be minimized. From this point of view, a decision to raise the retirement age appears a better measure than a future cut in benefits or an increase in taxes. Indeed, it may even lead to an increase in consumption (see, for example, Barrell et al. [2009] for an analysis applied to the United Kingdom).

Bang, Indeed!

The risk that no one talks about is the level of foreign investment in some of these countries and the consequent rollover risk. By this, we mean that when a bond comes due, you have to roll over that bond into another bond. If the party that bought the original bond wants cash to invest in something else or just does not want your bond risk anymore, you have to find someone to buy the new bond. Greece has a large number of bonds coming due soon. It is not just the new debt; they have to find someone to buy the old debt. And that is why they need so much money.

But it is not just a Greek problem. About 45 percent of Spain's debt is owned by non-Spaniards, and they need to roll over old debt and new debt of 190 billion euros this year alone. That is bigger than the entire GDP of Portugal. Spain cannot finance this internally. But will foreigners buy 90 billion euros and, if so, at what price if they are not convinced that Spain will enact serious austerity measures?

Listen to European Central Bank Governing Council President Jean-Claude Trichet:

> As regards fiscal policies, we call for decisive actions by governments to achieve a lasting and credible consolidation of public finances. The latest information shows that the correction of the large fiscal imbalances will, in general, require a stepping-up of current efforts. Fiscal consolidation will need to exceed substantially the annual structural adjustment of 0.5% of GDP set as a minimum requirement by the Stability and Growth Pact. . . .
>
> The longer the fiscal correction is postponed, the greater the adjustment needs become and the higher the risk of reputational and confidence losses. Instead, the swift implementation of frontloaded and comprehensive consolidation plans, focusing on the expenditure side and combined with structural reforms, will strengthen public confidence in the capacity of governments to regain sustainability of public finances, reduce risk premium in interest rates and thus support sustainable growth.[2]

This is a man who wants some serious austerity. No garden-variety cuts here and there. And that brings us to the heart of the problem. The chart a few pages ago showed the large fiscal deficits involved. If those are tackled seriously, it will put many countries into outright recessions and reduce the growth in others. Some, like Greece, will be in what can only be called a depression.

The entire Eurozone is at serious risk of another recession if it has not already entered into a second phase as this book is published. And one country after another is going to have to convince foreigners to buy its debt. But if they make the cuts, their GDP will fall, ironically increasing their debt-to-GDP ratio and making investors demand even higher rates, which becomes a very vicious spiral.

Again, as Reinhart and Rogoff wrote: "Highly indebted governments, banks, or corporations can seem to be merrily rolling along for an extended period, when **bang!**—confidence collapses, lenders disappear, and a crisis hits."[3]

The Center Cannot Hold

Sovereign debt as an investment for banks was a good idea only a little while ago. Take cheap money, lever up, and make a nice spread. No longer is it such a good idea. Credit spreads are widening all over Europe. Interest rates are rising for the European periphery.

We once again find ourselves on a Minsky journey to a rather distressing Minsky moment. Hyman Minsky famously taught us that stability breeds instability. The more things stay the same, the more complacent we get, until *Bang!* We get the Minsky moment. We always seem to think this time is different, and it never is.

The Minsky journey is where investment goes from what Minsky called a hedge unit, where the investment is its own source of repayment; to a speculative unit, where the investment only pays the interest; to a Ponzi unit, where the only way to repay the debt is for the value of the investment to rise. The end of the journey is always the Minsky moment of violent markets and unwanted volatility.

We had that Minsky journey and Minsky moment in 2008, when the financial systems of the world collapsed. No one wanted U.S. mortgage debt, and every financial institution worried what was on the balance sheet of other banks. The interbank lending system froze.

Greece is now at its Ponzi moment of financing. As John Hussman pointed out, if interest rates are at 15 percent when you roll over debt, and your country is not growing, you have no way to actually service the debt. And thus, the Minsky moment when the markets walk away. *Bang!* From Hussman's letter:

> The basic problem is that Greece has insufficient economic growth, enormous [fiscal] deficits (nearly 14% of GDP), a heavy existing debt burden as a proportion of GDP (over 120%), accruing at high interest rates (about 8%), payable in a currency that it is unable to devalue. This creates a violation of what economists call the "transversality" or "no-Ponzi" condition. In

order to credibly pay debt off, the debt has to have a well-defined present value (technically, the present value of the future debt should vanish if you look far enough into the future).

Without the transversality condition, the price of a security can be anything investors like. However arbitrary that price is, investors may be able to keep the asset on an upward path for some period of time, but the price will gradually bear less and less relation to the actual cash flows that will be delivered. At some point, the only reason to hold the asset will be the expectation of selling it to somebody else, even though it won't be delivering enough payments to justify the price.

Unless Greece implements enormous fiscal austerity, its debt will grow faster than the rate that investors use to discount it back to present value. Moreover, to bail out Greece for anything more than a short period of time, the rules of the game would have to be changed to allow for much larger budget deficits than those originally agreed upon in the Maastricht Treaty.[4]

And if Greece has further problems, the market will look at Spain (and Portugal and Ireland). For Spain to continue to get financing, the market must believe they are going to make a credible effort at austerity measures. And because they need so much foreign financing, that moment may be sooner than we now think, as their rollover risk is massive. If Spain gets slapped, then who will be next?

Who Takes the Loss?

There are examples of countries that have worked their way out of even worse problems and have done so without default. But those examples always came with currency devaluation and higher inflation. The Eurozone countries cannot devalue their currencies. The risk in Europe is that the austerity measures bring about deflation, which makes the debt an even greater burden.

The problem with having more liabilities than you can service means that someone has to take the loss. A report by Arnaud Marès at Morgan Stanley lays out the problem very well.

Debt/GDP ratios are too backward-looking and considerably underestimate the fiscal challenge faced by advanced economies' governments. On the basis of current policies, most governments are deep in negative equity.

This means governments will impose a loss on some of their stakeholders, in our view. The question is not whether they will renege on their promises, but rather upon which of their promises they will renege, and what form this default will take.

So far during the Great Recession, sovereign (and bank) senior unsecured bond holders have been the only constituency fully protected from partaking in this loss.

It is overly optimistic to assume that this can continue forever. The conflict that opposes bond holders to other government stakeholders is more intense than ever, and their interests are no longer sufficiently well aligned with those of influential political constituencies.[5]

The author of this report highlights that most of the obligations countries now have is to their pensioners and senior citizens. Naturally, governments could cut Social Security or Medicare and reduce the future liability. There is no way that would fly politically. The complication is that as countries grow older, most of the voters also happen to be senior citizens. As Figure 6.4 from the report shows, in the United States and Europe, older voters will be the majority of voters in 2020. Politically, governments have very little time to make adjustments to retirement and medical benefits.

If governments can't formally renege on their commitments and promises to seniors yet at the same time, they can't reasonably pay back bondholders, what can they do? As Marès points out, there is a well-known pattern in government behavior called *financial oppression*:

There exists an alternative to outright default. "Financial oppression" (imposing on creditors real rates of return that are

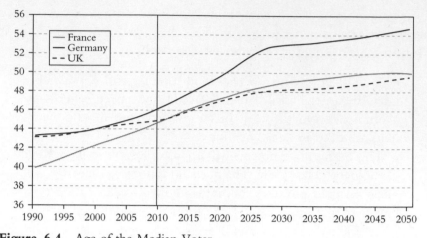

Figure 6.4   Age of the Median Voter
NOTE: Calculations assume stable turnout ratio for each age group, based on turnout at the most recent parliamentary election.
SOURCE: UN, Bundeswahlleiter, INSEE, Ipsos-Mori, Morgan Stanley Research.

either negative or artificially low) has been used repeatedly in history in similar circumstances.

Investors should be prepared to face financial oppression, a credible threat against which current yields provide little protection.

Financial oppression has taken place in the past as an alternative to default in countries that are generally considered to have a spotless sovereign credit record. Examples include: the revocation of gold clauses in bond contracts by the Roosevelt administration in 1934; the experience by then Chancellor of the Exchequer Hugh Dalton of issuing perpetual debt at an artificially low yield of 2.5% in the UK in 1946–47; and post-war inflationary episodes, notably in France (post both world wars), in the UK and in the US (post World War II). Each took place at a time when conflicting demands on finite government resources were high, and rentiers wielded reduced political power.[6]

Currently we're beginning to see the financial oppression in developed countries. In the United States, the United Kingdom, and

Europe, governments have forced their social security funds to only buy government bonds.

In the United States, for example, the Social Security dollars go to Treasury. Treasury issues so-called bonds against them. It would be incorrect to call these bonds because they're really IOUs. Social Security gets a so-called bond, but they can't sell it to anyone but the Treasury. A real bond can be marketed in the open market, but these securities issued to the Social Security Trust Fund are unmarketable and thus can only be redeemed at the U.S. Treasury. Even though the Treasury spends the Social Security money, it still counts these tax receipts against the federal deficit, masking the scale of the problems.

In Japan, government-controlled entities have been busy buying up Japanese government bonds (JGBs) for quite some time. The three largest holders of JGBs are Japan Post Bank, Japan Post Insurance, and Government Pension Investment Fund (GPIF). However, there is a limit to how much these public piggybanks can be abused to buy public debt. Japan Post Insurance will soon not be a likely buyer because insurance reserves have been on a steady decline, given Japan's demographics, and their year-over-year JGB holdings growth is almost 0 percent. At some stage, you run out of suckers to buy government debt.

What is certain is we will only see more efforts at financial oppression, but we will see increasing attempts to monetize deficits and reduce the future value of liabilities through inflation. It will not be pretty.

CHAPTER SEVEN

The Elements of Deflation

If Americans ever allow banks to control the issue of their currency, first by inflation and then by deflation, the banks will deprive the people of all property until their children will wake up homeless.
—Thomas Jefferson

G iven the enormous levels of debt globally and the massive amount of government spending, one of the more important questions of the moment is whether we will face inflation or deflation. The quick answer is yes.

Without trying to be too facile, in most (developed) countries, there is the potential for both, so the trick is to figure out in what order they will come. For the next two chapters, we will look first at deflation and then at inflation (and hyperinflation!). We'll explore what causes either economic event to happen.

The classic definition of *deflation* is a period of actual decline in the general price level and an economic environment that is characterized by inadequate or deficient aggregate demand.

The United States, the United Kingdom, Japan, and the European periphery are experiencing powerful, simultaneous deflationary forces that come from excessive debt and forced liquidation. This has created a classic balance sheet recession where after the bursting of a nation-wide asset price bubble, a large number of private-sector balance sheets are left with more liabilities than assets. In response, central banks and fiscal authorities have launched equally massive increases the size of their balance sheet and increased spending to compensate for the private sector retrenchment. Even so, they have only managed to slow down the deleveraging and disinflation. But as we will see, that can change.

The Supertrend Puzzle

I (John) am a big fan of puzzles of all kinds, especially picture puzzles. I love to figure out how the pieces fit together and watch the picture emerge, and I have spent many an enjoyable hour at the table struggling to find the missing piece that helps make sense of the pattern.

Perhaps that explains my fascination with economics and investing, as there are no greater puzzles (except possibly the great theological conundrums or the mind of a woman, about either of which I have only a few clues).

The great problem with economic puzzles is that the shapes of the pieces can and will change as they try to fit in against one another. One often finds that fitting two pieces together changes the way they meld with the other pieces you thought were already nailed down, which may of course change the pieces with which they are adjoined, and suddenly your neat economic picture no longer looks anything like the real world.*

There are two types of major economic puzzle pieces.

The first are those pieces that represent trends that are inexorable: trends that will not themselves change, or if they do, it will be slowly, but they will force every puzzle piece that touches them to shift, due to the force of their power. Demographic shifts or technology improvements over the long run are examples of this type of puzzle piece.

The second type is what we can think of as balancing trends, or trends that are not inevitable but, if they come about, will have

---

*This explains why all of the mathematical models make assumptions about variables that allow the models to work, except that what they end up showing is not related to the real world, which is composed of dynamic and not static variables.

significant implications. If you place that piece into the puzzle, it, too, changes the shape of all the pieces of the puzzle around it. And in the economic supertrend puzzle, balancing trends can change the shape of other pieces in ways that are not clear.

Deflation and inflation are in the latter category. They change the way almost all other variables behave.

Deflation and inflation are two sides of a coin, making some people winners and others losers. There is no way around it. Moderate inflation can help borrowers and hurts creditors, while moderate deflation hurts borrowers and helps creditors. (High levels of inflation or deflation hurt everyone as no one wants to borrow or lend.) As inflation eats away at debt, it punishes both savers and lenders. When faced with deflation, however, people change the way they consume, save, invest, and live.

When you become a Federal Reserve Bank governor, you are taken into a back room and are given a DNA transplant that makes you viscerally and at all times opposed to deflation. Deflation is a major economic game changer.

There are two kinds of deflation: good deflation and bad deflation. Good deflation that comes from increased productivity is desirable. In the late 1800s, the United States went through an almost 30-year period of deflation that saw massive improvements in agriculture (such as the McCormick reaper) and the ability of producers to get their products to markets through railroads. In fact, too many railroads were built, and a number of the companies that built them collapsed. Just as we experienced with the fiber-optic cable build-out, there was soon too much railroad capacity, and freight prices fell. That was bad for the shareholders but good for consumers. It was a time of great economic growth.

We all understand good deflation intuitively since we have experienced that in the world of technology, where we view it as normal that the price of a computer will fall, even as its quality rises over time. Indeed, we would all be surprised if our iPads did not fall rapidly in price and show greatly improved quality over the next decade. That is a kind of deflation we can all live with. In fact, in a world of rising productivity in any industry, prices *should* fall.

Even the good deflationary period of the late 1800s was not without its troubles. Many farmers suffered tremendously with falling prices, and there was significant social unrest. Most of them bought their farms with loans and borrowed money to buy seeds and machinery. As we know, deflation helps lenders and hurts borrowers. Falling prices and fixed debts became a terrible combination for farmers. Unsurprisingly, because of deflation, during the last 30 years of the nineteenth century, money dominated politics, and candidates like William Jennings Bryan suggested more inflationary alternatives to a hard gold standard.

Bad deflation comes from a lack of pricing power and lower final demand. It hurts the incomes of both employer and employee and discourages entrepreneurs from increasing their production capacity and thus employment. This is what we saw in the Great Depression, when prices collapsed by 25 percent, and we've seen this in Japan after the bubble burst in 1989. Once the deflationary dynamic is started, people form deflationary expectations. They expect prices to keep going down. They realize that goods will fall in price, and it creates the incentive to postpone spending.

Most of us have grown up experiencing only inflation, and many of us have seen firsthand the problems of rampant inflation in the 1970s. The threat of deflation, therefore, may seem like a fantasy to most readers. But the risks of deflation are real and cannot be easily dismissed. Currently, unemployment is almost 10 percent in the United States (and quite high throughout much of Europe), which is almost twice its average of the past two decades, and capacity utilization is at very low levels. The economy has started turning up, but any double dip or a later recession could easily tip prices below 0 percent and start a deflationary dynamic where we all suffer from the elements of deflation.

If we have a double dip recession in 2011 or one soon thereafter when inflation is already low, there is a real chance we could get deflation, so let's get familiar with it.

The Elements of Deflation: What Deflation Looks Like

Just as every schoolchild knows that water is formed by the two elements of hydrogen and oxygen in a very simple combination we all know as H_2O, so bad deflation has its own elements of composition. Let's look at some of them (in no particular order).

- **Excess capacity and unemployment**—First, deflation can happen because the real economy has tremendous slack and there is excess production capacity. It is hard to have pricing power when your competition also has more capacity than he wants, so he prices his product as low as he can to make a profit, but also to get the sale. The world is awash in excess capacity now. Eventually, we either grow the economy to utilize that capacity, or it will be taken off line through bankruptcy, a reduction in capacity (as when businesses lay off employees), or businesses simply exiting their industries. When the economy has excess slack, we see high and chronic unemployment. It reduces final demand, as people simply don't have the money to buy things.

  As Figure 7.1 shows, even after a strong bounce back from the lows following Lehman's bankruptcy, we are still below troughs of previous recessions.

  As Figure 7.2 shows, unemployment rates are near 10 percent in the United States and the European Union.
- **Wealth effect in reverse**—Deflation is also associated with massive wealth destruction. The events since the fall of 2007 have certainly provided that element. Home prices have dropped in many nations

Figure 7.1 U.S. and EU Capacity Utilization
SOURCE: Bloomberg, Variant Perception.

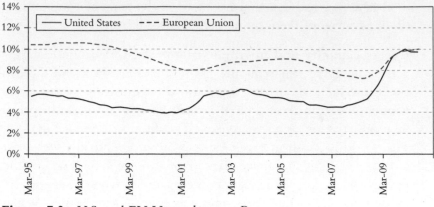

Figure 7.2 U.S. and EU Unemployment Rate
SOURCE: Bloomberg, Variant Perception.

all over the world, with some exceptions like Canada and Australia (which may be in its own housing bubble!). Trillions of dollars of wealth has evaporated, no longer available for use. Likewise, the bear market in equities in the developed world has wiped out trillions of dollars in valuation, resulting in rising savings rates as consumers, especially those close to a wanted retirement, try to repair their leaking balance sheets.

And while increased saving is good for an individual, it calls into play Keynes's paradox of thrift. That is, while it is good for one person to save, when everyone does it, it decreases consumer spending. Decreased consumer spending (or decreased final demand, in economic terms) means less pricing power for companies and is yet another element of deflation.

- **Collapsing home prices**—Falling home prices and a weak housing market are one more element of deflation. This is happening not just in the United States, but also much of Europe is suffering a real estate crisis. Japan has seen its real estate market fall almost 90 percent in nominal terms since 1989 in some cities, and that is part of the reason they have had 20 years with no job growth and that the nominal GDP is where it was 17 years ago.
- **Deleveraging**—Yet another element of deflation is the massive deleveraging that comes with a major credit crisis. Not only are consumers and businesses reducing their debt but also banks

are reducing their lending. Bank losses (at the last count we saw) are more than $2 trillion and rising. Deflation can lead to default, bankruptcy and restructurings, and ultimately financial distress. Deflation also reduces the nominal value of collateral, reducing the creditworthiness of firms and forcing companies to sell assets into falling prices.

As an aside, the European bank stress tests were a joke. They assumed no sovereign debt default. Evidently, the thought of Greece not paying its debt was just not in the realm of their thinking. There were other deficiencies as well, but that is the most glaring. European banks are still a concern unless the European Central Bank (ECB) goes ahead and buys all that sovereign debt from the banks, getting it off their balance sheets.

Irving Fisher, the great classical economist, tells us that the definition of *debt deflation* is when everyone in a market tries to reduce debt, which results in distress selling. This leads to a contraction of the money supply as bank loans are paid off. This in turn leads to a fall in the level of asset prices and a still greater fall in the net worth of businesses, precipitating bankruptcies, a fall in profits, and a reduction in output, trade, and employment. This then leads to loss of confidence, hoarding of money, and a fall in nominal interest rates and a rise in deflation-adjusted interest rates. It becomes a self-reinforcing process. Deflation becomes a vicious circle.

- **Collapse of money and lending**—When the money supply is falling in tandem with a slowing velocity of money, that brings up serious deflationary issues. And it is not just the United States. Global real broad money growth is close to zero (Figure 7.3). Deflationary pressures are the norm in the developed world (except for Britain, where inflation is the issue).

- **Government austerity**—In the short run, reducing government spending (in the United States at local, state, and federal levels) is deflationary, as noted in a previous chapter. Martin Wolf, in the *Financial Times,* wrote the following in July 2010 (arguing that the move to fiscal austerity is ill-advised):

We can see two huge threats in front of us. The first is the failure to recognize the strength of the deflationary pressures. . . .

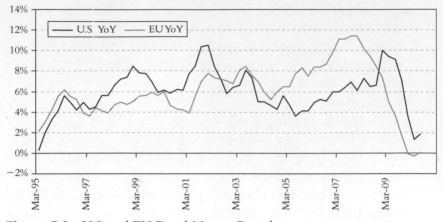

Figure 7.3   U.S. and EU Broad Money Growth
Source: Bloomberg, Variant Perception.

The danger that premature fiscal and monetary tightening will end up tipping the world economy back into recession is not small, even if the largest emerging countries should be well able to protect themselves. The second threat is failure to secure the medium-term structural shifts in fiscal positions, in management of the financial sector and in export-dependency, that are needed if a sustained and healthy global recovery is to occur.

We face the deflation of the depression era, and central bankers of the world are united in opposition. As Paul McCulley quipped this spring, when we asked him if he was concerned about inflation with all the stimulus and printing of money we were facing, "John, you better hope they can cause some inflation." And he is right. If we don't have a problem with inflation in the future, we are going to have far worse problems to deal with.

Saint Milton Friedman taught us that inflation is always and everywhere a monetary phenomenon. A central bank, by printing too much money, can bring about inflation and destroy a currency, all things being equal. But that is the tricky part of that equation, because not all things are equal. The pieces of the puzzle can change shape. When the elements of deflation combine in the right order, the central bank can print what seems a boatload of money without bringing about inflation. And we may now be watching that combination in a number of countries.

As my friend Lacy Hunt of Hoisington Asset Management points out, Friedman did not consider any increase in the money supply to be inflationary at all times. He considered excessive money growth to be inflationary and insufficient money growth to be deflationary. For this reason, Friedman advocated the Fed be replaced by a monetary rule in which money growth was held at a stationary rate of increase that was just sufficient to cover increases in the labor force and productivity. It is also important to recognize that Friedman then translated excessive or insufficient money growth into inflation or deflation, because he believed the velocity of money to be stable. This was true during the period when Friedman conducted the bulk of his empirical work (i.e., from about 1950 to 1980). However, after 1980, the velocity of money rose rapidly, reaching a peak in 1997, which exceeded the prior peak in 1918.

The Velocity of Money

What is the shape-shifting piece of the puzzle that Milton Friedman didn't count on when he said inflation was a monetary phenomenon? The piece is the velocity of money. If you print money but it doesn't go anywhere, you won't get inflation.

We all know intuitively from experience that when too much money chases too few goods, prices go up. And if there is too little money, prices go down.

During World War II in prisoner-of-war camps, goods and treats came largely through Red Cross parcels. Parcels contained cookies, chocolate, sugar, jam, butter, and the like. They also included cigarettes, which back in those days almost everyone smoked without thinking about. People traded jam for chocolate or cigarettes for cookies.

It was a barter economy, and a tin of jam was worth half a pound of margarine, for example. A cigarette was worth a few pieces of chocolates. Bartering isn't efficient, and the thing that was in highest supply and greatest demand was individual cigarettes. The cigarette started functioning as money; it became the unit of account and the medium of exchange (although it wasn't a store of value, as people eventually smoked them!).

Whenever the Red Cross parcels arrived, the quantity of money in the camp increased. Naturally, prices rose whenever the Red Cross parcels arrived. If the quantity of cigarettes declined, prices in the camp fell. Sometimes Red Cross parcels were interrupted due to the vagaries of war, and that meant fewer cigarettes in the camp. As some of the cigarettes were used for smoking, fewer were available to trade, and prices of various goods and services declined; that is, deflation occurred.[1]

This is the standard quantity theory of money. If you increase the quantity of cigarettes (i.e., money), prices rise. If you reduce the quantity of cigarettes or money, prices fall. So far, so simple. But the one thing that complicates matters is velocity.

Let's dig a little further and explore the concept of velocity of money. The velocity of money is the average frequency with which a unit of money is spent. For example, let's assume a very small economy of just you and me, which has a money supply of $100. I have the $100 and spend it to buy $100 of flowers from you. You in turn spend $100 to buy books from me. We have created $200 of our gross domestic product from a money supply of just $100. If we do that transaction every month (12 $\times$ $200), we would have $2,400 of GDP from our $100 monetary base.

What that means is that gross domestic product is a function of not just the money supply but how fast the money supply moves through the economy. Stated as an equation, it is P $=$ MV, where P is the price of your gross domestic product (nominal, so not inflation-adjusted here), M is the money supply, and V is the velocity of money.

Bear with us if this gets technical, but it's important.

Now, let's complicate our illustration just a bit, but not too much at first. This is very basic, and for those of you who will complain that we are being too simple, wait a few pages, please. Let's assume an island economy with 10 businesses and a money supply of $1 million. If each business does approximately $100,000 of business a quarter, then the gross domestic product for the island would be $4 million (4 times the $1 million quarterly production). The velocity of money in that economy is 4.

But what if our businesses got more productive? We introduce all sorts of interesting financial instruments, banking, new production capacity, computers, technical innovations, and robotics, and now everyone is doing $100,000 per month. Now our GDP is $12 million and the velocity of money is 12. But we have not increased the money supply. We're still trading with the same amount of money. Again, we assume that all businesses are static. They buy and sell the same amount every month. There are no winners and losers as of yet.

Now let's complicate matters. Two of the kids of the owners of the businesses decide to go into business for themselves. Having learned from their parents, they immediately become successful and start doing $100,000 a month themselves. The GDP potentially goes to $14 million. For everyone to stay at the same level of gross income, the velocity of money must increase to 14.

Now, this is important. In all our examples, the amount of money has stayed the same. What has changed is the velocity. But what if the velocity of money doesn't increase?

If the velocity of money does not increase, that means that each business is now going to buy and sell less in dollar terms each month. Remember, nominal GDP is money supply times velocity. If velocity does not increase, GDP will stay the same. The average business (there are now 12) goes from doing $1.2 million a year down to $1 million.

Each business now is doing around $80,000 per month. Overall, production is the same, but it is divided up among more businesses. For each of the businesses, it feels like a recession. They have fewer dollars, so they buy less and prices fall. This is a deflationary environment. In that world, the local central bank recognizes that the money supply needs to grow at some rate to make the demand for money neutral.

If the central bank of our island increases the money supply too much, you would have too much money chasing too few goods, and inflation would manifest its ugly head. (Remember, this is a very simplistic example. We assume static production from each business, running at full capacity.)

Let's say the central bank overshoots the increase in production and doubles the money supply to $2 million. If the velocity of money is still 12, then the GDP would grow to $24 million. That would be a good thing, wouldn't it?

No, because we only produce 20 percent more goods from the two new businesses. There is a relationship between production and price. Each business would now sell $200,000 per month or double their previous sales, which they would spend on goods and services, which only grew by 20 percent. They would start to bid up the price of the goods they want, and inflation sets in. Think of the 1970s.

Now, what about the velocity of money? Nobel laureate Milton Friedman taught us that inflation was always and everywhere a monetary phenomenon. That is, if inflation shows up, then the central bank has been printing too much money. Friedman assumed the velocity of money was constant in his work. And it was from about 1950 until 1978, when he was doing his seminal work. But then things changed. Let's look at two charts.

First, let's look at Figure 7.4, which shows the velocity of money for the last 108 years. Notice that the velocity of money fell during the Great Depression. And from 1953 to 1980, the velocity of money was almost exactly the average for the last 100 years. Note that the velocity of money *appears* to be mean reverting over long periods of time. That means one would expect the velocity of money to rise or fall over time back to the mean or average.

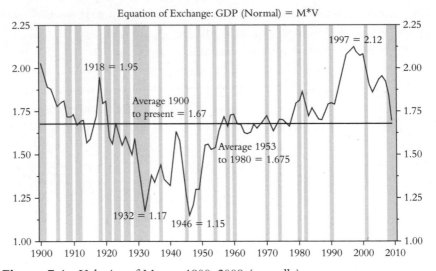

Figure 7.4 Velocity of Money 1900–2009 (annually)

NOTE: Through 2008. 2009; V = GDP/M, GDP = 14.3 trillion, M2 = 8.4 trillion, V = 1.69.
SOURCE: Hoisington Investment Management, Federal Reserve Board, Bureau of Economic Analysis, Bureau of the Census, Monetary Statistics of the United States.

Some would make the argument that we should use the mean from more modern times, since World War II, but even then, mean reversion would mean a slowing of the velocity of money (V), and mean reversion implies that V would go below (overcorrect) the mean. However you look at it, the clear implication is that V could drop if it mean reverts. In a few paragraphs, we will see why that is the case from a practical standpoint.

Now, let's look at the same chart since 1959 but with shaded gray areas that show us the times the economy is in recession. You can see this in Figure 7.5 (with recessions shaded). Note that with one exception in the 1970s, velocity drops during a recession. What is the response of the Federal Reserve Bank? An offsetting increase in the money supply to try to overcome the effects of the business cycle and the recession. If velocity falls, then money supply must rise for nominal GDP to grow. The Fed attempts to jump-start the economy back into growth by increasing the money supply.

The assumption is that GDP is $14.5 trillion, M2 is $8.5 trillion, and therefore velocity is 1.7, down from almost 1.95 just a few years ago. If velocity reverts to or below the mean, it could easily drop 10 percent from here. We will explore why this could happen in a minute.

But let's go back to our equation, P = MV. If velocity slows by 10 percent (which it well could), then money supply (M) would have

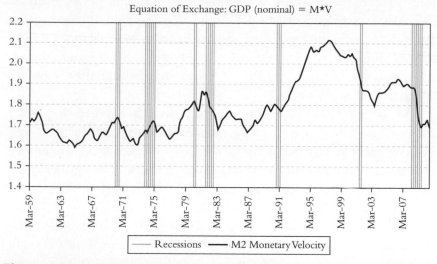

Figure 7.5   U.S. Monetary Velocity (quarterly)
SOURCE: Bloomberg, Variant Perception.

to rise by 10 percent just to maintain a static economy. But that assumes you do not have 1 percent population growth, 2 percent (or thereabouts) productivity growth, and a target inflation of 2 percent, which means M (money supply) needs to grow about 5 percent a year even if V was constant. And that is not particularly stimulative, given that we are in a relatively slow growth economy.

A Slowdown in Velocity

Now, why is the velocity of money slowing down? Notice the real rise in velocity from 1990 through about 1997. Growth in M2 was falling during most of that period, yet the economy was growing. That means that velocity had to rise faster than normal. Why? Primarily because of the financial innovations introduced in the early 1990s, like securitizations and CDOs. It is financial innovation that spurs above-trend growth in velocity.

And now we are watching the great unwinding of financial innovations, as they went to excess and caused a credit crisis. In principle, a CDO or subprime asset–backed security should be a good thing. And in the beginning, they were. But then standards got loose, greed kicked in, and Wall Street began to game the system. End of game.

What drove velocity (financial innovation) to new highs is no longer part of the equation. We no longer have all sorts of fancy vehicles like ABCP programs, SIVs, CDOs, and CMBSs making money move around the economy faster. The absence of these financial innovations is slowing things down. If the money supply did not rise significantly to offset that slowdown in velocity, the economy would already be in a much deeper recession.

While the Fed does not have control over M2, when they lower interest rates, it is supposed to make us want to take on more risk, borrow money, and boost the economy. So, they have an indirect influence. And notice in Figure 7.6 that M2 has not been growing that much lately, after shooting up in late 2008 as the Fed flooded the market with liquidity.

Bottom line? Expect money-supply growth well north of what the economy could normally tolerate for the next few years. Is that enough? Too much? About right? We won't know for a long time. This will allow armchair economists (and that is most of us) to sit back and Monday-morning quarterback for many years.

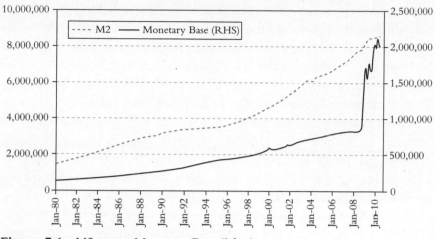

Figure 7.6 M2 versus Monetary Base ($ bns)
SOURCE: Bloomberg, Variant Perception.

The concept of the velocity of money is something that drives the gold bugs nuts. A gold bug is someone for whom the answer to the question "Where should I invest?" is almost always gold, with a smattering of natural resources. They assume that fiat currencies (paper money) will go the way of all flesh, which is historically not an unrealistic assumption. The question is when, and the when can be a long way off, making gold a boring investment for long periods of time. Most gold bugs subscribe to the Austrian school of economics founded by Ludwig von Mises. Von Mises did not factor the velocity of money into his equations.

When gold bugs see a rise in the supply of money, they think that translates into a rise in the price of gold, as that should bring about inflation. And they would be right if monetary velocity remained constant.

If you assume a constant number of transactions, then the prices paid would be a *direct* function of the supply of money and velocity. But if velocity falls, you could have the supply of money rising, perhaps substantially, and prices paid actually falling if the velocity of money is falling faster than the rise in the money supply. As we said, this drives the gold bugs nuts.

As an aside, both your humble authors are believers in owning gold, and in some countries and currencies, owning more than a small insurance portfolio is well recommended. For us, gold is not so much an inflation hedge as a currency hedge. The odd fact is that in at least dollar terms, gold has not correlated all that well with inflation, although all the gold-oriented web sites and books seem to focus on gold as an inflation hedge. In fact, in the 1970s, the last real inflationary period we had, soy and lumber did better. But neither soy nor lumber is easy to buy or hold. People don't tend to accumulate soybeans when they distrust their Zimbabwean dollars or German reichsmarks.

Gold is a very useful instrument when people lose confidence in a currency or in the central bank that controls that currency to maintain a reasonable purchasing power. Gold of late has gone up against the U.S. dollar, but it has gone up much more percentage-wise against the euro and the pound sterling.

Now, the central bank has some control over this process by controlling how much money they put into the system, by regulating how much actual reserves a bank must have, and by adjusting the price at which the central bank will make money available to the bank, plus a host of other factors. But in our simple world, we just need to know that an increase in lending will increase the money supply.

So, one way to think of the money supply is all of the cash plus all loans and credit available. (For the world, that is about $2 trillion in cash and $50 trillion in loans and credit.) And for the entire last 60-plus years, the amount of money supply, debt, and leverage in the system has been rising, steadily at first and then at a much faster pace. But now the shadow banking system has collapsed, and all the dynamics that kept debt going up have reversed gears.

Notice in Figure 7.7 that a dollar of debt buys less and less GDP growth as time goes on, until debt has become a drag on the economy. Why? Go back to the chapter on Rogoff and Reinhart's book. The increase in debt of late has been government debt, which is a drag on the economy. Government debt crowds out savings and investments.

The Fed's balance sheet may have doubled, but now the leverage in the system is shrinking. Individuals and businesses are paying down their debts and taking fewer loans. Banks are reducing their lending. This is a phenomenon all over the developed world. The governments are stepping in to take up some of the slack on the debt side, but there is a limit to how much even large governments can borrow, as we are finding out. Velocity falls when companies and individuals deleverage.

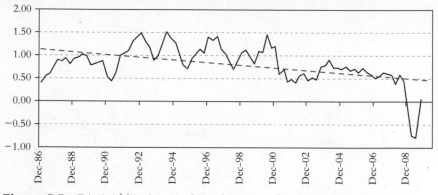

Figure 7.7 Diminishing Marginal Productivity of Debt in the U.S. Economy (in $)
SOURCE: Bloomberg, Variant Perception.

It is the end of the debt supercycle. It is endgame. As leverage and debt are taken off the table, there is real downward pressure on the money supply and the velocity of money. It is one of the most deflationary forces at work in the world today. Just look at the charts below of M3 money supply for various countries. It is turning negative, something not witnessed for a long time.

This is true for Europe, as you can see from Figure 7.8.

Figure 7.8 Europe M3, Year over Year
SOURCE: Bloomberg, Variant Perception.

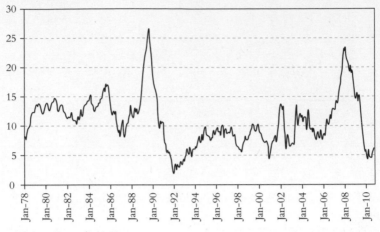

Figure 7.9   Australia M3
SOURCE: Bloomberg, Variant Perception.

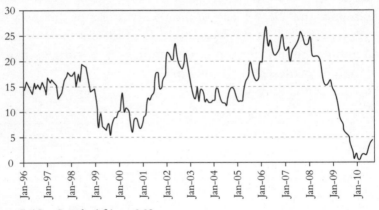

Figure 7.10   South African M3
SOURCE: Bloomberg, Variant Perception.

And for Australia, as you can see in Figure 7.9.

And even emerging markets like South Africa, as you can see in Figure 7.10.

The Roadmap Ahead: Bernanke's Helicopter Speech

The current trend, as noted previously, is for lower inflation and falling velocity. That is why it will be important to watch the consumer price index (CPI) numbers even more closely in the coming months.

If the United States and/or Europe gets into outright deflation, we expect the respective central banks to react by increasing their asset purchases and by outright monetization of government debt, buying treasuries from insurance companies and pension funds. Putting more money into banks when they are not lending does not seem to be helpful as far as deflation is concerned. More mortgages? Corporate debt? Moving out the yield curve? All are options both the Fed and the ECB will consider. We need to be paying attention.

The good news is that we do have a road map of sorts. One of the most memorable scenes in the film *Patton* is when George C. Scott defeats the Germans and yells, "Rommel, you magnificent bastard! I read your book!" If an investor were to utter that today, they would have read the speech by Ben Bernanke. In November 2002, Bernanke gave a now-famous speech, which has come to be known as his helicopter speech, titled "Deflation: Making Sure 'It' Doesn't Happen Here."[2] By the way, I (John) have always been convinced that his remark about printing presses and helicopters was a failed attempt at economist humor. This explains why we don't get many offers from comedy clubs.

Let's sum up the helicopter section: You can create inflation by printing a lot of money. But that is not the interesting part of the speech.

Let's look at what Bernanke really said. First, he begins by telling us that he believes the likelihood of deflation is remote. But since it did happen in Japan and seems to be the cause of the current Japanese problems, we cannot dismiss the possibility outright. Therefore, we need to see what policies can be brought to bear on the problem.

He then goes on to say that the most important thing is to prevent deflation **before** it happens. He says that a central bank should allow for some "cushion" and should not target zero inflation, and he speculates that this is over 1 percent. Typically, central banks target inflation of 1 percent to 3 percent, although this means that in normal times inflation is more likely to rise above the acceptable target than fall below zero in poor times.

Central banks can usually influence this by raising and lowering interest rates. But what if the Fed funds rate falls to zero? Not to worry, there are still policy levers that can be pulled. Quoting Bernanke:

So what then might the Fed do if its target interest rate, the overnight federal funds rate, fell to zero? One relatively straightforward extension of current procedures would be to try to stimulate spending by lowering rates further out along the Treasury term structure—that is, rates on government bonds of longer maturities. . . .

A more direct method, which I personally prefer, would be for the Fed to begin announcing explicit ceilings for yields on longer-maturity Treasury debt (say, bonds maturing within the next two years). The Fed could enforce these interest-rate ceilings by committing to make unlimited purchases of securities up to two years from maturity at prices consistent with the targeted yields. If this program were successful, not only would yields on medium-term Treasury securities fall, but (because of links operating through expectations of future interest rates) yields on longer-term public and private debt (such as mortgages) would likely fall as well.

Lower rates over the maturity spectrum of public and private securities should strengthen aggregate demand in the usual ways and thus help to end deflation. Of course, if operating in relatively short-dated Treasury debt proved insufficient, the Fed could also attempt to cap yields of Treasury securities at still longer maturities, say three to six years.

He then proceeds to outline what could be done if the economy falls into outright deflation and uses the examples, and others, cited previously. It seems clear to me from the context that he is making an academic list of potential policies the Fed could pursue if outright deflation became a reality. He was not suggesting they be used, nor do we believe he thinks we will ever get to the place where they would be contemplated. He was simply pointing out that the Fed can fight deflation if it wants to. (And now, in late 2010, that question might become more than academic.)

With this as background, we can begin to look at what we believe is the true import of the speech. Read these sentences, noting our boldface words:

A central bank, either alone or in cooperation with other parts of the government, retains considerable power to expand aggregate demand and economic activity **even when its accustomed policy rate is at zero**.

The basic prescription for preventing deflation is therefore straightforward, at least in principle: Use monetary and fiscal policy as needed to support aggregate spending. . . . [As Keynesian as you can get.]

Some observers have concluded that when the central bank's policy rate falls to zero—its practical minimum—monetary policy loses its ability to further stimulate aggregate demand and the economy.

To **stimulate aggregate spending** when short-term interest rates have reached zero, the Fed must expand the scale of its asset purchases or, possibly, expand the menu of assets that it buys.

Now, let us go to his conclusion:

Sustained deflation can be highly destructive to a modern economy and should be strongly resisted. Fortunately, for the foreseeable future, the chances of a serious deflation in the United States appear remote indeed, in large part because of our economy's underlying strengths but also because of the determination of the Federal Reserve and other U.S. policymakers to act preemptively against deflationary pressures. Moreover, as I have discussed today, a variety of policy responses are available should deflation appear to be taking hold. Because some of these alternative policy tools are relatively less familiar, they may raise practical problems of implementation and of calibration of their likely economic effects. **For this reason, as I have emphasized, prevention of deflation is preferable to cure.** Nevertheless, I hope to have persuaded you that the Federal Reserve and other economic policymakers would be far from helpless in the face of deflation, even should the federal funds rate hit its zero bound.

And there you have it. All the data pointing to a slowing economy? It puts us (in the United States) closer to deflation. It is not the headline data per se we need to think about. We need to start thinking about what the Fed will do if we have a double-dip recession and start to fall into deflation. Will they move out the yield curve, as he suggested? Buy more and varied assets, like mortgages and corporate debt? What will that do to markets and investments?

Note that last bolded line: **"For this reason, as I have emphasized, prevention of deflation is preferable to cure."** If Bernanke is true to his words, that means he may act in advance of the next recession if the data continue to come in weak and deflation starts to actually become a threat. That is the thing we don't see in all the economic data—the potential for new Fed action. Let's hope that, like the deflation scare in 2002, it doesn't come about. Stay tuned.

If great contractions are caused by excessive debt and these contractions lead to deflation, then the Fed can only temporarily offset the inevitable deflation. Quantitative easing (QE) will only work by inducing another borrowing and lending cycle. This will mean that the economy will add more leverage to an already overleveraged economy. Thus, the QE buys the economy some additional growth but only for a limited time. Why limited? The additional leverage leads to economic deterioration and increased systemic risk. Thus, the only fundamental fix for an economy plagued by extreme overindebtedness is time and austerity. There is no lasting monetary policy fix.

One final thought before we close this chapter on deflation. Recessions are by definition deflationary. One of the things we learned from *This Time Is Different* by Rogoff and Reinhart is that economies are more fragile and volatile and that recessions are more frequent after a credit crisis. Further, spending cuts are better than tax increases at improving the health of an economy after a credit crisis.

We think we can take it as a given that there is another recession in front of the United States and/or Europe at some point. That is the natural order of things. But it would be better to have that inevitable recession as far into the future as possible, and preferably with a little inflationary cushion and some room for active policy responses. A recession in 2011 or 2012 would be problematic, if not catastrophic. Rates are as low as they can go. Higher deficit spending, as a way to address recession, is not in the political cards without very serious consequences. Yet unemployment would shoot up and tax collections go down at all levels of government if there were another recession.

That is why we worry so much about taking the Bush tax cuts away when the economy is weak. When you read this, we will know what Congress did about them. Today, as we write, it is up in the air. Now, maybe those who argue that tax increases don't matter are right. They have their academic studies. But the preponderance of work suggests those studies are flawed and at worst are guilty of data mining (looking for data that support your already-developed conclusions).

Professor Michael Boskin wrote in July in the *Wall Street Journal:* "The president does not say that economists agree that the high future taxes to finance the stimulus will hurt the economy. (The University of Chicago's Harald Uhlig estimates $3.40 of lost output for every dollar of government spending.) Either the president is not being told of serious alternative viewpoints, or serious viewpoints are defined as only those that support his position. In either case, he is being ill-served by his staff."

There Are No Good Choices

As we finalize this book, the Fed has announced that it will buy $600 billion in Treasury debt by June 2010 and reserves the right to buy more. The theories that Bernanke invoked in the speech are about to be tested in the reality of the world economy.

We are in a period when the Fed is in the process of reflating the economy, or at least attempting to do so. They will eventually be successful if they persist (though at what cost to the value of the dollar, one can only guess). One can have a theoretical argument about whether that is the right thing to do (we are most vocal that it isn't!) or whether the Fed should just leave things alone, let the banks fail, and let the system purge itself. We find that a boring and almost pointless argument.

The people in control don't buy Austrian economics. It makes for nice polemics but is never going to be policy. We are much more interested in learning what the Fed and Congress will actually do and then shaping our portfolio accordingly. (And the same goes if you live in Europe or Britain or Japan!)

A mentor of mine once told me that the market would do whatever it could to cause the most pain to the most people. One way to do that would be to allow deflation to develop over the next few quarters or years, thereby probably affecting many investment classes, before inflation and then stagflation become (hopefully) the end of our perilous journey. Which, of course, would be good for gold. If you can hold on in the meantime.

Is it possible that we can find some Goldilocks end to this crisis? That the Fed can find the right mix, and Congress wakes up and puts some fiscal adults in control? All things are possible, but that is not the way we would bet.

While there are some who are very sure of our near future, we are not. There are just too many variables. Let us give you one scenario that worries us. Congress shows no discipline and lets the budget run through a few more trillion in the next two years. The Fed has been successful in reflating the economy after it has embarked on even more aggressive quantitative easing. The bond markets get very nervous, and longer-term rates start to rise. What little recovery we are seeing is threatened by higher rates in a period of high unemployment.

Does the Fed monetize the debt and bring on real inflation and further destruction of the dollar? Or allow interest rates to rise and once again push us into recession? (A triple dip?) The Fed is faced with a dual mandate, unlike other central banks. They are supposed to maintain price equilibrium and also set policy that will encourage full employment. At that point, they will have to choose one over the other. There are no good choices.

CHAPTER EIGHT

Inflation and Hyperinflation

Bankruptcies of governments have, on the whole, done less harm to mankind than their ability to raise loans.

—R. H. Tawney,
Religion and the Rise of Capitalism, 1926

By a continuing process of inflation, government can confiscate, secretly and unobserved, an important part of the wealth of their citizens.

—John Maynard Keynes,
Economic Consequences of Peace

Unemployed men took one or two rucksacks and went from peasant to peasant. They even took the train to favorable locations to get foodstuffs illegally which they sold afterwards in the town at three or fourfold the prices they had paid themselves. First the peasants were happy about the great amount of paper money which rained into their houses for their eggs and butter.... However, when they came to town with their full briefcases to buy goods, they discovered to their chagrin that, whereas they had only asked for a fivefold price for their produce, the prices for scythe, hammer and cauldron, which they wanted to buy, had risen by a factor of 50.

—Stefan Zweig,
The World of Yesterday, 1944[1]

n the previous chapter, we looked at deflation. Now let's look at the opposite: inflation and even hyperinflation. Hyperinflation is an extreme case of inflation and a nightmare for anyone living it.

We know that the world is drowning in too much debt, and it is unlikely that households and governments everywhere will be able to pay down that debt. Doing so in some cases is impossible, and in other cases it will condemn people to many hard years of labor to be debt-free. Inflation, by comparison, appears to be the easy way out for many policy makers.

Companies and households typically deal with excessive debt by defaulting; countries overwhelmingly usually deal with excessive debt by inflating it away. While debt is fixed, prices and wages can go up, making the total debt burden smaller. People can't increase prices and wages through inflation, but governments can create inflation, and they've been pretty good at it over the years. Inflation, debt monetization, and currency debasement are not new. They have been used for the past few thousand years as means to get rid of debt. In fact, they work pretty well.

The average person thinks that inflation comes from printing money. There is some truth to this, and indeed the most vivid images of hyperinflation are of printed German reichsmarks being burned for heat in the 1920s or Hungarian pengös being swept up in the streets in 1945.

You don't even have to go that far back to see hyperinflation and how brilliantly it works at eliminating debt. Let's look at the example of Brazil, which is one of the world's most recent examples of hyperinflation. This happened within our lifetimes. In the late 1980s and 1990s, it very successfully got rid of most of its debt.

Today, Brazil has very little debt, as it has all been inflated away. Its economy is booming, people trust the central bank, and the country is a success story. Much like the United States had high inflation in the 1970s and then got a diligent central banker like Paul Volcker, in Brazil a new government came in, beat inflation, produced strong real GDP growth, and set the stage for one of the greatest economic success stories of the past two decades. Indeed, the same could be said of other countries like Turkey that had hyperinflation, devaluation, and then found monetary and fiscal rectitude.

In 1993, Brazilian inflation was roughly 2,000 percent. Only four years later, in 1997 it was 7 percent. Almost as if by magic, the debt disappeared. Imagine if the United States increased its money supply, which is currently $900 billion, by a factor of 10,000 times, as Brazil did between 1991 and 1996. We would have 9 quadrillion U.S. dollars on the Fed's balance sheet. That is a lot of zeros. It would also mean that our current debt of 13 trillion would be chump change. A critic of this strategy for getting rid of our debt could point out that no one would lend to us again if we did that. Hardly. Investors, sadly, have very short memories. Markets always forgive default and inflation. Just look at Brazil, Bolivia, and Russia today. Foreigners are delighted to invest in these countries.*

Endgame is not complicated under inflation and hyperinflation. Deflation is not inevitable. Money printing and monetization of government debt work when real growth fails. It has worked in countless emerging market economies (Zimbabwe, Ukraine, Tajikistan, Taiwan, Brazil, etc.). We could even use it in the United States to get rid of all our debts. It would take a few years, and then we could get a new central banker like Volcker to kill inflation. We could then be a real success story like Brazil.

Honestly, recommending hyperinflation is tongue in cheek. But now even serious economists are recommending inflation as a solution. Given the powerful deflationary forces in the world, inflation will stay low in the near term. This gives some comfort to mainstream economists who think we can create inflation to solve the debt problem in the short run. The International Monetary Fund's top economist, Olivier Blanchard, has argued that central banks should target a higher inflation rate than they do at present to avoid the possibility of deflation. Economists like Paul Krugman, a Nobel Prize winner, and Blanchard argue that central banks should raise their inflation targets to as high as 4 percent. Paul McCulley argues that central banks should be "responsibly irresponsible." There are, however, problems with inflation as a policy tool.

In this chapter, we'll examine inflation and hyperinflation, what they are, how they're different, and how hyperinflation ends.

---

*As a quick aside, that is why we expect the current attempts by the Fed at quantitative easing 2 to be probably ineffective: $600 billion is not all that much in the grand scheme of things. Now, if they start talking $6 trillion, that would get our attention.

A Dose of Inflation

In the previous chapter, we discussed why the current crisis presents the real risk of deflation if monetary velocity falls and does not rise. However, there are many reasons to believe that we will not see deflation.

The major mistake that deflationists now make is their focus on spare capacity. Central bankers and most economists assume that because of the huge deleveraging we're seeing, governments can print money and borrow like crazy without provoking inflation because of slack in productive capacity created by the recession.

The severity of the recession means that they are wrong. During a normal downturn, production slows, but spare capacity isn't destroyed, and it is able to create extra supply when demand returns. A severe credit squeeze, though, does lasting structural damage, as the evaporation of bank lending destroys firms' longer-term ability to produce at given levels.

People who think inflation isn't possible point to high unemployment in the United States, the United Kingdom, and Europe. But as we've shown earlier in this book, many of the unemployed in the developed world are unskilled or will be unemployed long enough that their skills will be totally rusty and, hence, they will be unemployable. The slack, in other word is imaginary.

According to a major study by Athanasios Orphanides, now central banker in Cyprus, the "ex-post revisions of the output gap are of the same order of magnitude as the output gap itself, that these ex post revisions are highly persistent and that real-time estimates tend to be severely biased around business cycle turning points, when the cost of policy induced errors due to incorrect measurement is at its greatest. . . . The bulk of the problem is due to the pervasive unreliability of end-of-sample estimates of the trend in output."[2] The English translation is: Economists and central bankers are very, very bad at estimating output gaps. No surprise there!

The output gap is often subject to considerable measurement error, and it is often revised because of revisions to real GDP and to estimates of the economy's underlying rate of productivity growth. So output gap estimates and capacity utilization estimates are almost worthless in real time. Not only are they worthless but also revisions turn out to be bigger even than the output gap itself. (As we've written before, anyone can make mistakes, but it takes an expert with a computer to really foul things up.)

Even Federal Reserve governors understand the problem. As Charles Plosser of the Philadelphia Federal Reserve has noted, "The data uncertainties are not just theoretical curiosities. They have caused actual problems when policy has been based on mis-measured gaps, resulting in unnecessary economic instability. **A particularly poignant example is the Great Inflation of the 1970s in the U.S.** [emphasis added]."[3]

I have written before that when you become a Federal Reserve Bank governor, you are taken into a back room and are given a DNA transplant that makes you viscerally and at all times opposed to deflation. Modern central bankers are much happier with inflation. They're pretty good at producing it, in fact.

Figure 8.1 shows U.S. inflation historically, going back to the late 1600s. (How economic historians know what prices were centuries ago always amazes us, but that is the story for another fascinating book.) As you can see from Figure 8.1, when the United States and the rest of the world used a gold standard, periods of inflation alternated with periods of deflation. On average, the price level didn't go anywhere. One year's inflation was usually canceled out by the next year's deflation. But if you look to the right on the chart, you see that suddenly we don't get deflation anymore. After the Bretton Woods Agreement in 1948, when the world moved to a dollar standard only nominally backed by gold,

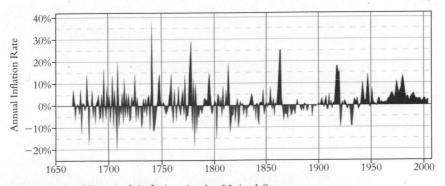

Figure 8.1 Historical Inflation in the United States
SOURCE: John J. McCusker, *How Much Is That in Real Money? A Historical Price Index for Use as a Deflator of Money Values in the Economy of the United States* (Oak Knoll Press, 1992; 2nd ed., rev., 2001).

and then after 1971, when the United States no longer made the dollar exchangeable for gold, something happened: We only got inflation.

Figure 8.1 shows that inflation is the norm in a world of paper currencies. Central banks and governments have an inflationary bias. They can regulate monetary policy much more easily when interest rates are positive, so they prefer always to have some inflation in the system. In fact, there are very, very few examples of deflation after 1948 or 1971.

In the previous chapter, we looked at the elements of deflation. Deflation can happen right after banking crises and property busts. It happened, for example, after the Japanese bubble burst and as the Japanese banks started going bust. It also happened after the housing bubble burst in Hong Kong in 1997, the banking bust in Ireland in 2008, and the Baltics after their housing bust in 2008. These examples are the only examples we know of deflation after 1971. Almost all of these cases happened because the countries had given up control of their monetary policy. Hong Kong, Ireland, and the Baltics did not control their own money supply. They operated pegs that fixed their exchange rate to the U.S. dollar or the euro (in Ireland's case, it was in fact already *inside* the euro). **Japan is the one and only case of deflation in a country that is not pegged to another currency or in a currency union.**

As Reinhart and Rogoff have shown us, the typical pattern is for banking crises to lead to sovereign defaults and for sovereign defaults to lead to inflation.

BANKING CRISIS → DEFAULT → INFLATION

The simple explanation is that banking crises unleash powerful deflationary forces of deleveraging and falling monetary velocity. In this environment, people, corporations, and eventually governments are unable to pay their debts and default. Government defaults typically lead foreigners to sell the local currency, and you get a currency devaluation. A devaluation makes prices for imported goods more expensive and leads to inflation. At the same time, governments and central banks fight the downturn with more expansive monetary policies, which leads to higher inflation.

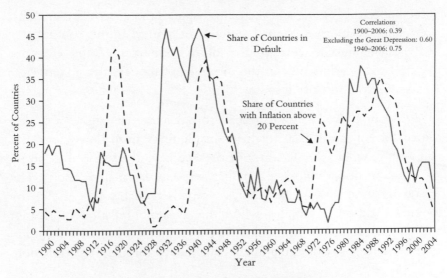

Figure 8.2   Inflation and External Default 1900–2006
SOURCE: Reinhart and Rogoff, "Banking Crises: An Equal Opportunity Menace," www.bresserpereira
.org.br/terceiros/cursos/Rogoff.Banking_Crises.pdf.

The previous paragraph is a highly simplified (or if you're an economist, it is a highly stylized) version of what typically happens. But it is accurate. Figure 8.2, by Reinhart and Rogoff, captures very well how inflation typically follows external defaults, which typically follow banking crises.

It is easy to see why this is the case. Every week, you can read a very respectable professor recommending monetizing deficits and having a free lunch. If only the world worked that way. The following was written by Ricardo Caballero, a brilliant professor at MIT:

> What we need is a fiscal expansion (e.g. a temporary and large cut of sales taxes) that does not raise public debt in equal amount. This can be done with a "helicopter drop" targeted at the Treasury. That is, a monetary gift from the Fed to the Treasury.
>
> Critics may argue that this is simply voodoo accounting, as it is still the case that the consolidated balance sheet of the government, which includes the Fed, has incurred a liability. But this argument misses the point that the economy is in

liquidity-trap range, and once this happens the system becomes willing to absorb unlimited amounts of money. In this context, by changing the composition of the liabilities of the consolidated public sector in the direction of money, the government gets a sort of "free lunch."[4]

Of course, in Professor Caballero's defense, he argues that we should have a mechanism to drain this liquidity from the system, but realistically, would the Treasury or the Fed have the wisdom to do it?

Inflation doesn't work as a policy response for many reasons. The reason inflation only makes things worse is probably best shown by looking at extreme examples, where the ravages of inflation are clearest and most evident. We will look at hyperinflations, which is a lot of fun for the reader, but not much fun if you've lived through hyperinflation.

The Characteristics of Hyperinflations

Just as Reinhart and Rogoff wrote the book on banking and debt crises, there is one book that is the bible on hyperinflations. Professor Peter Bernholz, from the University of Basel, has written *Monetary Regimes and Inflation,* which provides an overview of every inflationary episode that has ever happened, and he explains the origins and characteristics of hyperinflation. It is well worth your time if you are interested in the mechanics of hyperinflation.

As Professor Bernholz points out, you can get inflationary episodes without printing money. Under the Greeks and Romans, rulers often made gold and silver coins smaller or put bad coins into circulation to debase their currency. **However, true hyperinflation only happens with paper currencies.**[5]

As you can see from Table 8.1, almost all hyperinflations have happened in the twentieth century. (Note: he wrote the book before the episode in Zimbabwe.)

The only hyperinflation prior to the twentieth century was during the French Revolution, when the French monetary regime, too, was based on the paper money standard.

We don't have very long-term inflation data for most countries, but as you can see in the case of the United Kingdom, where we have

Table 8.1 Hyperinflations in History

Country	Year	Highest Inflation per Month %	Country	Year	Highest Inflation per Month %
Argentina	1989/90	196	Hungary	1945/46	$1.295*10^{16}$
Armenia	1993/94	438	Kazakhstan	1994	57
Austria	1921/22	124	Kyrgyzstan	1992	157
Azerbaijan	1991/94	118	Nicaragua	1986/89	127
Belarus	1994	53	Peru	1921/24	114
Bolivia	1984/86	120	Poland	1989/90	188
Brazil	1989/93	84	Poland	1992/94	77
Bulgaria	1997	242	Serbia	1922/24	309,000,000
China	1947/49	4,209	Soviet Union	1945/49	279
Congo (Zaire)	1991/94	225	Taiwan	1995	399
France	1789/96	143	Tajikistan	1993/96	78
Georgia	1993/94	197	Turkmenistan	1992/94	63
Germany	1920/23	29,500	Ukraine	1990	249
Greece	1942/45	11,288	Yugoslavia		59
Hungary	1923/24	82			

SOURCE: Peter Bernholz, *Monetary Regimes and Inflation: History, Economic and Political Relationships* (Edward Elgar Publishing, March 27, 2006).

historical data, inflation was relatively stable for about 600 years. It was only after the United Kingdom moved toward paper money that inflation has really taken off. Unfortunately, this is true of every country with a paper currency (see Figure 8.3). *Interestingly, after countries abandoned the gold standard, there are more cases of hyperinflation than deflation.*

Figure 8.3 shows inflation, but we need to distinguish between *inflation* and *hyperinflation*. Many countries have high inflation, but hyperinflation is a very special case in which money grows greater than 50 percent from one month to the next. When money starts growing that quickly, the numbers become truly astronomical.

To give you a sense of just how crazy inflation can get once it gets going, Figure 8.4 shows inflation in Weimar Germany. You can see that toward the end of 1923, inflation was growing at 16 million percent per year.

What kinds of prices does 16 million percent inflation give you? The highest-value banknote issued by the Weimar government's Reichsbank

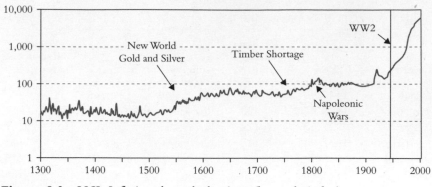

Figure 8.3   U.K. Inflation through the Ages (log-scale index)
SOURCE: Societe Generale, Phelps-Brown & Hopkins.

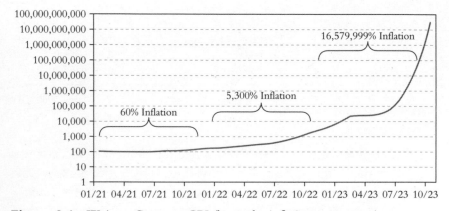

Figure 8.4   Weimar Germany CPI (log scale; inflation per annum)
SOURCE: Societe Generale, "Popular Delusions: Some Useful Things I've Learned about Germany's Hyperinflation," February 26, 2010, Bresciani-Turroni (1931), SG Cross Asset Research.

had a face value of 100 trillion marks (100,000,000,000,000; 100 billion on the log scale).[6] At the height of the inflation, one U.S. dollar was worth 4 trillion German marks. One of the firms printing these notes submitted an invoice for the work to the Reichsbank for 32,776,899,763,734,490,417.05 (3.28 × 1019, or 33 quintillion) marks.[7]

What causes such a spectacular increase in prices? Bernholz has explained the process very elegantly. He argues that governments have a bias toward inflation. The evidence doesn't disagree with him. The only thing that limits a government's desire for inflation is an independent central bank. After looking at inflation across all countries and analyzing all hyperinflationary episodes, the lessons are the following:

- Metallic standards like gold or silver show no or a much smaller inflationary tendency than discretionary paper money standards.
- Paper money standards with central banks independent of political authorities are less inflation based than those with dependent central banks.
- Currencies based on discretionary paper standards and bound by a regime of a fixed exchange rate to currencies, which either enjoy a metallic standard or, with a discretionary paper money standard, an independent central bank, show also a smaller tendency toward inflation, whether their central banks are independent or not.[8]

Bernholz examined 12 of the 29 hyperinflationary episodes where significant data exist. Every hyperinflation looked the same. "Hyperinflations are always caused by public budget deficits which are largely financed by money creation." But even more interestingly, Bernholz identified the level at which hyperinflations can start. He concluded that "the figures demonstrate clearly that deficits amounting to 40 percent or more of expenditures cannot be maintained. They lead to high inflation and hyperinflations...."[9] Interestingly, even lower levels of government deficits can cause inflation. For example, 20 percent deficits were behind all but four cases of hyperinflation.

Stay with us here, because this is an important point. Most analysts quote government deficits as a percentage of GDP. They'll say, "The United States has a government deficit of 10 percent of GDP." While this measure makes some sense, it doesn't tell you how big the deficit is relative to expenditures. *The deficit may be 10 percent of the size of the U.S. economy; currently the U.S. deficit is over 30 percent of all government spending.* That is a big difference.

Figure 8.5 shows the level of deficits relative to expenditures before hyperinflationary periods.

Interestingly, currently Japan and the United States are not far from levels that have preceded hyperinflations. The big difference between

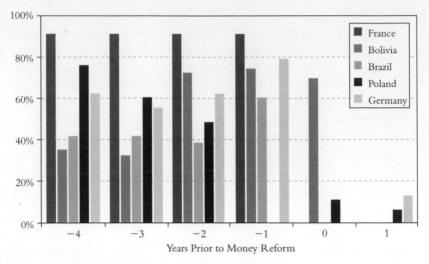

Figure 8.5 Budget Deficits before Hyperinflations
SOURCE: Societe Generale.

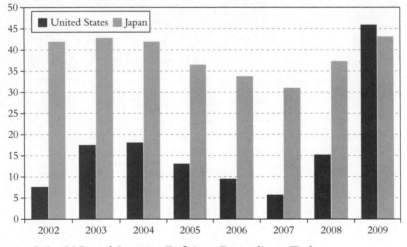

Figure 8.6 U.S. and Japanese Deficit to Expenditure Today
SOURCE: Societe Generale.

Japan or the United States and countries that have experienced hyperinflations is that the central banks are not monetizing most of the deficit. If they were to do that, then we would be one step away from paying quadrillions of dollars for a stamp or a sandwich (see Figure 8.6).

It is extremely important to note Bernholz's conclusion. Hyperinflations are not caused by aggressive central banks. They are caused by irresponsible and profligate legislatures that spend far beyond their means and by accommodative central banks that lend a helping hand to governments.

What are the implications for the present day? Fiscal liabilities are the real threat that will lead to higher inflation, if central banks continue to monetize government liabilities. In the case of a monetization, governments with independently authorized central banks disavow the overly convenient slippery slope option of paying their bills by printing new currency. A government must pay down its liabilities with currency already in circulation or else finance deficits by issuing new bonds and selling them to the public or to their central bank to acquire the necessary money. For the bonds to end up in the central bank, it must conduct an open market purchase. This action increases the monetary base through the money creation process. This process of financing government spending is called monetizing the debt. Monetizing debt is thus a two-step process where the government issues debt to finance its spending and the central bank purchases the debt from the public. The public is left with an increased supply of base money.

Although now with quantitative easing (QE2), some would argue that the United States is on such a path. Mohamed El-Erian writes:

> The unfortunate conclusion is that QE2 will be of limited success in sustaining high growth and job creation in the US, and will complicate life for many other countries. With domestic outcomes again falling short of policy expectations, it is just a matter of time until the Fed will be expected to do even more. And this means Wednesday's QE2 announcement is unlikely to be the end of unusual Fed policy activism.

Do we think the Fed will abandon its responsibility to control inflation and resort to total monetization of U.S. debt? No. But in the attempt to get mild inflation, it is possible the controlled fire they hope to kindle could get out of control, forcing them to act to take back the excess reserves and bring about a recession, as did Volcker. Let's hope it does not come to that.

The Dangers of Inflation

If inflation is the cure for too much debt, as we suggested earlier in our tongue-in-cheek example of Brazil, why is it that high inflation and eventually hyperinflation made things worse? Governments have to spend money all year round, but typically they collect tax revenues at the end of the year. So the value of the government's revenue in real terms is constantly diminished until the money is spent. Indeed, plugging a hole with inflation merely makes the hole bigger. Digging yourself deeper in an inflationary situation is what economists call the Tanzi effect, after the economist who discovered it.

Hyperinflations are all very similar. At first, bad money drives out the good. Under the Greeks and Romans, when gold coins were debased, few people were dumb enough to want to exchange their old coins that had high gold content for newer ones that had low gold content, so older good coins disappeared as people hid them. This is called Gresham's law: Bad money drives out good money.

In modern hyperinflations where gold coins don't exist, people begin to barter and exchange goods and services to avoid having to use devalued paper. Then, if they can get their hands on a foreign currency that is perceived to be hard and unlikely to lose its value, like dollars or deutschmarks, they will start to use the foreign currency. At first, they'll use the foreign currency as a unit of account to settle wages and price negotiations, then as a means of exchange, and finally as a store of value. Once enough people use the hard currency, Gresham's law reverses itself and hyperinflations come full circle. The good foreign money drives out the bad, and the inflating currency becomes totally worthless. This is called Their's law.

This happened in Argentina. If you are buying a home, you literally come to the closing with large bags of physical U.S. dollars. One side counts the cash while the other checks the paperwork.

The consequences to this pattern are dreadful. Hyperinflation completely destroys the purchasing power of private and public savings. No one wants to hold paper money, so it leads to excessive consumption and the hoarding of real assets. Investors face uncertainty and refuse to invest, unemployment skyrockets, and savings flee the country. The best-performing stock market in 2008 was Zimbabwe, which offered people a way to hedge their currency risks, even as their economy plummeted.

The Problems of Inflation

It's tempting to think that highly indebted countries can inflate their way out of their fiscal problems. Inflation would erode the real value of debt. Debts are fixed, while workers, companies, and governments could earn higher income as wages and prices could be indexed to inflation.

The main drawback of high inflation or hyperinflation is that most people become poorer through reduced real income. If we look at the real incomes, we can see that periods of high inflation, for example in the late seventies and in the last few years, have led to negative real wages. On the other hand, periods of disinflation and deflation have led to periods of positive real wage growth. Simply put, prices go up faster than wages, so the things you need to buy tend to go up faster in price than your salary (see Figure 8.7).

There are three main problems with trying to use inflation to get rid of the value of real debt. Investors would recognize even a stealth inflation policy and quickly push up yields. Many governments around the world have tied pensions and salaries to inflation measures, so increases in government spending would rise with inflation.

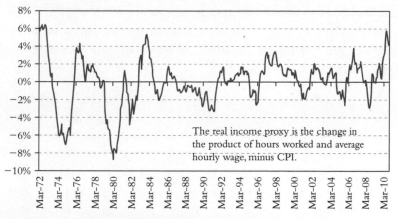

Figure 8.7   Real Income Proxy Year over Year
Source: Bloomberg, Variant Perception.

Nearly half of federal outlays are linked to inflation, so higher inflation means higher deficits. Social Security, which represents about 25 percent of federal spending outlays, is officially indexed, and Medicare and Medicaid are unofficially indexed. Indeed, over the period 2009 to 2020, the Congressional Budget Office (CBO) estimates that these three programs will account for 72 percent of the growth in total federal outlays and about the same share of the growth in debt. If anything, CBO's assumptions may be conservative, as they are required under current law to assume a sharp cutback in physician reimbursement payments under the Medicare program. Those cuts have been delayed every year since 2003. Any increase in inflation will erode the value of existing debt, but it will make deficits much larger going forward and even possibly increase the real burden of debt as a percentage of GDP. The CBO estimates that if inflation is 1 percentage point higher over the next decade than the rate CBO has projected, budget deficits during those years would be roughly $700 billion larger.[10]

Hyperinflation in the United States?

Congress likes spending more than a drunken sailor on shore leave, and the Federal Reserve sees the answer to any problem as providing more liquidity. Given this unfortunate dynamic, what is the likelihood that the United States will suffer from higher inflation and hyperinflation?

Who better to answer the question than the world's foremost expert on hyperinflation? Given all the fiscal problems and the monetary response, Bernholz sees many potential problems, but he currently sees no danger in the United States:

> But does this mean that inflation may evolve into a hyperinflation in the United States? I believe not. Though it is true that budget deficits with government expenditures covered by 40 percent or more through credits have historically led to hyperinflation, it has been stressed in Monetary Regimes and Inflation that it is not only the size of these credits but also their composition that is important. This is noted in the book thus: **"It will be demonstrated by looking at 12 hyperinflations**

that they have all been caused by the financing of huge budget deficits through money creation" [emphasis added]. This expresses the fact that only credit extended directly or indirectly by the monetary authorities to the government leads to the creation of money, that is, an increase of the monetary base. This is not true for borrowings taken up in the capital markets if they are not resold to the Fed. Looking from this perspective at the U.S. deficit, by far not all of the credits borrowed by the government were financed by the Fed. According to preliminary and rough estimates, not 40 percent but "only" about 13 percent of U.S. expenditures are presently financed this way. Moreover, in discussing this problem it has to be taken into account that about two-thirds of dollar bills are estimated to circulate abroad. This—together with the fact that incredibly huge holdings of dollar assets are owned especially by the central banks of China, India, and the Gulf States—may pose other and later dangers. But these dangers will be, except for a return of the dollar bills and a purchase of foreign-owned dollar assets by the Fed, of a different nature. Inflation may rise more or less strongly during the next years, but there is presently no danger of a hyperinflation in the United States.[11]

Bernholz is likely being far too generous to the Fed and Congress. He is not counting more than $700 billion worth of mortgage bonds by Fannie and Freddie that the Fed bought with money it printed. Arguably, if other central banks had not been dumping their mortgage-backed securities, the Fed would have monetized 100 percent of the U.S. deficit through Treasury purchases. Interestingly, the only country in the world that currently fits the bill for hyperinflation is the United Kingdom, where 100 percent of the budget deficit was monetized by the central bank. Unsurprisingly, ever since, inflation in the United Kingdom has consistently overshot the Bank of England's own forecasts. Apparently, they don't see a connection.

While it is unlikely that the United States, Japan, or any other country will soon enter hyperinflation, the situation could change in the future if any of the central banks were to lose their independence or continue to coordinate their actions with their treasuries. Central banks have lost a lot of independence through quantitative easing. They may say they are keeping an arm's length from the legislature and the Treasury, but few are fooled. Central banks in the United Kingdom, Europe, and the United States are now effectively working alongside the Treasury to pump money into the economy, so far with limited results due to the massive deleveraging in the private sector. They may continue to try this on a greater scale, and the larger the scale, the greater the need for coordination and the less the independence. If we go into a downturn, we hope central banks will be wise enough not to monetize government debt in any fiscal crisis. Sadly, they probably will.

The Federal Reserve has made spectacular mistakes over the past few decades. Under Alan Greenspan, the Fed's only solution to any problem was to provide more liquidity. To a man who only has a hammer, everything looks like a nail. Under Bernanke, the Federal Reserve effectively monetized government debt and monetized mortgage bonds held by quasi-government entities like Fannie Mae and Freddie Mac.

If we go into another downturn, will the Fed use its hammer again and provide more liquidity by monetizing even greater quantities of government liabilities? We hope not. Debt deflation is a terrible thing, but hyperinflation is even worse. We must remain vigilant that central banks maintain their independence.

PART TWO

A WORLD TOUR: WHO WILL FACE ENDGAME FIRST?

From a Bayesian standpoint, if you always observe a certain combination of information when X occurs, and never observe that same data when X is not present, then even if X is hidden under a hat, you would conclude that X is most likely there. If I see clowns walking around the grocery store buying peanuts, and there's a big top tent with two unicycles in front of it in the middle of what is usually an open field, I'm sorry, I'm going to conclude that the circus is in town.

—John Hussman

In the following sections of the book, we look at some of the more troubled countries in the world. Some of the countries are very small, and you may not know where to find them on the map. Others are large and well known. What they all have in common are extraordinary challenges of too much debt and large imbalances that need to be corrected.

Guessing which countries will have crises in advance is not as hard as it seems. There are a few factors that make countries vulnerable to debt crises and a few telltale signs that a country will have trouble down the line. On their own, each individual sign doesn't mean much, but taken together, they are always present before financial crises.

Why is it that people are pretty good at spotting problems around them, but economists are very bad at seeing blowups before they happen? Let's answer this practically. If you had a neighbor who was always running up credit card bills and who constantly borrowed money from neighbors to help pay the credit card bills, would you conclude your neighbor was a high bankruptcy risk? Common sense tells you they're in trouble. Responsible people don't borrow and pay back their borrowings with more borrowings. You would be right to guess that they have a problem. People whose finances are in order don't do those things. Likewise, countries that borrow too much from their neighbors end up in trouble, yet economists never seem to figure out which countries will blow up in advance.

To see how this happens, let's look at one of the most spectacular (although smallest) blowups in recent years: Iceland.

Iceland has fewer people than Wichita, Kansas, but it managed to accumulate about €50 billion in debts to foreign banks. That was about 10 times its GDP. To put that in perspective, total U.S. debt (public and private) is about three and a half times GDP.

Like many other small European countries, it borrowed money very cheaply from abroad and paid very high interest rates on foreign deposits. Icelanders could borrow Japanese yen for close to 0 percent, and they paid foreign investors very high rates. For instance, Kaupthing Bank's (an Icelandic bank) Isle of Man subsidiary offered 7.15 percent on one-year deposits denominated in British pounds, and if you deposited money in Iceland as Icelandic kronor, you could get up to 15 percent.

Iceland's extremely strong currency created tremendous imbalances. The very high interest rate differential, the carry trade, made the krona appreciate. The strengthening of the Icelandic krona meant that Icelanders could buy more and more cars, flat screens, and expensive watches from abroad. The buying spree was so large that Iceland's current account deficit was 25 percent of GDP in 2006. America's dangerously large current account deficit was about 7 percent that year, to put it in perspective.

The imbalances were so large that Iceland was an accident waiting to happen. As long as foreign money kept flowing into Iceland to finance the current account deficit and to roll the bank loans, everything was okay. But like any other bubble, as soon as the financing was pulled, the house of cards would collapse. That is exactly what happened right after Lehman Brothers, when all Icelandic banks went bust.

Let's rewind, though, and see what foreign central bankers had to say about Iceland. None of them saw it.

In 2006, former Fed economist and later Federal Reserve Governor Fred Mishkin co-authored "Financial Stability in Iceland." The report maintained that Iceland's economic fundamentals were strong.

> [Iceland's] financial regulation and supervision is considered to be of high quality. Iceland also has a strong fiscal position that is far superior to what is seen in the United States, Japan and Europe. Iceland's financial sector has undergone a substantial liberalization, which was complete over a decade ago, and its banking sector has been transformed from one focused mainly on domestic markets to one providing financial intermediation services to the rest of the world, particularly Scandinavia and the UK.
>
> There are three traditional routes to financial instability that have manifested themselves in recent financial crises: 1) financial liberalization with weak prudential regulation and supervision, 2) severe fiscal imbalances, and 3) imprudent monetary policy. None of these routes describe the current situation in Iceland. The economy has already adjusted to financial liberalization, which was already completed a long time ago, while prudential regulation and supervision is generally quite strong.[1]

Talk about the blind leading the blind. Mishkin is a close confidant of Bernanke and worked at the Fed from 2006 to 2008. He even wrote a book with Bernanke on inflation targeting.

Contrast this cavalier approach with what happened back in 2006 when a professor of economics at the University of Chicago, Bob Aliber, took an interest in Iceland. As Michael Lewis brilliantly describes the scene, "Aliber found himself at the London Business School, listening to a talk on Iceland, about which he knew nothing. He recognized instantly the signs. Digging into the data, he found in Iceland the outlines of what was so clearly a historic act of financial madness that it belonged in a textbook. 'The Perfect Bubble,' Aliber calls Iceland's financial rise, and he has the textbook in the works: an updated version of Charles Kindleberger's 1978 classic, *Manias, Panics, and Crashes*, a new edition of which he's currently editing. In it, Iceland, he decided back in 2006, would now have its own little box, along with the South Sea Bubble and the Tulip Craze—even though Iceland had yet to crash. For him the actual crash was a mere formality."[2]

How did Miskin totally miss the crisis, and how did Aliber immediately understand what was going on? How did Mishkin—a member of the Federal Reserve Board of Governors, a man who visited Iceland, who was supposed to be charged with guarding financial stability—miss the telltale signs, yet a professor who had never been to Iceland was able to spot the bubble?

Economic Aunt Minnies

The answer is simple. Mishkin failed to spot an Aunt Minnie.

In medicine, an Aunt Minnie is a particular set of symptoms that is pathognomonic, or distinctly characteristic of a specific disease. (The word comes from the Greek *pathognomonikos,* meaning skilled in judging diseases.) Even if each of the individual symptoms might be fairly common, when you have such a set of symptoms, its presence means that a particular disease is present beyond any doubt.

In the next few chapters, we'll be looking at countries around the world and spotting the telltale signs of economic disease. We'll look at what factors make it likely you'll face a crisis and what factors determine whether a crisis will turn out well. We'll look at how endgame will work around the world.

The following list comes from Michael Pettis, a very incisive commentator on global economics. It is probably one of the best single pieces you can read on how to identify problem countries in advance. Here is a slightly edited version of Michael Pettis's five things that matter.[3]

1. Debt levels matter. The best way to measure them is as total debt to GDP or external debt to exports. As a general rule, the more debt you have, the more difficulty you are going to have servicing it. Coupons matter, too. Low rates are much more serviceable than high rates.

2. The structure of the balance sheet matters, and this may be much more important than the actual level of debt. Not all debt is equal. An investor has to distinguish between inverted debt and hedged debt. With inverted debt, the value of liabilities is positively correlated with the value of assets, so that the debt burden and servicing costs decline in good times and rise in bad times. With hedged debt, they are negatively correlated.

    Foreign currency and short-term borrowings are examples of inverted debt. This makes the good times better and the bad times worse. Long-term fixed-rate local-currency borrowing is an example of hedged debt. During an inflation or currency crisis, the cost of servicing the debt actually declines in real terms, providing the borrower with some automatic relief, and this relief increases the worse conditions become.

    Highly inverted debt structures are very dangerous because they reinforce negative shocks and can cause events to spiral out of control, but unfortunately they are very popular because in good times, when debt levels typically rise, they magnify positive shocks.

3. The economy's underlying volatility matters. Less volatile economies are less subject to violent fluctuations, especially if the performance of the economy is correlated with financing ability. This is especially a problem for countries whose economies are highly dependent on commodities. Typically, commodity prices go down in bad times, making it that much harder to export profitably.

4. The structure of the investor base matters. Contagion is caused not so much by fear, as most people assume, but by large amounts of highly leveraged positions, which force investors into various forms of delta hedging, that is, buy when prices rise, and sell when they drop.

5. The composition of the investor base also matters. A sovereign default is always a political decision, and it is easier to default if the creditors have little domestic political power or influence. Unless

foreign investors have old-fashioned gunboats or a monopoly of new financing, for example, it is generally safer to default on foreigners than on locals. It is also easier to default on households via financial repression than it is to default on wealthy and powerful locals.

As you can see, the structure and ownership are almost more important than absolute debt levels themselves. This has very important implications, which we will go into as we go country by country around the world.

The insight that it is better to borrow in local currency versus foreign currency is critical. The United States and the United Kingdom, for example, are able to borrow exclusively in their own currency. This acts as an important shock absorber in bad times. It also creates an incentive to use devaluation and inflation as a means of financial repression. Devaluation hurts foreign bondholders, and inflation eases payments in your own currency in the short run.

Smaller countries are less able to borrow in their own currency. In the case of Iceland and Hungary, for example, borrowing large amounts of money in foreign currency means that they are trapped in a vicious circle that is usually only cured by default. For larger countries that can borrow in their own currency, like the United States, we'll most likely see inflation as central banks come to the aid of cash-strapped governments who insist on spending.

The tour of the world won't be pretty, but at least we hope it will be informative.

CHAPTER NINE

The United States

The Mess We Find Ourselves In

We are hurtling irreversibly toward a budgetary crack-up that will generate the mother of all crises in global bond and currency markets.
—David Stockman, director of the Office of Management and Budget under President Ronald Reagan

Something that can't go on, will stop.
—Herb Stein, chairman of the Council of Economic Advisers under President Richard Nixon

When we started writing this book, we purposefully set out to write so simply that even a politician could understand the nature of our problems. If there is any chapter in this book that is specifically written for congressmen, it is this chapter. We hope they will read it. We hope it will add something positive to the national conversation.

After the collapse of Lehman Brothers and AIG, almost all Americans hated Wall Street, yet surprisingly, one institution in America had a lower poll rating. No points for guessing. It is too easy.

Congress is the most reviled institution in America and with reason. According to a report by the Pew Center for People and the Press, "When asked for a single word that best describes their impression of Congress, 'dysfunctional,' 'corrupt,' 'self-serving' and 'inept' are volunteered most frequently. Of people offering a one-word description, 86% have something negative to say, while only 4% say something positive. Just 12% believe that Republicans and Democrats are working together in dealing with important issues facing the country—81% don't think so."[1] (Interestingly, when you poll people about their representative, the numbers are much higher. Evidently, it is the idiots from the other districts they do not like. So for the representatives reading this chapter, it is all those other guys and not you. Your constituents love you.)

Why is it that Congress is so looked down on? As this chapter will show, Congress, along with successive presidents, have done nothing to resolve long-term problems that will haunt us in years to come. Everyone knows we are on an unsustainable path of spending, yet not enough politicians have the foresight, let alone the courage, to do anything about it, with some notable exceptions.

Unfortunately, the debate in Washington is partisan and poisoned. Any serious effort at fiscal reform goes nowhere, and every congressperson is in favor in principle of reducing spending and curtailing entitlements, but few are willing to do so in practice.

Putting politics aside, in this chapter, we'll look at the evidence from nonpartisan, independent analysts about the ruinous road ahead if we do not do something to reform ourselves. The verdict is unanimous. Many nonpartisan, independent studies and reports have highlighted the pathetic state the United States finds itself in. We'll look at a few in this chapter to show how any sane person should recognize that the United States currently is like a car speeding 100 miles an hour heading toward a brick wall.

This is not a Republican issue, it is not a Democratic issue, and it is not even a Tea Party issue. It is an issue that concerns all of us. How we deal with our problems and what choices we make will determine what kind of Social Security we'll get when we're older, what kind of medical care we'll receive, and how much we'll be taxed. Unfortunately, we'll probably get a lot less of what we want and we'll pay a lot more.

Yes, We're Screwed

In recent testimony before Congress, Chairman Bernanke pointed out the unsustainable fiscal situation the United States was in and the need to make difficult choices. He stated:

> The recent projections from the Social Security and Medicare trustees show that, in the absence of programmatic changes, Social Security and Medicare outlays will together increase from about 8½ percent of GDP today to 10 percent by 2020 and 12½ percent by 2030. With the ratio of debt to GDP already elevated, we will not be able to continue borrowing indefinitely to meet these demands. **Addressing the country's fiscal problems will require a willingness to make difficult choices** [Emphasis added]. In the end, the fundamental decision that the Congress, the Administration, and the American people must confront is how large a share of the nation's economic resources to devote to federal government programs, including entitlement programs.[2]

In July 2010, the International Monetary Fund issued its annual review of U.S. economic policy. In language only a bureaucrat could write, "Directors welcomed the authorities' commitment to fiscal stabilization, but noted that a larger than budgeted adjustment would be required to stabilize debt-to-GDP."[3] That is a smack-down in bureaucrat-speak.

If you read ahead, though, it gets much better. The IMF is really saying that the U.S. debt is much like Greece's. In Section 6 of the July 2010 Selected Issues Paper, the IMF writes, **"The U.S. fiscal gap associated with today's federal fiscal policy is huge for plausible discount rates"** [Emphasis added].

Translation: We're pretty much bankrupt, and it is extremely unlikely we'll be able to close the gap between what we collect and what we'll spend. It adds that "closing the fiscal gap requires a permanent annual fiscal adjustment equal to about 14 percent of U.S. GDP." Fourteen percent is huge. That is more than a trillion dollars to save a year to get our fiscal house in order.

The IMF isn't the only one pointing out that we're screwed (*screwed* is a technical economic term). In an earlier chapter, we quoted from the

BIS report showing how most developed countries are on an unsus-tainable path. American observers recognize it as well. For example, the Committee on the Fiscal Future of the United States was established under the auspices of the National Academy of Sciences and the National Academy of Public Administration, supported by the MacArthur Foundation, to carry out a comprehensive study leading to a set of plausible scenarios for the federal budget, to put it on a path toward a stable fiscal future. The report is not a Republican or Tea Party or Democratic report. The committee that wrote it was staffed by experts of all political persuasions. As the document says:

> Members of the committee have quite varied backgrounds and perspectives on the budget. We disagree on many policy mat-ters; but we are unanimous that forceful, even painful, action must be taken soon to alter the nation's fiscal course.
>
> The federal government is currently spending far more than it collects in revenues, and if current policies are continued, will do so for the foreseeable future. Over the long term, three major programs—Medicare, Medicaid, and Social Security—account for the projected faster growth in federal spending relative to revenues. No reasonably foreseeable rate of economic growth would overcome this structural deficit. . . .
>
> **The current trajectory of the federal budget cannot be sustained. Without a course change, the nation faces the risk of a disruptive fiscal crisis, a risk that increases each year that action to address the growing structural deficit is delayed** [Emphasis added]. With delay, the available options become more extreme and therefore more difficult, and even more pain is shifted to future generations.
>
> The cumulative effect of the fundamental mismatch between expected revenues and the spending implied by the federal government's policies and commitments will be a very large and rapid increase in the amounts that the United States must borrow to finance current spending. This spending will include growing interest payments. . . . In addition to this fundamental imbalance, there has been a surge of spending and a drop in revenues because of the 2008–2009 economic downturn, which added

more than $1.5 trillion of debt in just 1 year, about $4,500 of additional borrowing for each U.S. resident. **This temporary borrowing surge is of concern, of course; however, it is the much larger longer term mismatch between projected spending and projected revenues implied by current policies that is the greater concern and the focus of this report.**[4]

Failure to prepare for the future prevents us from taking steps today. For Keynesians who want greater fiscal spending and deficits in the short run to stimulate the economy, the irony is that if we actually got our fiscal house in order, we'd have greater flexibility to boost spending in a downturn. As Frederic Mishkin, a Columbia University professor and former U.S. Federal Reserve governor, has pointed out, if the United States took concrete steps to address future deficits right now, the government would have more freedom to run deficits in the short run if needed. As he wrote, "There really is a need for the Congress to get serious about long-run fiscal sustainability."[5]

Another nonpartisan, independent analysis of our finances comes from the Congressional Budget Office, which is charged with studying bills that come before Congress. It paints a very dire picture. First, it shows what happens under a baseline scenario, which we'll call the rosy scenario. It assumes everything goes well. You can see it in Figure 9.1.

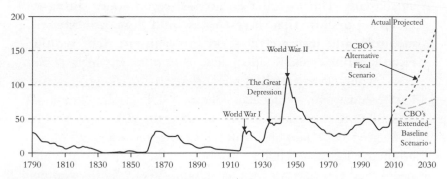

Figure 9.1   Federal Debt Held by the Public 1790–2035 (percentage of GDP)
SOURCE: Congressional Budget Office, *The Long-Term Budget Outlook* (June 2010) and *Historical Data on Federal Debt Held by the Public* (July 2010).

It also has an alternative fiscal scenario, which is much more plausible. As you can see, we become like Japan, with debt to GDP of 200 percent in 20 years.

The alternative scenario assumes the following: "Therefore, CBO also developed an alternative fiscal scenario, in which most of the tax cuts originally enacted in 2001 and 2003 are extended (rather than allowed to expire at the end of this year as scheduled under current law); the alternative minimum tax is indexed for inflation (halting its growing reach under current law); Medicare's payments to physicians rise over time (which would not happen under current law); tax law evolves in the long run so that tax revenues remain at about 19 percent of GDP; and some other aspects of current law are adjusted in coming years."

The potential problems of rising debt for the United States are hardly reassuring:

> **Beyond those gradual consequences, a growing level of federal debt would also increase the probability of a sudden fiscal crisis, during which investors would lose confidence in the government's ability to manage its budget, and the government would thereby lose its ability to borrow at affordable rates.** It is possible that interest rates would rise gradually as investors' confidence declined, giving legislators advance warning of the worsening situation and sufficient time to make policy choices that could avert a crisis. **But as other countries' experiences show, it is also possible that investors would lose confidence abruptly and interest rates on government debt would rise sharply** [Emphasis added]. The exact point at which such a crisis might occur for the United States is unknown, in part because the ratio of federal debt to GDP is climbing into unfamiliar territory and in part because the risk of a crisis is influenced by a number of other factors, including the government's long-term budget outlook, its near-term borrowing needs, and the health of the economy. When fiscal crises do occur, they often happen during an economic downturn, which amplifies the difficulties of adjusting fiscal policy in response.[6]

The CBO points out something very important, and it relates to the sand piles and fingers of instability. Collapses happen suddenly and unexpectedly. They happen because of underlying instability, and they can be triggered by even small events.

My [John] good friend Niall Ferguson wrote about how unexpected and nonlinear collapses happen:

> Imperial collapse may come much more suddenly than many historians imagine. A combination of fiscal deficits and military overstretch suggests that the United States may be the next empire on the precipice.
>
> If empires are complex systems that sooner or later succumb to sudden and catastrophic malfunctions, rather than cycling sedately from Arcadia to Apogee to Armageddon, what are the implications for the United States today? First, debating the stages of decline may be a waste of time—it is a precipitous and unexpected fall that should most concern policymakers and citizens. Second, most imperial falls are associated with fiscal crises. All the above cases were marked by sharp imbalances between revenues and expenditures, as well as difficulties with financing public debt. Alarm bells should therefore be ringing very loudly, indeed, as the United States contemplates a deficit for 2009 of more than $1.4 trillion—about 11.2 percent of GDP, the biggest deficit in 60 years—and another for 2010 that will not be much smaller. Public debt, meanwhile, is set to more than double in the coming decade, from $5.8 trillion in 2008 to $14.3 trillion in 2019. Within the same timeframe, interest payments on that debt are forecast to leap from eight percent of federal revenues to 17 percent. . . .
>
> These numbers are bad, but in the realm of political entities, the role of perception is just as crucial, if not more so. In imperial crises, it is not the material underpinnings of power that really matter but expectations about future power. The fiscal numbers cited above cannot erode U.S. strength on their own, but they can work to weaken a long-assumed faith in the United States' ability to weather any crisis. For now, the world still expects the United States to muddle through, eventually

confronting its problems when, as Churchill famously said, all the alternatives have been exhausted. Through this lens, past alarms about the deficit seem overblown, and 2080—when the U.S. debt may reach staggering proportions—seems a long way off, leaving plenty of time to plug the fiscal hole. But one day, a seemingly random piece of bad news—perhaps a negative report by a rating agency—will make the headlines during an otherwise quiet news cycle. Suddenly, it will be not just a few policy wonks who worry about the sustainability of U.S. fiscal policy but also the public at large, not to mention investors abroad. It is this shift that is crucial: a complex adaptive system is in big trouble when its component parts lose faith in its viability.[7]

When people suddenly and unexpectedly lose faith in U.S. debt, we will not see a slow increase in interest rates and a slow decline of the dollar. We will be unlikely to have time to take the right steps. By that stage, it will be too late. The decline will happen quickly and unexpectedly.

Congress: Blind, Ignorant, and Indifferent

You would think that the combined wisdom of the Congressional Budget Office, the Bank of International Settlements, the Committee on the Fiscal Future of the United States, and scores of other organizations would be enough for Congress to see how unsustainable our fiscal path is. And you'd be wrong. Perhaps some members of Congress read these reports. We know that some of them care. But the bottom line is that they collectively are doing nothing about it. Touching Social Security, Medicare, and health care is the political third rail. You will get elected only if you do not touch them. And because of that, we have no reform.

Congress displays little to no regard for even the slightest show of fiscal restraint. We can see this in how federal salaries have increased at a faster rate than salaries in the private sector, and we can see it in how quickly benefits have expanded for federal workers. While workers' earnings have gone nowhere, federal employees' average compensation has grown to more than double what private-sector workers earn (that is not a typo!). The total irresponsibility is not recent. For the last nine years, federal workers have been awarded bigger average pay and benefit increases than private employees. Because of the sustained increases, the compensation gap between federal and private workers has doubled in the past decade.

Federal civil servants earned average pay and benefits of $123,049 in 2009 while private workers made $61,051 in total compensation, according to the Bureau of Economic Analysis (Figure 9.2). The data are the latest available. The federal compensation advantage has grown from $30,415 in 2000 to $61,998 last year.[8]

The fiscal problems in the United States are not purely confined to the federal government. At least 46 states had enormous troubles covering huge budget shortfalls for fiscal year 2011 (Figure 9.3). These came on top of the large shortfalls that 48 states faced in fiscal years 2009 and 2010.[9]

As Figure 9.4 shows, the budget shortfalls are gapingly large. Some states have shortfalls of 40 and 50 percent of their spending. If the states were countries, they would be prime candidates for bankruptcy or hyperinflation.

Unfortunately, the very large budget shortfalls are not only due to the downturn. Before the Great Recession started, almost all states were

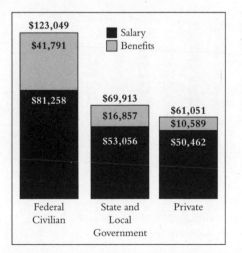

Figure 9.2 Average Compensation in the United States (2009)
SOURCE: Bureau of Economic Analysis (Julie Snider, *USA Today*).

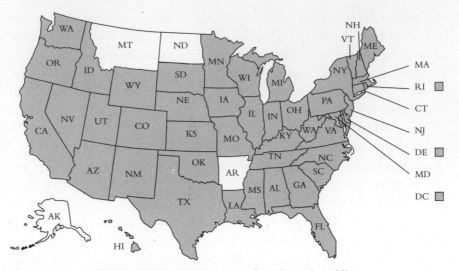

Figure 9.3   This Year 46 States Have Faced Budget Shortfalls

NOTE: Includes states with shortfalls in fiscal 2010.
SOURCE: Center on Budget and Policy Priorities survey (cbpp.org).

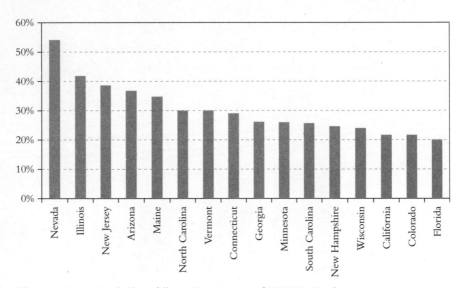

Figure 9.4   Total Shortfalls as Percentage of FY2011 Budget
SOURCE: Center on Budget and Policy Priorities.

running sizable budget deficits. Complacent financial markets let them do that. Things got much worse in the downturn, but things aren't getting any better going forward.

We don't know what each state will pass as a budget in 2012, but we do have estimates for their shortfalls. As Figure 9.5 shows, Nevada and Illinois are going to have shortfalls of 40 percent going forward.

These insanely high budget shortfalls are simply not sustainable. Herb Stein, chairman of the Council of Economic Advisers under President Richard Nixon, said, "Something that can't go on, will stop." One day completely out-of-control spending by state and local governments will come to an end. It is a matter of *when,* not if. That day of reckoning will probably come with a crisis.

In the short run, crises have been postponed due to the federal government bailing out the states. Figure 9.6 shows the growth in federal payouts to state and local governments, also known as grants-in-aid.

According to Bloomberg News:

> [Grants in aid] have increased almost three times as fast as overall spending during the period, according to data compiled by the Commerce Department. Funds were provided at a $525

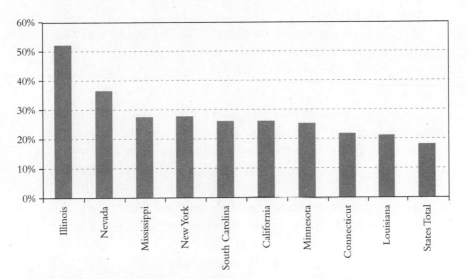

Figure 9.5   FY2012 Shortfall as Percentage of FY2011 Budget
SOURCE: Center on Budget and Policy Priorities.

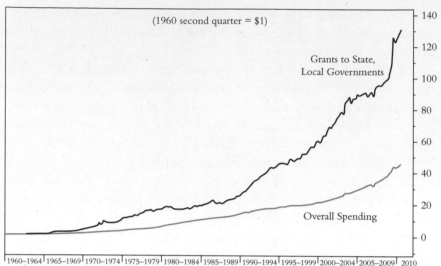

(1960 second quarter = $1)

Grants to State, Local Governments

Overall Spending

1960–1964 1965–1969 1970–1974 1975–1979 1980–1984 1985–1989 1990–1994 1995–1999 2000–2004 2005–2009 2010

Figure 9.6   Growth in Grants in Aid versus Total Spending
SOURCE: Bloomberg Chart of the Day, Commerce Department.

billion annual rate in the second quarter, a 33 percent jump
from two years ago. Most of the money went to pay health-care
expenses under the Medicaid insurance program and to cover
educational costs. . . .

The federal government provided $131.25 of state and local
aid last quarter for every dollar spent 50 years ago. For total
expenditures, the second-quarter figure was only $45.75. . . .[10]

To put this very simplistically, the states are like children who are
vastly overspending, and daddy, that is, the federal government, is
having to step in to bail them out. This cannot go on forever. At a
certain stage, a good parent has to let the children suffer the consequences of their own actions. Actually, the parent really is you,
the taxpayer, and other states. So the responsible states are bailing out
the irresponsible states. And you, the taxpayer, will ultimately bail out
your profligate government.

What is interesting is that this crisis is not evenly spread. In fact, it
will be the fiscally conservative states and the fiscally conservative taxpayers who will bail out the fiscally profligate ones. Table 9.1 is
extremely eye-opening. States where voters feel the government should
do more for them end up with bigger debts. States that believe in

smaller government typically have smaller debts. All the states that voted for McCain have very small debt/GDP while those that voted for Obama have very high debt/GDP.

The problem is probably much bigger than the numbers suggest. Much like the United States, individual states have tremendous hidden liabilities. The total debt of California might look manageable at 8 percent of its

Table 9.1 Per Capita Debt by State

McCain States	Per Capita State Debt	Obama States	Per Capita State Debt
Kentucky	$1,685	Connecticut	$4,859
Mississippi	$1,478	Massachusetts	$4,606
Alaska	$1,345	Hawaii	$3,996
Louisiana	$1,271	New Jersey	$3,669
Kansas	$1,140	New York	$3,135
Georgia	$1,120	Delaware	$2,489
West Virginia	$1,079	California	$2,362
Utah	$ 957	Washington	$2,226
South Carolina	$ 917	Rhode Island	$2,127
Alabama	$ 796	Oregon	$1,859
Missouri	$ 780	Illinois	$1,856
Arizona	$ 736	Wisconsin	$1,720
Oklahoma	$ 570	Maryland	$1,608
Idaho	$ 532	New Mexico	$1,398
Texas	$ 520	Florida	$1,123
Montana	$ 358	Minnesota	$1,037
North Dakota	$ 327	Pennsylvania	$ 938
Tennessee	$ 318	Ohio	$ 933
Arkansas	$ 312	Nevada	$ 925
South Dakota	$ 135	Virginia	$ 895
Wyoming	$ 77	North Carolina	$ 765
Nebraska	$ 15	Maine	$ 760
Average per capita state debt	**$ 749**	Michigan	$ 748
		Vermont	$ 709
		New Hampshire	$ 665
		Indiana	$ 493
		Colorado	$ 400
		Iowa	$ 73
		Average per capita state debt	**$1,728**

SOURCE: Marc Faber, Gloom Boom & Doom Report; Chuck Devore, Big Government, http://biggovernment.com.

economy. But if you include the fair value of the shortfall in California's pension funds, the total liability jumps to 37 percent of its GDP.

We have earlier discussed the problems of Greece and the European periphery. Many U.S. states are in a terrible position, and if they were European countries, the fair value of their pension obligations would exceed the debt/GDP level of 60 percent as set out in the European Maastricht Treaty, according to Andrew Biggs, an economist with the American Enterprise Institute.

Some economists think the last straw for states and cities will be debt hidden in their pension obligations. As Figure 9.7 shows, even though pension obligations are not reported as debt on a state's budget, the obligations are real, and when added to the existing debt, they show that the real burden states face is three to four times as large.

According to the *New York Times*, "Joshua Rauh, an economist at Northwestern University, and Robert Novy-Marx of the University of Chicago, recently recalculated the value of the 50 states' pension obligations the way the bond markets value debt. They put the number at $5.17 trillion. After the $1.94 trillion set aside in state pension funds was subtracted, there was a gap of $3.23 trillion—more than three times the amount the states owe their bondholders."[11] This $3 trillion dollar number has been duplicated in two other studies using different methodology.

The United States has similar unstated liabilities. Our total debt is a little less than our GDP, but our long-term liabilities are much, much higher. As Professor of Economics Laurence Kotlikoff at Boston University has pointed out:

> [The] gargantuan discrepancy between our "official" debt and our actual net indebtedness isn't surprising. It reflects what economists call the labeling problem. Congress has been very careful over the years to label most of its liabilities "unofficial" to keep them off the books and far in the future. . . . The fiscal gap isn't affected by fiscal labeling. It's the only theoretically correct measure of our long-run fiscal condition because it considers all spending, no matter how labeled, and incorporates long-term and short-term policy.[12]

The official U.S. deficit and debt numbers are based on cash accounting, which tracks what comes into your checking account and

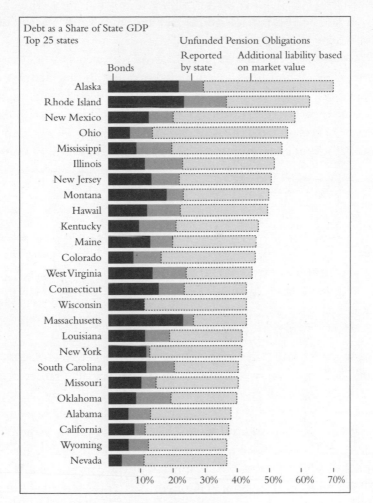

Figure 9.7 Overloaded with Unseen Debts

NOTE: While states' explicit debts—the value of their bonds outstanding—may look manageable, those amounts do not include shortfalls in their pension funds. Currently, public pension funds are not required to disclose the market value of their pension obligations, though some say that is the more meaningful measure. States also share the burden of the national debt, which can further balloon a state's total debt load.

SOURCE: © Andrew G. Biggs. Reprinted with permission of the American Enterprise Institute for Public Policy Research, Washington, DC.

what goes out. For the average person, that works fine for paying today's bills, but it's a poor way to measure a financial condition that could include credit card debt, car loans, a mortgage, and an overdue electric bill. Companies and complex institutions, for this reason, use accrual accounting, which does not judge how well you're doing by your checking account. It measures income and expenses when they occur, or accrue. Accrual accounting gives a much more accurate picture of where your finances are.

The supreme irony is that federal law requires companies that have revenue of $1 million or more to use accrual accounting. If any private company used cash accounting instead of accrual accounting, its executives would be prosecuted by the government. It is illegal for businesses to keep their books the way the government does, hiding long-term obligations the way the government hides its indebtedness from voters.

What Does It All Mean?

One outcome that is extremely likely is that our taxes will go up. Some of these new taxes will be good. They'll simply be reversing the ridiculous situation we currently find where special interests receive money from the government via subsidies. Other taxes, though, will be very poor for growth.

As Martin Feldstein has written:

> Most federal nondefense spending, other than Social Security and Medicare, is now done through special tax rules rather than by direct cash outlays. . . . These tax rules—because they result in the loss of revenue that would otherwise be collected by the government—are equivalent to direct government expenditures. . . . This year tax expenditures will raise the federal deficit by about $1 trillion, according to estimates by the congressional Joint Committee on Taxation. If Congress is serious about cutting government spending, it has to go after many of them. . . .[13]

Indeed, the tax burden in the United States is actually low compared with other countries around the world. As Figure 9.8 shows, it is lower than almost every other major country.

The Kindness of Strangers

The United States has depended on foreigners to buy very large amounts of our debt. The largest buyers have been the Chinese, the Japanese, the Russians, and the Saudis. The Chinese and the Japanese

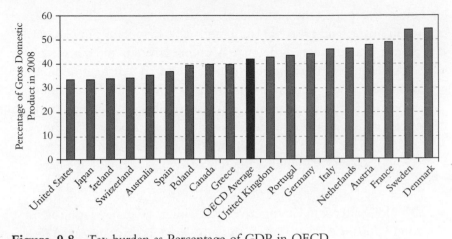

Figure 9.8 Tax burden as Percentage of GDP in OECD
SOURCE: "Choosing the Nation's Fiscal Future," Committee on the Fiscal Future of the United States, National Research Council and National Academy of Public Administration.

recycle their dollars. We buy their products, and rather than selling the dollars we give them, they buy U.S. government bonds to keep the yuan and the yen from appreciating. The Saudis and the Russians do the same when we buy their oil. It's an odd form of vendor financing.

Foreigners, however, are becoming less and less comfortable buying our bonds. They know that our fiscal situation is untenable. Here is a small episode that gives a real insight into what foreigners think about our debt.

The British daily newspaper the *Telegraph* reported on Tim Geithner's first trip to China: "In his first official visit to China since becoming Treasury Secretary, Mr. Geithner told politicians and academics in Beijing that he still supports a strong US dollar, and insisted that the trillions of dollars of Chinese investments would not be unduly damaged by the economic crisis. Speaking at Peking University, Mr. Geithner said: 'Chinese assets are very safe.' The comment provoked loud laughter from the audience of students."[14] Even Chinese students know how unlikely any fiscal reform is in the United States.

In the words of David Stockman, director of the Office of Management and Budget under President Ronald Reagan:

A while back, when Tim Geithner told a group of Beijing students that Washington would get its fiscal house in order over the next five years, they guffawed. It is no wonder. The U.S. economy is comprised of an aging, debt-burdened population which manufactures little that is competitive in today's over-capacitated global economy. In fact, we are down to 8 million manufacturing production jobs in an economy with 150 million workers. Such an economy must drastically cut spending and ramp-up savings and reinvestment to ever regain a healthy footing. That means public-sector savings in the form of budget surpluses, along with higher household savings rates than we have had for decades.[15]

Not long after Tim Geithner visited Beijing, a Chinese rating agency, Dagong Global Credit Rating Company, used its first entry into sovereign debt rating to paint a disturbing portrait of global sovereign creditworthiness, giving much greater weight to "wealth creating capacity" and foreign reserves than Fitch, Standard & Poor's, or Moody's. The United States falls to AA, while Britain and France slipped to AA−. Belgium, Spain, and Italy are ranked at A−, along with Malaysia. Table 9.2 shows that the United States is number 13 in the global ranking.

Let's hear their rationale in slightly mangled English:

In the normal credit and debt relationship, the cash flow newly created by the debtor, rather than that newly borrowed, should be the fundamental of debt repayment, on the basis of which, the credit relation can exist and develop stably. The way of over-reliance on financing income and debt roll-over will ultimately lead to a strong reaction of bond market, thus when the borrowing costs and difficulties increase, the credit risks will burst dramatically.

Therefore, Dagong holds that the countries with current fiscal revenue sufficient to cover the debt service, have stronger fiscal strength than those countries which mainly depend on financing income to repay debts in the same circumstance, even sometimes the financing incomes of latter seem stable in the short term.[16]

Simply put, because U.S. debt is growing with no end in sight, we're not paying down our debt. We simply roll it. We issue new debt

Table 9.2 Dagong Ratings

Number	Sovereigns	Local Currency		Foreign Currency	
		Ratings	Outlooks	Ratings	Outlooks
1	Norway	AAA	Stable	AAA	Stable
2	Denmark	AAA	Stable	AAA	Stable
3	Luxembourg	AAA	Stable	AAA	Stable
4	Switzerland	AAA	Stable	AAA	Stable
5	Singapore	AAA	Stable	AAA	Stable
6	Australia	AAA	Stable	AA+	Stable
7	New Zealand	AAA	Stable	AA+	Stable
8	Canada	AA+	Stable	AA+	Stable
9	Netherlands	AA+	Stable	AA+	Stable
10	China	AA+	Stable	AAA	Stable
11	Germany	AA+	Stable	AA+	Stable
12	Saudi Arabia	AA	Stable	AA	Stable
13	United States	AA	Negative	AA	Negative
14	South Korea	AA−	Stable	AA−	Stable
15	Japan	AA−	Negative	AA	Stable
16	Britain	AA−	Negative	AA−	Negative
17	France	AA−	Negative	AA−	Negative
18	Belgium	A+	Stable	A+	Stable
19	Chile	A+	Stable	A+	Stable
20	South Africa	A	Stable	A	Stable

SOURCE: Sovereign Credit Rating Report of 50 Countries in 2010, Dagong Credit Rating Company.

to pay off the old and borrow a little more each time. As we have pointed out before, this violates the transversality or no-Ponzi condition. Without any meaningful fiscal reform, the only reason to hold a government bond is because someone else might pay more for it than you bought it for; that is, there might be a greater fool out there somewhere. The problem is that eventually markets run out of fools.

You will not be surprised to learn that Dagong International Credit Rating Company of China has been prohibited by the U.S. government from entering the U.S. market. Perhaps the reason is that the company is headquartered at Beijing without a branch in the United States and not involved in rating U.S.-based companies. It did not have any subscribers in the United States. The simpler explanation is that it is always easier to shoot the messenger than fix things.

Endgame for the United States

As Reinhart and Rogoff have pointed out, when it comes to the various types of crises, there is very little difference between developed and emerging-market countries, especially as to the fallout. It seems that the developed world has no corner on special wisdom that would allow crises to be avoided or to be recovered from more quickly. In fact, because of their overconfidence—because they actually feel they have superior systems—developed countries can dig deeper holes for themselves than emerging markets. That is what is happening to the United States now. Our complacency is preventing us from making necessary fiscal adjustments. The United States has difficult choices ahead if we do not want to become like so many emerging-market countries that have faced debt and currency crises.

Again, when *people* have too much debt, they typically default. When *countries* have too much debt, you have one of three options:

1. They can inflate away the debt.
2. They can default on it.
3. They can devalue and hurt any foreigners who are holding the debt.

The Present Contains All Possible Futures

Let's quickly review. Like teenagers, we as a U.S. polity have made a number of bad choices over the past decade. We allowed banks to overleverage and, in the case of AIG (and others), sell what were essentially naked call options of credit default swaps, based on their firm balance sheets, far in excess of their net worth, and that put our entire financial system at risk. We gave mortgages to people who could not pay them and did so in such large amounts that we again brought down the entire world financial system to the point that only with staggering amounts of taxpayer money was it brought back from the brink of

Armageddon. We assumed that home prices were not in a bubble but were a permanent fixture of ever-rising value, and we borrowed against our homes to finance what seemed like the perfect lifestyle. We did not regulate the mortgage markets. We ran large and growing government deficits. We did not save enough. We allowed rating agencies to degrade their ratings to a point where they no longer meant anything. The list is much longer, but you get the idea.

Now, we are faced with a continuing crisis and the aftermath of multiple bubbles bursting. We are left with a massive government deficit and growing public debt, recent record unemployment, and consumers who are desperately trying to repair their balance sheets.

As we have seen in previous chapters, if present trends are left unchecked, we will need to find $15 trillion in the next 10 years, just to pay for U.S. government debt, without counting state, county, and city debt. And perhaps some loans for business will be needed? A few mortgages? Where can all this money come from? The answer is that it can't be found. Long before we get to 2019, there will be an upheaval in the bond market, forcing what could be unpleasant changes.

We are left with no good choices, only difficult or bad ones. We have created a situation that is going to cause a lot of pain. It is not a question of pain or no pain; it is just when and how we decide (or are forced) to take it. There are no easy paths, but some bad choices are less bad than others. So, let's review some of the choices we can make. (Again, we are being very general here.)

Argentinean Disease

One way to deal with the deficit is to do what Argentina and other countries have done: simply print the money needed to cover the deficits. Of course, that eventually means hyperinflation and the collapse of the currency and all debt. There are analysts who think this is an inevitable outcome. How else, they ask, can we deal with the debt? Where is the political willpower?

One large hedge-fund manager in Brazil humorously remarked that Argentina is a binomial country. When faced with two choices (hence binomial), they always made the bad choice. Could it happen here?

As we discussed earlier, hyperinflation is not an economic event; it is a political choice. The current political season is a sign that the voter population is beginning to pay attention to the need for something more than talk of change. There is growing discomfort with the size of the deficits. Further, the Fed would have to cooperate for there to be hyperinflation, and we think there is only a very slight (as in almost zero) chance of that happening. Could Congress change the rules and take over the Fed? Anything's possible, but I seriously doubt there is any appetite in saner circles for such a thing to happen.

We think the chances of hyperinflation in the United States are quite low. Even given the recent bout of QE2, it is hard to conceive of the Fed actually monetizing the debt to allow the U.S. government to run large deficits, as opposed to the ostensible reason of fighting deflation. It would be the worst of all possible bad choices.

The Austrian Solution

Here I refer to the Austrian school of economic theory, based on the work of Ludwig von Mises and Friedrich Hayek. There are those in the Austrian camp who argue for the need to do away with the Fed; return to the gold standard; allow the banks that are now deemed too big to fail to go ahead and fail, along with any businesses that are also mismanaged (such as GM and Chrysler); and leave the high ground to new and more properly run businesses and banks.

In their model, government spending is slashed to the bone, as are (in most cases) taxes. The advantage is that, in theory, you get all your pain at once and then can begin to recover from what would be a very bad and deep recession. The bad news is that you risk getting 30 percent unemployment and another depression that could take a very long time to climb out of.

Now, let us say that we have *greatly* simplified their argument. If you want to learn more, you can go to www.mises.org. It is an excellent web site for all things Austrian. While I (John's) am not Austrian, I have spent a lot of time reading the literature and have certain sympathies for this view.

That being said, this also has almost no chance of such a solution being implemented. In Congress, only my (John's) friend Ron Paul is its advocate and now his son Rand in the Senate. Most Austrian followers are Libertarian by nature, and that is just not a political reality for the coming decade.

The Eastern European Solution

As it turned out, Niall Ferguson (author of the brilliant book *The Ascent of Money* and Harvard professor) was in Dallas last spring, and I (John) was graciously invited to hear him speak. He gave a great speech and signed books, and then we went to a local dive and proceeded to solve the world's problems over scotch (Niall) and tequila (me), much further into the night than we originally intended. He's a very funny and knowledgeable guy.

As we were talking about possible paths, he brought one to mind that I hadn't thought of. He reminded me of the period after the fall of the Berlin Wall, as the nations of Eastern Europe broke from the former Soviet Union. They started with very weak economies and simply overhauled their entire governments and economies in a rather short period of time, though not in lockstep with one another. Privatization, lowered taxes, and the like were the order of the day.

We here in the United States are always talking about the need for reform. We need to reform health care or education or energy. In Eastern Europe, they did not *reform* in the sense that we use the word. In many cases, they simply started from scratch and built new systems. They had the advantage that there was general agreement that things did not work the way they had been, so there was more room for change.

Today in the United States, there are large constituencies that resist change. We only get to tinker around the edges, when real structural change is needed. Sadly, we agreed that here there is not much chance of major change. We can't even get the obvious changes needed in the financial regulatory world.

Japanese Disease

In a few chapters, we will visit at length the problems facing Japan, but a quick tutorial is needed here. Their population is shrinking, as is their workforce. They are running massive fiscal deficits and have done so for almost 20 years. Government debt-to-GDP is now up to 200 percent and projected to rise to over 220 percent within a few years. They started their lost decades with a savings rate of almost 16 percent and are now down to 2 percent, as their aging population spends its savings in retirement. They have had no new job creation for 20 years, and nominal GDP is where it was 17 years ago.

As bad as our problems are here in the United States, their bubble was far more massive. Values of commercial property fell 87 percent! Their stock market is still down 70 percent 20 years later. They had twice as much bank leverage to GDP as the United States. (Think about how bad off we would be if bank lending was twice as large and had even worse defaults and capital shortfalls!)

And yet, they muddle through. Productivity has kept their standard of living very high. Up until recently, their exports were strong. The trading floors of the world are littered with the bodies of traders who have shorted Japanese government debt in the belief that it simply must implode. While we believe that it eventually will, if they stay on the path they are on, Japan is a very clear demonstration that things that don't make sense can go on longer than we think.

Richard Koo (chief economist of Nomura Securities, in Tokyo) argues passionately that Japan had a balance sheet recession and that the only way for Japan to fight it was to run massive deficits. Banks were not lending and businesses were not borrowing, as both groups were trying to repair their balance sheets, which were savaged by the bursting of the bubble. It is said that at one time the value of the land on which the Emperor's Palace sits in Tokyo was worth more than all of California. Clearly, this was a bubble that puts our housing bubble to shame.

We understand the point that there are differences between Japan and the United States. But there are also similarities. We, too, have had a balance sheet recession, although here it was mostly individuals and financial institutions that have had to retrench and repair their balance sheets.

Japan elected to run large deficits and raise taxes. A few chapters back, we covered the literature that suggests that government stimulus and deficits have no long-run positive effect on GDP.

Back in Chapter 3, we learned that if you increase government spending (the G in our equation), it will have a positive effect in the short run on GDP, but not in the long run. In essence, the increase in G must be made up by savings from consumers and businesses and foreigners.

But an increase in G does not enhance overall productivity. Government spending may be necessary, but it is not especially productive. You increase productivity when private businesses invest and create jobs and products. But if government soaks up the investment capital, there is less for private business.

And that is Japanese disease. You run large deficits, sucking the air out of the room, and you raise taxes, taking the money from productive businesses and reducing the ability of consumers to save. Then you go for 20 years with little or no economic or job growth.

This is the path we currently seem to be on. The Japanese experience says that it could last a lot longer than people think before we hit the wall because if savings rise in the United States, and if banks, instead of lending, put that money on deposit with the Fed, as they are now doing (to repair their balance sheets), the United States could run large deficits for longer than most observers (and we probably should include ourselves in that group) currently believe.

We will need 15 to 18 million new jobs in the next five years, just to get back to where we were only a few years ago. Without the creation of whole new industries, that is not going to happen. Nearly 20 percent of Americans are not paying anything close to the amount of taxes they paid a few years ago, and at least 10 million are now collecting some kind of unemployment benefits or welfare.

The jobs we need will not come from government transfer payments. As we saw earlier, they can only come from private businesses. And in reality, as we discussed in previous chapters, it is business start-ups that are needed, as that is where the real growth in net new jobs are. And that means investment. But if we allocate our investment money to government bonds, if we tax the capital needed by entrepreneurs who invest in and start businesses, we delay that return to growth.

Choosing large deficits does not reduce the amount of pain we will experience; it just seemingly reduces it in the short term and creates the potential for a serious economic upheaval when the bond market finally decides to opt for higher rates. This path is a bad choice, but sadly, in reality, it is one we could take without a serious move to curtail federal spending.

As we will see in a few chapters, Japan will soon be faced with its own Greek moment of truth. If we in the United States choose to continue to run large deficits, we will face that same end all too soon. It will mean high interest rates, ever larger deficits, worse unemployment, and a very diminished standard of living. This is not a wise choice.

The Glide Path Option

A glide path is the final path followed by an aircraft as it is landing. We need to establish a glide path to sustainable deficits—could we dream of surpluses? That is because at some point there will be recognition, either proactively or forced on us by the bond market, that large deficits are unsustainable in the long term.

If Congress and the president decided to lay out a real (and credible) plan to reduce the deficit over time, say five or six years, to where it was less than nominal GDP, the bond market would (we think) behave. Reducing deficits by $150 billion a year through a combination of cuts in growth and spending would get us there in five years.

The problem is that there is real temporary pain associated with this option. Remember that equation back in Chapter 3?

GDP (Gross Domestic Product) is defined as Consumption (C) plus Investment (I) plus Government Spending (G) plus [Exports (E) minus Imports (I)]

or:

$$GDP = C + I + G + (E - I)$$

Absent a growing private sector, if you reduce G (government spending), you also reduce GDP in the short run. You have to take some pain today to do that. But you avoid worse pain down the road: a bubble of massive federal debt that has to be serviced will be very painful when it blows up, as all bubbles do.

The glide path option means that structural unemployment is going to be higher than we like (which is actually the case with all the options). And the large tax increases that come with this option will by their very nature be a drag on growth. And of course, then we will eventually have to deal with the $70 trillion in our off-balance-sheet liabilities in Medicare and Social Security and pensions. We can debate tax increases all we want, but we sadly think we will soon have a VAT tax if we want to preserve some semblance of Medicare. And let's be certain that an increase in taxes of the magnitude needed is not a pro-growth policy.

There are no easy or good options. Let's just hope that we cut corporate taxes enough when we do create a VAT, that it will make our corporations more competitive on a global basis, which will be a boost for jobs.

That's pretty much it. This is not a problem we can grow ourselves out of in the next few years. We have simply dug ourselves into a huge hole. This is not a normal recession. There is not a V ending to this recession. We are going to have to deal with the pain. It will be the pain of reduced returns on traditional stock market investments, eventually a lower dollar against most currencies (other than the euro, the pound, and the yen), low returns on bonds, European-like unemployment, lower corporate profits over the long term, and a very slow-growth environment. But if we choose this path, we will get through it in the fullness of time.

We can repair our national balance sheet. We can get deficits under control over time. We made it through the 1970s, which was not easy. There are whole new industries and technologies that promise an increase in jobs.

One last thought: Let's assume that we find the political will to begin the process of creating some version of the glide path option, which we admit is not easy. That means the most important election in this whole process was not the one last November, nor will it be the one in 2012. Rather, it will be the one in 2014.

It is doubtful that unemployment will be back around 5 percent or that economic growth will be robust, if the future reveals itself to be somewhere on the line of the arguments we are making in this book. That is typically not a good atmosphere for incumbents. If voters react by demanding yet another round of stimulus and deficits from Congress, we will be training our politicians that we do not have the discipline to stay the course and will not allow them to make the hard choices.

Our leaders need to be candid with the American people. There are no magic answers, no easy solutions. The time for the blame game is over. We need to get on with the job of setting a course back to a sustainable economy that will grow and produce the jobs and opportunities that we have had in the past and we want for our children. It will mean some years of difficulty, but we can get through it if we choose to.

If we do not choose to act prudently, far more difficult times will be forced on us. Let's hope we can be proactive.

Some Policy Suggestions

It is beyond the scope of this book to suggest specific ideas on how we cut our spending or raise taxes. That we in the United States must get the fiscal deficit below nominal GDP and, even better, run a surplus is the case we have tried to make. The recent proposals by the chairmen of the President's Commission on the Deficit were interesting. They are possibly a political nonstarter, but it is ideas like these that are going to be needed. To get to a reasonable deficit, there are going to have to be hard choices and real trade-offs.

In general, the heavy lifting should be done by spending cuts more than tax increases. As we saw from earlier chapters, tax increases have a growth cost, and it is growth that we need. And as we tinker with our tax code, let's make sure we position our corporations to be more competitive. And for Pete's sake, figure out a way to lower taxes on offshore income so that the corporations will bring it home and spend it here on job-creating business rather than investing it offshore.

Now, a few outside-the-box policy thoughts that might help.

Let's Target Our Legal Immigration

We bring in about 1 million people a year from foreign countries, usually relatives of people already here. These are not typically people with degrees and money. Why not take a cue from Canada and think about letting in people with money and education for a few years?

Specifically, if you buy a house for cash and pay for health care two years in advance, you get a temporary green card. Keep your act together for four years, and you get to keep it. Let 250,000 people a year (and one or two of their family) come in and buy homes until we have gone through the excess inventory in homes, which would happen within a few years. It puts a floor in the housing market and gets the homebuilding businesses back to building a lot sooner, and that is a lot of jobs. That would seriously help get GDP back in the right direction.

Further, every one of those new immigrants is going to need to buy furniture, food, clothing, a car, and more. What a boost to the economy! And it helps support the dollar. If the average home purchase was $200,000, that would be $50 billion, with at least another $10 billion in other purchases, all of which has to be converted into dollars and is a direct stimulus to the economy. With not one penny in taxes, except that the new owners will, of course, pay taxes.

And these people are going to have to figure out how to make a living. Going on welfare gives up the right to the green card. So many of them will start small businesses (which hire people) or become part of the productive workforce.

Remember, this does not bring in any more people than we are already admitting; it just changes the component for a few years. And as we saw in Chapter 3, the only way you can grow your economy is to increase your population or increase your productivity. That's it. We could do a lot better by choosing the people we want to come in by some metric other than simply being a relative. (We are not saying that we totally abandon that policy, just reduce the numbers in that program for a while.)

As a corollary to that concept, why not give every foreign graduate with an advanced degree a temporary green card, especially in the hard sciences? We train these people and then send them back to make their country more productive? We need them. Silicon Valley would still be a backwater if not for immigrants. Again, we need to give some thought to admitting immigrants who can help our return to a booming, productive economy.

There will be some high irony in a few years when not only the United States but also developed countries all over the world realize that they are competing on a worldwide stage for the best and brightest and that the real competition is to attract more of the best and brightest immigrants and keep more of their own people at home.

Getting Our Energy Policy Right

As we noted in a previous chapter, consumers and businesses can deleverage, the government can decide to run smaller deficits, and you can run large trade deficits, but you can only do two of them at any one time. (As we discussed, this is an accounting identity. It is not up for debate.). If we are serious about wanting to get our fiscal deficit under control, we must deal with our trade deficit. And that means getting real about our energy dependence on foreign oil. Short of making Alberta the 51st state, it will require some real changes.

We imported (on a net basis) $204 billion in petroleum-related products, which is well over half of our 2009 trade deficit of $380 billion, which itself was down from almost $700 billion in 2008.

Many economists (including us) speak of rising oil prices as a tax on the U.S. consumer, as it takes discretionary dollars that could be used for other goods and services and instead send them overseas. What if we could take that tax and spend it here in the United States on things we need?

As we said earlier in the book, we suggest a $0.30 a gallon gas tax increase every year until we are no longer dependent on foreign oil (phased in at 2.5 cents a month). If we start to become a net energy exporter, the tax would go back down. As in Europe, people would begin to opt for smaller, more fuel-efficient cars. A national miles per gallon that looked like Europe would get us a long way toward oil independence, if not all the way there.

We use about 140 billion gallons of gasoline a year in the United States, or about 72 percent of our total petroleum consumption. That would create a tax revenue stream of about $40 billion the first year, $80 billion the second year, and so on. That's a lot of money.

We would not put that tax money back into federal coffers. We suggest using the entire tax for rebuilding our infrastructure, which is deteriorating badly. Bridges, roads, water systems, smart electric grids, self-sustaining public transportation (no subsidies!), and so on. The large bulk of the money should stay local where the taxes are paid, with a much lesser amount for national projects.

For what it is worth, those projects will create a lot of jobs, and this is a tax that will benefit our kids as they can use the improved infrastructure.

Let's be clear. This is really a tax shift. By changing consumer preferences, and this will, we are taking money we are sending to oil-exporting nations and putting it to use here.

Next we would take a page from T. Boone Pickens and convert our national truck fleet to natural gas, a fuel we have in abundance. We could take some of the money from the gasoline tax to step in and build the needed infrastructure, but then it could be leased to operators and pay for itself over time.

As U.S. gas consumption slowed, it would have the benefit of reducing oil prices relative to what they would have been. It helps us in our fight to control the fiscal deficit and reduce our dependence on foreign energy.

And since we will eventually be shifting to an electric car fleet in the 2020s, we need to think about how we are going to create that electricity. While coal can certainly do the job, a much cleaner and more efficient way is modern nuclear power. We need to build (pick a number) 50, 75, or 100 nuclear power plants as we build a smart grid that reduces our dependence on fossil fuels.

Getting the Right Job Policies

Every day elected officials and the bureaucrats they are in charge of should wake up and ask themselves, "What can I do to make it easier for jobs to be created in my area of responsibility?" It should not be lost on anyone that states that have high taxes and lots of regulations are seeing people and businesses move to lower-tax states, which of course makes it harder for those states to collect enough taxes to pay for the services they provide.

There have to be rules, of course. But the rules and regulations should be the minimum needed to keep the barriers to entry for new businesses as low as possible. It is one thing to set rules for public safety. It is another to require dozens of forms and lawyers to open a small business. Running a business is hard enough without extra paperwork required by bureaucrats who don't have any skin in the game and can respond when they are ready and not when needed.

A proper job policy begins with educational opportunities, and that means a proper education in schools that get that their job is teaching children. I (John) have seven kids (five adopted), and their education needs have been widely divergent. I have had to shop schools more than once to find a school where one particular kid could thrive. Schools that teach to one size fits all or, at the most, a few sizes are outmoded in a modern world. Schools that are organized for the benefits of teachers' unions don't work at the primary job. We need to recognize that we need schools that cater to the diverse learning styles of the kids.

We have to recognize that we have to compete with China, India, Indonesia, and Germany (and a hundred other countries). At one time, we were up to the task, but we seem more hesitant these days. We need to recognize that unique skill that is the young American entrepreneur and work to train and find more of them, and it is in our schools that we find the breeding grounds for tomorrow's jobs.

Think about Tax Policies to Encourage New Businesses

Without jobs and lower unemployment, we have no real chance to get our fiscal house in order without really significant pain. The first order of business is to find ways to create new jobs. Since business start-ups are the true source of net new job creation, let's figure out what we can do to encourage them. Why not tell anyone who starts a business within the next three years that if he sells his business after five years, and has created some minimum number of new jobs, that he can sell his business when he wants for zero capital gains? That seems to us an incentive we can believe in.

And let's compete for global jobs. Let's offer international companies the opportunity to create a company in the United States and have their corporate taxes only be a low number for 10 years and then rise slowly after that. Why not 12 percent to compete with Ireland? Of course, that might give them an advantage with existing companies, so why not cut corporate taxes to where we can compete internationally?

There have to be taxes, but we can figure out how to restructure our tax code. As we finish this book, Erskine Bowles and Alan Simpson have put together a proposal to restructure the tax code, putting a top rate at 23 percent, but taxing capital gains and dividends at the same rate. They have a very interesting table with their release that shows what keeping certain tax expenditures would cost. For instance, if we decided that we wanted to keep the child tax credit and the earned income credit, it would cost an extra 1 percent of tax rate for everyone. The mortgage interest tax deduction would cost another 4 percent of tax rate for everyone. Considering that 40 percent of Americans do not own homes and a large percentage of those who do own owe nothing or very little, maybe it is something to consider.*

Another bipartisan group, headed by former Senator Pete Domenici and President Clinton's Office of Management and Budget Director Alice Rivlin, put forth a plan with two rates of 15 percent and 27 percent and a sales tax of 6.5 percent.

We hope that as more proposals are offered that the designers use the same format as Erskine Bowles. Show us what each large item in the tax code costs, and let us decide what we think is a good investment of our tax dollars and what we don't.

We won't go into details on these plans because there will be lots of others coming out soon. But it is refreshing to perhaps be at the beginning of a real conversation on reforming taxes in such a way as to encourage savings and new business while also getting the fiscal deficit under control.

We are dealing with the aftermath of the third bubble in the last 10 years, the last one being in government. And it is the one that is going to create the most problems as we try to solve how to shrink the government (at all levels) back down to a size that we can afford and that will not crowd out new business and private investment. It will not be easy, but the fact that we are seeing bipartisan proposals (which are bringing howls from both sides of the aisle) is encouraging. It shows that there are people who are beginning to get it.

Finally, we are optimistic that we will in fact figure it out. Over time, those new jobs will come as a new generation of American entrepreneurs

---

*John's daughter Tiffani and son Henry with new mortgages would probably vigorously disagree!

figure out how to create a business that gives us goods and services we want. Just as we had personal computers and the Internet come along, we are going to see revolutions in the biotech, wireless telecom (you ain't seen nothing yet!—there is a whole new wireless build-out coming), robotics, electric cars, smart infrastructure, and so much more.

As a reminder, in the late 1970s, when the Japanese were kicking our brains in, inflation was roaring, interest rates were pushing 20 percent, unemployment was almost 10 percent, and businesses were struggling, the correct answer to the question "Where will the jobs come from?" was "I don't know, but they will."

It is what we do.

CHAPTER TEN

The European Periphery

A Modern-Day Gold Standard

Europe exemplifies a situation unfavorable to a common currency. It is composed of separate nations, speaking different languages, with different customs, and having citizens feeling far greater loyalty and attachment to their own country than to a common market or to the idea of Europe.
> —Professor Milton Friedman,
> *The Times*, November 19, 1997

There is no example in history of a lasting monetary union that was not linked to one State.

> —Otmar Issuing,
> Chief Economist of the German Bundesbank in 1991

The countries of the European periphery are falling like dominoes due to too much debt. Greece required a bailout from the European Union and the IMF in May 2010. Ireland required one a few months later in November 2010. As we write this book, Portugal and Spain are next in the sights of the speculators. Much like the subprime crisis in the United States took down the mortgage lenders first, then Bear Stearns and then Lehman Brothers, the problems of too much debt are threatening to bring down European states.

During the good years, Portugal, Ireland, Italy, and Greece enjoyed the benefits of being in the euro, but now all the imbalances that have built up over time need to be redressed. This chapter deals with how these countries got there, what the current problems are, and possible ways out.

The Euro: A Suboptimal Currency Union

It may seem obvious to state it, but Europe is not a country. Europe is many things. It is a continent. It is an idea of better things to come for many immigrants who come to its shores from Africa and the Middle East. But it is also a currency area. And it is not a good one.

Many of us take our national currencies for granted, and we assume that we have always had dollars, pounds, yen, or euros. In fact, for a long time, individual banks issued notes promising the holder to exchange the notes for gold. The idea that a currency should exactly equal national territory is really one that came about very late in history.

Before the euro was created, Robert Mundell, an economist, wrote about what made an optimal currency area. His writing was so important that he won a Nobel Prize for his work. He wrote that a currency area is *optimal* when it has:

- Mobility of capital and labor
- Flexibility of wages and prices
- Similar business cycles
- Fiscal transfers to cushion the blows of recession to any region

Europe has almost none of these. Very bluntly, that means it is not a good currency area.

The United States is a good currency union. It has the same coins and money in Alaska as it does in Florida and the same in California as it does in Maine. If you look at economic shocks, the United States absorbs them pretty well. If you're unemployed in southern California in the early 1990s after the end of the Cold War defense cutbacks or in Texas in the early 1980s after the oil boom turned to bust, you can pack your bags and go to a state that is growing. That is exactly what happened. This doesn't happen in Europe. Greeks don't pack up and move to Finland. Greeks don't speak Finnish (no one does outside of Finland). And if Americans had stayed in California or Texas, they would have received fiscal transfers from the central government to cushion the blow. There is no central European government that can make fiscal transfers. So the United States works because it has mobility of labor and capital, as well as fiscal shock absorbers.

The modern euro is like a gold standard. Obviously, the euro isn't exchangeable for gold, but it is similar in many important ways. Like the gold standard, the euro forces adjustment in real prices and wages instead of exchange rates. And much like the gold standard, it has a recessionary bias. Under a gold standard, the burden of adjustment is always placed on the weak-currency country, not on the strong countries.

Under a classical gold standard, countries that experience downward pressure on the value of their currency are forced to contract their economies, which typically raises unemployment because wages don't fall fast enough to deal with reduced demand. Interestingly, the gold standard doesn't work the other way. It doesn't impose any adjustment burden on countries seeing upward market pressure on currency values. This one-way adjustment mechanism creates a deflationary bias for countries in a recession. The deflationary bias also makes it likely, at least by historical measures, that we will catch hell from the Austrians.

Economists like Barry Eichengreen, arguably one of the great experts on the gold standard and writer of the tour de force *Golden Fetters,* argues that sticking to the gold standard was a major factor in preventing governments from fighting the Great Depression. Sticking to the gold standard turned what could have been a minor recession following the crash of 1929 into the Great Depression. Countries that were not on the gold standard in 1929 or that quickly abandoned it escaped the Great Depression with far less drawdown of economic output.

Before we begin, we need to introduce a very important distinction. In Europe, the so-called core is Germany, France, Netherlands, and Belgium. They are in general wealthier, have higher price stability, and have much more integrated economies. The periphery is Portugal, Ireland, Italy, Greece, and Spain (known often as the PIIGS). These countries historically are poorer (or regions within them are), have less price stability, are not well integrated with Germany and France, and have less coordinated business cycles. The difference between the core and periphery leads to all sorts of problems that we'll explain in this chapter.

Over the past 10 years, the European periphery has experienced large increases in wages and prices compared with the core. While prices and wages were stagnant in Germany, they were increasing at a rapid rate in the periphery. This made the periphery very uncompetitive relative to Germany and the rest of the core. The result? The periphery countries were importing a lot more than they were exporting and were running large current account deficits. The only way to fix this is through a real cut in wages and prices, an internal devaluation, or deflation. This is hugely contractionary and poses tremendous problems.

Rapidly rising prices with low interest rates created the problem of negative real interest rates in the periphery. In plain English, that means that if the borrowing rate is 3 percent while inflation is 4 percent, you're effectively borrowing for 1 percent less than inflation. You're being paid to borrow. And borrow they did. The European peripheral countries racked up enormous debts in euros, a currency that they can't print.

The United States, the United Kingdom, and Switzerland have monetized liabilities to provide liquidity to banks, ease fiscal expansion, influence long-end rates, and weaken their currency. The European periphery (the proverbial PIIGS: Portugal, Ireland, Italy, Greece, and Spain) does not have that option. The only historical analogy to the situation of the European periphery is countries that experienced deflation while under a gold standard: where debts had to be paid down in a currency—that is, gold—that they could not print.

Germany refuses to reduce its enormous trade surplus and increase its domestic consumption to rebalance Europe and help the weaker economies grow out of their difficulties. Remember, for every deficit, there has to be a surplus. Instead, Germany is busy cutting spending and reducing domestic demand, just as much as its periphery neighbors. Because the euro is like a gold standard, it is a regime with a strong deflationary bias. The burden of adjustment falls on the deficit countries in the periphery who are forced to deflate.

Unlike the gold standard, it is almost impossible to leave the euro. The Maastricht treaty was very clear about how to get into the euro but said nothing about how to get out. Indeed, the mechanics of a country leaving the euro would be so messy that even if it were the right policy in the long run, most politicians and businesspeople would oppose it in the short run. Consider the following in the event of a breakup of Italy leaving the Eurozone:

> Market participants would be aware of this fact. Households and firms anticipating that domestic deposits would be redenominated into the lira, which would then lose value against the euro, would shift their deposits to other euro-area banks. A system-wide bank run would follow. Investors anticipating that their claims on the Italian government would be redenominated into lira would shift into claims on other euro-area governments, leading to a bond-market crisis. If the precipitating factor was parliamentary debate over abandoning the lira, it would be unlikely that the ECB would provide extensive lender-of-last-resort support. And if the government was already in a weak fiscal position, it would not be able to borrow to bail out the banks and buy back its debt. This would be the mother of all financial crises.[1] [Not unlike the process Greece is in!]

The consequences are too dire for most politicians to even consider. That is why the euro most likely will plod along as politicians do everything they can to keep the project going. This will have profound implications for economic growth, deflation, and financial markets.

The euro is not an economic currency. It is a political one, and as long as there is the political will, it will remain a currency. Ironically, it is the well-off nations like Germany or the Netherlands (where we sit today editing yet another final draft of this book) who could exit without their own internal crisis. Not that either country would, and their banks do own a lot of peripheral country debt.

What does the evidence for deflation and contraction show so far? European inflation is running below that of most other countries. Arguably, we will see inflation in countries that can monetize debt and

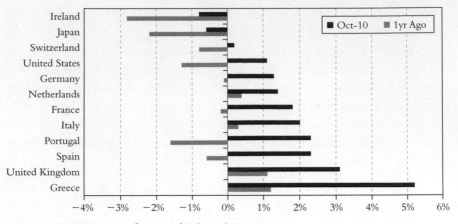

Figure 10.1 Core Inflation of Selected Countries
SOURCE: Bloomberg, Variant Perception.

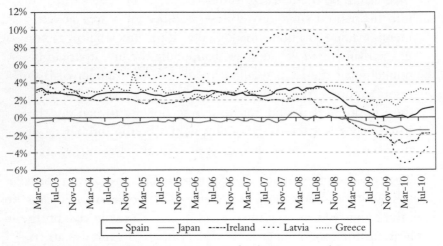

Figure 10.2 Core CPI: Spain, Latvia, Ireland, Greece, and Japan
SOURCE: Bloomberg, Variant Perception.

see deflation in those that can't. Unsurprisingly, Figure 10.1 shows that the highest rates of inflation are in the United States and the United Kingdom, while the lowest are in the Eurozone countries and in Japan, which is trapped in deflation.

It is worth noting that the European periphery has the prime candidates for protracted deflations. (See Figure 10.2.)

Figure 10.3 German versus European Periphery Bond Spreads
SOURCE: Bloomberg, Variant Perception.

One of the main things investors and journalists have wanted to talk about this past year is the unfolding situation in Greece and the periphery. Figure 10.3 shows this starkly. The problems are not new, but the markets are now realizing the depth of the problem.

Let's look at an excerpt from the September 2010 issue of *Vanity Fair* by Michael Lewis.[2]

> As it turned out, what the Greeks wanted to do, once the lights went out and they were alone in the dark with a pile of borrowed money, was turn their government into a piñata stuffed with fantastic sums and give as many citizens as possible a whack at it. In just the past decade the wage bill of the Greek public sector has doubled, in real terms—and that number doesn't take into account the bribes collected by public officials. The average government job pays almost three times the average private-sector job.
>
> The national railroad has annual revenues of 100 million euros against an annual wage bill of 400 million, plus 300 million euros in other expenses. The average state railroad employee earns 65,000 euros a year. Twenty years ago a successful businessman turned minister of finance named Stefanos

Manos pointed out that it would be cheaper to put all Greece's rail passengers into taxicabs: it's still true. "We have a railroad company which is bankrupt beyond comprehension," Manos put it to me. "And yet there isn't a single private company in Greece with that kind of average pay."

The Greek public-school system is the site of breathtaking inefficiency: one of the lowest-ranked systems in Europe, it nonetheless employs four times as many teachers per pupil as the highest-ranked, Finland's. Greeks who send their children to public schools simply assume that they will need to hire private tutors to make sure they actually learn something. There are three government-owned defense companies: together they have billions of euros in debts, and mounting losses.

The retirement age for Greek jobs classified as "arduous" is as early as 55 for men and 50 for women. As this is also the moment when the state begins to shovel out generous pensions, more than 600 Greek professions somehow managed to get themselves classified as arduous: hairdressers, radio announcers, waiters, musicians, and on and on and on. The Greek public health-care system spends far more on supplies than the European average—and it is not uncommon, several Greeks tell me, to see nurses and doctors leaving the job with their arms filled with paper towels and diapers and whatever else they can plunder from the supply closets.

The Greek people never learned to pay their taxes . . . because no one is ever punished. It's like a gentleman not opening a door for a lady.

Where waste ends and theft begins almost doesn't matter; the one masks and thus enables the other. It's simply assumed, for instance, that anyone who is working for the government is meant to be bribed. People who go to public health clinics assume they will need to bribe doctors to actually take care of them. Government ministers who have spent their lives in public service emerge from office able to afford multi-million-dollar mansions and two or three country homes.

The level of change that will be needed in Greece is almost beyond description. As Lewis points out, it is more than just balancing a few budgets and making some cuts. It demands a change in the national character—in the way of doing things that everyone has gotten used to.

The leaders of Europe make brave statements that no European Union member can be allowed to default. There *must* be a way. And yet, the reality is that the solution is for the Greeks to borrow even more money that they cannot pay. Default is not only possible; it is likely.

Greece is a disaster, but it is a small one. Greece is a gnat on an elephant's backside. Greek nominal GDP is about 2 percent of the euro area total. Spain's GDP is over 12 percent of the euro area.

Spain had the mother of all housing bubbles. To put things in perspective, Spain now has as many unsold homes as the United States, even though the United States is about six times bigger. Spain is roughly 12 percent of the EU GDP, yet it accounted for 30 percent of all new homes built since 2000 in the EU. Most of the new homes were financed with capital from abroad, so Spain's housing crisis is closely tied in with a financing crisis.

The impact on the banking sector will be severe. Consider this: The value of outstanding loans to Spanish developers has gone from just €33.5 billion in 2000 to €318 billion in 2008, a rise of 850 percent in eight years. If you add in construction sector debts, the overall value of outstanding loans to developers and construction companies rises to €470 billion. That's almost 50 percent of Spanish GDP.

The magnitude of the Spanish problem is staggering and will overwhelm all the benefits of dynamic provisioning. Spain has 613,512 homes that are finished but unsold as of December 2008, according to the Spanish Housing Ministry. To that number, you'd have to add 626,691 homes that were under construction as of that date. Of those, 250,000 were sold (but subject to cancellation), and the others were ready to hit the market. So conservatively, Spain has more than 1 million unsold homes. Unfortunately, many of the homes are on the coast, and without a return of overleveraged British tourists, they are likely to remain unsold. Spain's homes are all in the wrong places.

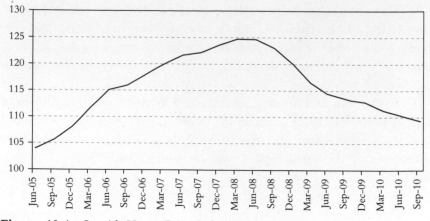

Figure 10.4 Spanish House Price Index (Housing Ministry data)
SOURCE: Bloomberg, Variant Perception.

Spain's building stocks bubble looks very much like the U.S. bubble and other classic bubbles. It went up tenfold and then went down 90 percent. The math is very simple.

Given this woeful state of affairs, you might assume Spanish house prices had suffered like U.S. house prices. This is not the case. As Figure 10.4 shows, according to official statistics, Spanish house prices are down little more than 10 percent from their peaks.

Given the mother of all housing bubbles and a lack of competitiveness, Spain is likely to face a prolonged downturn and very large budget deficits for some time to come. The Spanish unemployment rate is double the average of a core country like France, as Figure 10.5 shows. Even with recent labor market reforms, the structural problems remain.

The problems of the core versus the periphery, however, will not go away. Irrespective of the current Greek crisis, European spreads should fundamentally trade much wider than they did during the quiet period of 2000 to 2010. As we write in late 2010, interest rate spreads of the periphery countries are once again rising back to crisis levels, signaling another sovereign debt crisis. Investors have been complacent for too long and willing to lend at the periphery at rates that made no sense, based on their poor fiscal credibility and their dim outlook for growth following a decade of inflation, excess consumption, and living beyond their means.

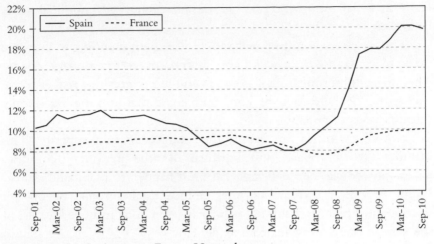

Figure 10.5 Spain versus France Unemployment
SOURCE: Bloomberg, Variant Perception.

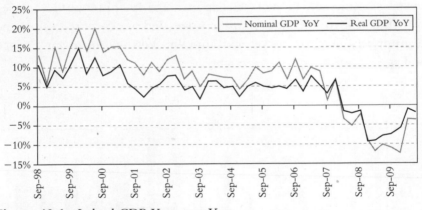

Figure 10.6 Ireland GDP Year over Year
SOURCE: Bloomberg, Variant Perception.

What is ahead for the European periphery? The European periphery is likely to follow in the footsteps of Ireland. Of all European countries, Ireland is now the most advanced in its own deflationary drama. Ireland is experiencing severe deflation, and even though GDP growth is turning up quarter on quarter, it is still deflating nominally (Figure 10.6).

Deflation will exacerbate government deficits in the long run, as companies pay nominal, not real, taxes. (In a deflationary environment, real—after deflation—taxes could be increasing, yet nominal taxes decreasing.)

The periphery countries will slash government spending to keep the markets at bay, which will have short-term contractionary effects. The longer-term squeeze will come from their overvalued real effective exchange rates and lack of competitiveness that can be fixed only through years of deflation.

Not all countries can export their way back to prosperity. This includes Greece, Spain, and Portugal. As the periphery countries necessarily reduce their deficits, what must happen to maintain balance? Either European surplus countries reduce their surplus, or on net Europe must reduce its surplus, in which case China must reduce its, or the United States must increase its deficit.

A weak euro will not help the European periphery. As Figure 10.7 shows, exports outside the Eurozone as a percentage of GDP are very low for Greece, Spain, and Portugal. Except for Ireland, the PIIGS are not very open economies, and most of their exports are to other European countries.

Only internal measures to make wages and prices more flexible and to improve the labor market and improve skills will have any impact, and these cannot happen overnight.

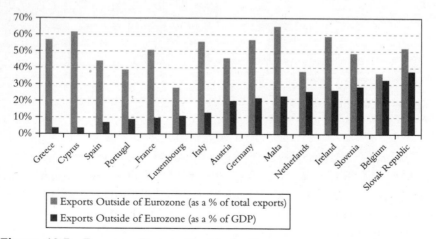

Figure 10.7 European Exports Outside the Eurozone
SOURCE: Jacob Funk Kirkegaard, "The Role of External Demand in the Eurozone," Peterson Institute for International Economics, May 27, 2010, www.petersoninstitute.org/realtime/index.cfm?p=1595.

The European periphery faces a period of debt deflation. As we have pointed out elsewhere, the public sector and private sector in periphery economies cannot deleverage at the same time without running a trade surplus. (The problem is that Germany and China aren't about to start running deficits.) This is true for mathematical reasons that are inescapable. Earlier, we showed that the following relationship is true:

Domestic Private Sector Financial Balance + Fiscal Balance

+ Foreign Financial Balance = 0

This is an economic identity that can't be violated. Simply put, the changes in one sector's financial balance cannot be viewed in isolation. If government wants to run a fiscal surplus and reduce government debt, it needs to run an even larger trade surplus, or else the domestic private sector will need to engage in deficit spending. The only way that both the government and the private sector can deleverage is if the countries run large current account surpluses; in other words, your demand has to come from another country.

The map in Figure 10.8 is illuminating.

What does this mean for Europe? In Europe governments by treaty are not supposed to run deficits of more than 3 percent of GDP

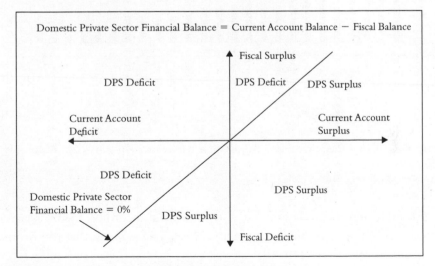

Figure 10.8   Three-Sector Financial Balances Map
SOURCE: Rob Parenteau, MacroStrategy Edge, www.creditwritedowns.com/2010/03/leading-piigs-to-slaughter.html.

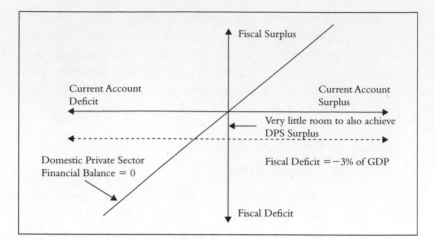

Figure 10.9 The EMU Triangle: When FX Policy Is Constrained and Current Account Surplus Is Unachievable

SOURCE: Rob Parenteau, MacroStrategy Edge, www.creditwritedowns.com/2010/03/leading-piigs -to-slaughter.html.

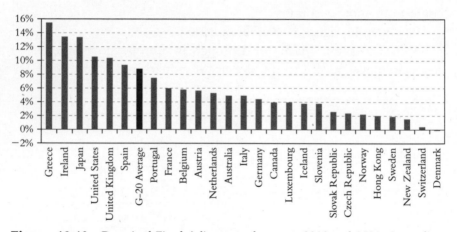

Figure 10.10 Required Fiscal Adjustment between 2010 and 2020, According to IMF

SOURCE: Bloomberg, Variant Perception.

(although they routinely do). If you look at it according to the Maastricht deficit criteria, as seen in Figure 10.9, you will see that the room for maneuver is very limited.[3]

The room for adjustment is simply too small. As Figure 10.10 shows, the required fiscal adjustment in most European countries is simply too large. There is literally no chance that almost any of the

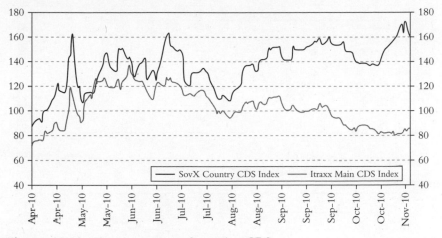

Figure 10.11 Corporate versus Sovereign CDSs
SOURCE: Bloomberg, Variant Perception.

European periphery countries (with the exception of Italy, which has a path if it has the political will) will succeed in their goal of abiding by the Maastricht criteria and deleveraging at the same time. To do so will require that these countries reduce their trade deficits by enough that it could only mean a local depression for some time. It would mean depressed incomes and wages, lower tax revenues, and in short, a very ugly picture.

The extremely low likelihood for success is already reflected in the marketplace. Market participants are beginning to believe governments will not pay back their debts. Governments are now held in such low regard by investors that in many countries, corporate bonds trade at tighter spreads than their equivalent sovereigns. Figure 10.11 shows that for the first time ever, corporate CDSs (credit default swaps, a way to hedge your bond holdings) are tighter than sovereign CDSs.

Some Countries Recover; Others Don't

Currently, the world is caught in a tug-of-war between deflation and inflation. The world faces powerful deflationary forces that have induced equally powerful inflationary responses from governments around the

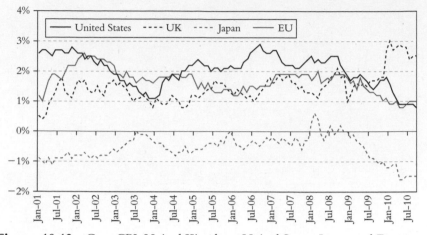

Figure 10.12   Core CPI: United Kingdom, United States, Japan, and European Union
SOURCE: National Statistics, Variant Perception.

world. The effects will not happen everywhere and to all assets at the same time. Some regions of the world will experience growing inflation, while other parts will be trapped in a deflationary spiral; some assets will move up in price, while others stagnate or even deflate.

Interestingly, so far only Japan is showing negative core inflation, but the United States, United Kingdom, Germany, and France all have relatively high core inflation, as Figure 10.12 shows.

On the other hand, the countries that are genuinely experiencing the beginning of what will be a prolonged deflationary period are Spain, Ireland, Greece, Japan, and Baltic countries like Latvia (Figure 10.13). These are the countries with the greatest imbalances. So far, they have had no meaningful reforms.

Central banks are overwhelmingly more concerned about deflation than about inflation. It is precisely the deflationary fear—the fear of the liquidity trap—that will drive central banks to be extremely loose with their monetary policies. Central banks are afraid of the fall in monetary velocity, and because of this, they will continue to flood the world with money until they are convinced velocity will rise. The current low levels of CPI—itself only one measure of inflation—will give them false confidence that they have a sweet spot in which they can print money with impunity without causing inflation.

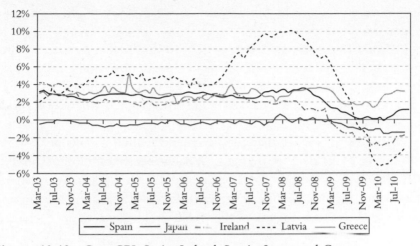

Figure 10.13   Core CPI: Spain, Ireland, Latvia, Japan, and Greece
SOURCE: National Statistics, Variant Perception.

Bottom line? We expect Greece to default on its debt at some point. You cannot keep on adding to debt when too much debt was the original problem. Greece cannot grow its way out of its problems. Germany has begun to make it known that they expect bondholders and not just German taxpayers to take some of the pain of restructuring.

Sadly, we must say the same for Portugal. They just don't seem to get it. But in the end, the market will force them to.

Spain? It is hard to see a way out, short of willingly throwing themselves into a major depression, which does not really solve the problem. Spanish debt is going to suffer a haircut, and that is both government and private debt. It is just too much. For more in-depth information on the Spanish problem and the problems of other peripheral countries, you can go to www.johnmauldin.com/PIGS and see research from Jonathan Tepper of Variant Perception and other related material. Just type in your e-mail address as your name and Endgame as the password.

And Mother Ireland (at least to John)? They are making the right and difficult efforts, as opposed to Greece. Their hearts (as all Irish hearts are) are in the right place. But it is a very deep hole in which they find themselves. One way or another, they will muddle through. That is what the Irish have done for centuries. We would not want to bet on their government bonds, but a home in the country might be a good wager.

Want a European success story? Go to tiny Malta, an island full of history in the Mediterranean. Not really the population of a decent city, they are a demonstration of what can happen when politicians of all sides can come together. Malta is really a small town where everybody knows everybody.

Malta seems to get that they have no natural advantage. So the business of Malta became business. Whatever it takes to attract investments and jobs is the first order of the day. Like politicians everywhere, they fight. But they seemingly get what it takes to keep their economy growing. Would that the rest of the world could take a lesson. Seriously.

CHAPTER ELEVEN

Eastern European Problems

We must pay the debt precisely and punctually, even if we destroy the economy in so doing.

—Katalin Botos, Secretary of State in the
Hungarian Finance Ministry (1990–1993)

E astern Europe faces daunting structural issues. A decade of excess lending, wage and price growth, and large current account deficits has created major imbalances. To make things worse, most of the borrowing for the Baltics, Romania, Bulgaria, and Hungary was in foreign currencies.

Eastern Europe, much like Spain and Ireland, will face deflation and high unemployment for some time. At best, we are likely to see an L-shaped recovery for Eastern Europe. Figure 11.1 shows the real effective exchange rates of Eastern European countries. It is clear that they have become far less competitive against a benchmark country of the European core, like Germany. (This is the same problem Portugal, Ireland, Greece, and Spain face, but on a smaller scale.)

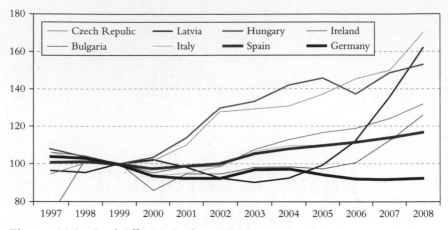

Figure 11.1   Real Effective Exchange Rates in Europe
SOURCE: Eurostat, Variant Perception.

In this chapter, we look at the Baltics and Hungary, the two poster children of what can go wrong when you have too much lending and housing bubbles.

Hungary: Damned If They Do, Damned If They Don't

One of the outcomes of the economic crisis is that we all became a little more financially literate. As economic news suddenly moved to the top of news bulletins and migrated from the graveyard pages of newspapers to become front-page headlines, the jargon of finance began to enter the common lexicon. Obscure terms such as *collaterized debt obligation, LIBOR, securitization,* and *credit default swap* became fairly commonplace. One of these terms was the so-called *carry trade.* This usually referred to the Japanese carry trade. In essence, investors exploited Japan's very low interest rates by borrowing in yen and using the funds to buy assets in another country, such as the United Kingdom or the United States (remember those days?), that earned a much higher rate of interest.

Much less discussed, though, was the Eastern Europe carry trade. Several Eastern European countries had very high interest rates in the years leading up to the banking crisis, largely a legacy of trying to bring down uncomfortably high rates of inflation. Hungary's rates, for instance, reached 12.5 percent in 2004 to try to combat a rising inflation rate that eventually peaked out at well over 7 percent.

This made borrowing in Hungary very expensive. In neighboring Austria, the banks there had started to offer loans and mortgages to their customers in Swiss francs. Rates in Austria, at 2 percent, may have been lower than in Hungary, but in Switzerland, they were even lower, at around 0.50 percent. Why would Austrians borrow at 2 percent when they could just as easily borrow at 0.50 percent? The same question applied to Hungarians, except the difference was much bigger. So the Austrian banks, many of which also had branches in Hungary (a throwback to the days of the Austro-Hungarian Empire), began to engage in the same business there, lending Swiss francs to Hungarian borrowers.

Unsurprisingly, this proved to be very popular in Hungary. All of a sudden, people who were unable to afford a mortgage in Hungarian forints because of the prohibitively high interest rates were able to get a seemingly great deal in Swiss francs (or euros, but most of the borrowing was from Switzerland). Property prices surged, and the economy appeared to flourish. It was not long before the majority of debt in Hungary was denominated in a foreign currency. Indeed, as Figure 11.2 shows, Hungary was one of the worst offenders in this respect, with almost two-thirds of household debt (mortgages and consumer loans) in a foreign currency.

As we have learned throughout this book, there is no such thing as a free lunch. Sure, you can borrow much cheaper in a foreign currency and save a lot of money to begin with. But what of the extra risks, many of which your average borrower is blissfully unaware of until it is too late?

Well, when borrowing in a foreign currency, you are exposed to the foreign exchange movements of the two currencies. Imagine as a Hungarian you borrowed in Swiss francs to buy a house in Hungary. When you came to repay the loan, if the Hungarian forint had weakened significantly against the Swiss franc, you would have to find more forints to pay back what you owe in francs. As exchange rates can move

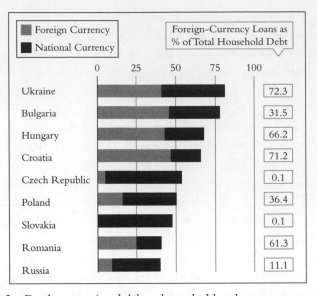

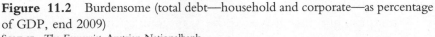

Figure 11.2 Burdensome (total debt—household and corporate—as percentage of GDP, end 2009)
SOURCE: *The Economist*, Austrian Nationalbank.

fast and far, doing so could be very costly. This means Hungary's net external debt/GDP ratio has the ability to balloon instantly with any weakness in the Hungarian forint. Indeed, the debt almost doubled overnight as the forint weakened in late 2008, as Figure 11.3 shows.

This is a risk that has far from disappeared. As the exchange rates of the Swiss franc against the Hungarian forint in Figure 11.4 show, servicing foreign debt in Hungary is as difficult as it has ever been:

Hungary's fiscal situation deteriorated fast during the financial crisis. Output collapsed, and the government, in common with many other countries across the globe, had to ramp up borrowing to make up for the shortfall in tax revenues. The result? Despite getting its budget deficit down to one of the lowest in Europe, Hungary now has one of the highest debt-to-GDP ratios in the region. (See Figure 11.5.)

It was thus no surprise that Hungary, along with Latvia, became one of the first countries postcrisis to call in the IMF for financial aid, obtaining a $15 billion loan from the organization in November 2008. The loan had the usual tough conditions that would ensure the country's fiscal health was restored so further bailouts could be avoided. There is

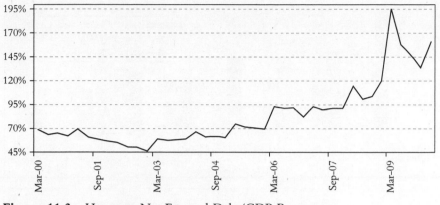

Figure 11.3   Hungary: Net External Debt/GDP Percentage
SOURCE: National Statistics, Variant Perception.

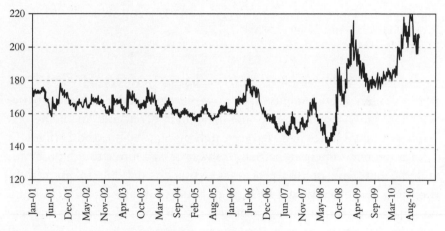

Figure 11.4   Hungarian Forint per Swiss Franc
SOURCE: Bloomberg, Variant Perception.

no doubt the loan helped stabilize the country's finances through the darkest hours of the crisis. Lately, however, there has been friction between the current Hungarian government and the IMF. This is where Hungary becomes very important and why we should pay close attention.

Hungary has had austerity measures in place from as early as 2006—well before the IMF came in with its loan—as the government fought

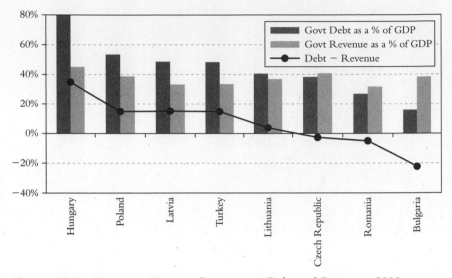

Figure 11.5   Emerging Europe: Government Debt and Revenue 2009
SOURCE: National Statistics, Variant Perception.

to reduce a swelling budget deficit to be ready to comply with European Union requirements. But now we are seeing reform fatigue, which is fairly usual in response to tough economic medicine. As Barclays Capital notes in a 2010 research piece, "'Stabilisation fatigue' is a common phenomenon that sets in a year or two into a tough program, and the outcome of that process is extremely difficult to predict. In short, the recent early success of the Greeks' courageous efforts should be applauded, but investors would be well advised to keep in perspective that sovereign risks very much remain a reality."[1]

So although it may appear that countries like Greece have taken the steps necessary to solve their problems and we can all go back to sleep, it is very unlikely that we are in the clear yet, as Hungary makes clear. If we watch Hungary, we will have a good idea how things will play out in many other parts of the world.

But ongoing austerity fatigue is only one of Hungary's problems. With a heavily indebted private and public sector, Hungary is going to have to look to its export sector to rejuvenate its economy and reduce its foreign debt. There are several problems associated with this. First, Hungary's export sector is too small on its own to pull the economy forward. Second, Hungary will be trying to increase exports at the same time countries all over the world, from China to Spain, from the United Kingdom to Greece, are trying to do the same. Competition is intense.

However, the most crushing problem of Hungary's is directly a result of having so much of its debt denominated in a foreign currency. If the Hungarian central bank cuts rates to try to make the forint cheaper and thus make Hungary's exports more competitive, it risks a wave of private-sector defaults. Remember all those mortgages in Swiss francs we mentioned? Well, those loans would suddenly balloon in value to the extent that many borrowers would have to throw in the towel. Property prices would collapse, and the economy would sink.

And there would be a risk that trouble could spread abroad. The banks in Austria who had originally made the loans would be at risk of going under, creating all sorts of problems in Austria and further afield. It would not be pretty. (Remember, it was the default of a little-known Austrian bank called Credit Anstalt that triggered the global financial crisis in 1931.)

The European Central Bank (ECB) has determined that Greece is too big to fail and is stepping in. But if there is a further crisis in Hungary and other Eastern European countries, the bank problems in Austria would be so massive that the banking sector in Austria would be too big to save for the Austrian government, not dissimilar to the situation in Iceland.

The Austrian banks have lent approximately 140 percent of the country's GDP to Eastern Europe. There is no way the Austrian government could bail them out in the event of a real crisis. The ECB would have to step in, and that, gentle reader, will not bode well for the euro. Nor will it sit well with voters in Germany and other core countries.

But neither can the central bank in Hungary risk maintaining rates at their current high level for too long. This will mean choking off the competitiveness the country needs to boost its export sector and repair its economy. Policy makers in Hungary are in an impossible position; they are damned if they do and damned if they don't.

Hungary will be important to watch as we move toward endgame. The country will remain a potential hand grenade in the European region—and perhaps further afield—as long as its foreign exchange–

denominated loans remain so high. It wouldn't take much to kick off a wave of defaults in Hungary, which would mean grave problems for European banks. And as we have learned so starkly throughout this crisis, when banks have a problem, we all have a problem.

Yet the greater implications of Hungary's plight lie in its bid to cut costs and restore fiscal order. Hungary is a leading indicator when it comes to experiencing the effects of austerity, having lived through such circumstances for more than four years now. Reform, or stabilization, fatigue is common one to two years into public belt-tightening programs. We should not be so complacent as to think austerity programs recently agreed to in countries like Greece and Ireland will be the end of the matter. Remember, the light at the end of the tunnel is sometimes another train.

The Baltics: How to Destroy Your Economy and Keep Your Peg

The Baltic countries—Latvia, Lithuania, and Estonia—lie on the Baltic Sea in the far eastern fringes of Europe. Their economies are very small, even smaller than Greece's, but like Greece, they matter. It was even before Greece came under scrutiny that the Baltic countries, especially Latvia, came under the spotlight. Indeed, it was really the Baltics that first alerted investors to what Ken Rogoff and Carmen Reinhart so elegantly demonstrated in their book *This Time Is Different,* that what normally follows a financial crisis are sovereign crises.

It isn't always obvious after the initial financial cataclysm where the first domino will fall. The financial crisis in the 1930s after the Wall Street crash of 1929 started in Austria, of all places. The Asian crisis in 1997 could have had many triggers, given the enormous economic imbalances in the region at that time, yet it was a sell-off in the Thai baht that proved to be the catalyst. In our fingers of instability analogy that we discussed in Chapter 2, it is not the grain of sand that's the real cause for the avalanche, but the level of instability in the overall system. After a financial collapse, the system is in a very fragile state; we know it might only take one grain of sand to create an avalanche, but heaven knows which one! After Lehman fell, there were many candidates for the first sovereign to get into trouble. It turned out to be Latvia (closely followed by its Baltic neighbors) that would earn the dubious distinction of being one of the first countries postcrisis to have to call in the IMF for assistance.

First, let's look at why the guns of the world's investors turned to the Baltics during and after the financial crisis. Then, we'll look at what this means for other potential sovereign mishaps waiting to happen around the globe.

The Baltic countries regained their independence from the Soviet Union in the early 1990s following the collapse of communism. They were enthusiastic in leaving their Soviet past behind and embracing the West, with all three countries first joining NATO and then the European Union. A further ambition of Latvia, Lithuania, and Estonia was to join the euro, so all three adopted currency pegs with the euro, a precondition for joining the common currency.

A currency peg is when a country agrees to fix its exchange rate to another. For example, the Latvians fixed the lats at 1 EUR = 0.702804 LVL. If people want lati at a higher price than that, the central bank has to print them and buy euros. If people want to exchange their euros at a higher price than that, then the central bank has to raise interest rates and withdraw money from the local economy to strengthen the currency. Effectively, pegs imply giving up control of your own money supply and handing it over to the market or to a foreign central bank. However, it can provide a higher degree of stability in good times.

Here's where Baltic countries' problems started. By fixing their currencies to the euro, it made it a lot easier for foreign banks to start lending to people in the Baltics. The peg eliminated exchange rate risk. Take Swedish banks as an example. They had a lot of spare cash—deposited by conservative Swedish savers—that they wanted to lend out. Sweden has many historical ties with Latvia (and the other Baltic countries) and is one of its largest trading partners. This has led to Swedish banks having subsidiaries in Baltic countries. Once the peg came into being, the Swedish banks went into overdrive, lending euros to their subsidiaries, who exchanged them for local currencies at the fixed peg level. The subsidiaries then lent out the local currency to Latvians, Lithuanians, and Estonians, fueling property prices, funding flashy cars, and creating a latterly unheard-of consumer boom. Suddenly, the modest

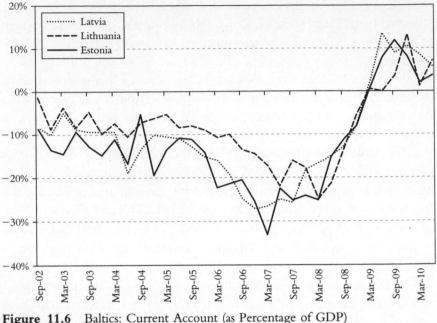

Figure 11.6   Baltics: Current Account (as Percentage of GDP)
SOURCE: National Statistics, Variant Perception.

economies of the Baltic nations looked like they were able to generate a lot of wealth, often ostentatious.

The result? As Baltic residents spent like they'd never spent before, current account (trade) deficits reached eye-watering levels, as Figure 11.6 shows.

All three countries managed to run up current account deficits of more than 20 percent in 2006 and 2007. This makes the current account deficits seen in the run-up to the Asian crisis of the late 1990s look like Mini-Mes. However, as we've seen over and over again in examples throughout this book, markets abhor an imbalance and will move to correct it. The borrowing and spending binge couldn't continue. Worldwide, fear throttled liquidity as the financial crisis tightened its grip.

Wages had risen in Baltic countries as their credit-driven prosperity increased. This made goods and labor from Baltic countries less competitive. When global growth began to seriously slow in the aftermath of the financial crisis, growth in the Baltic states started to take a serious hit. Government deficits in the Baltic countries grew fast, and it wasn't long before Latvia had to call in the IMF to formulate a rescue package. This is, of course, when Latvia earned the dubious honor of being the first potential sovereign hand grenade to go off as a result of the financial crisis. The other Baltic countries came under intense scrutiny at the same time, as the three economies were very tightly linked. They were closely followed by the Balkan countries (Romania, Bulgaria, etc.), Dubai, and then the European periphery countries (Iceland, Spain, Greece, Portugal, Ireland). Will there be more to come? We defer to the wicked-smart Professors Rogoff and Reinhart here, who have shown that sovereign crises tend to cluster. So we are pretty sure they would say, resoundingly, "Yes."

But back to the Baltics. What is the outlook for them now? Well, Latvia is going through one of the most drastic austerity programs we've ever heard of. Teachers have seen their wages slashed by almost half, some government employees have had to take pay cuts of 20 percent, and pensioners who work have seen the value of their pensions decimated by up to 70 percent. It makes most other austerity measures attempted elsewhere look like mere tweaking.

To compound the misery, the authorities in Latvia are refusing to drop the currency peg. This would involve a lot of short-term pain, especially for the Swedish banks we mentioned earlier, who have lent heavily in Latvia and the other Baltic countries. However, the end of the currency peg would also mean the government could reverse some of the savage cuts it has made. Breaking the peg would cause the currency to devalue, instantly making Latvian goods and services much cheaper and more competitive. The Latvian economy would grow very quickly, and the fiscal situation would greatly improve. As it stands, nominal GDP has bounced back from the lows in the Baltic countries, but it is still close to zero (Figure 11.7). This is crucial as it means tax revenues will remain depressed, and cutbacks will have to continue.

As it is, it's the teacher, the pensioner, and the government employee—the little people—who will continue to take the brunt of the adjustment. Instead, the political elites, who would have the most to directly gain from entry to the euro, cling to the peg at all costs. Resentment simmers and threatens to boil over at any time. Not only that, but people are leaving in search of a better life. One survey

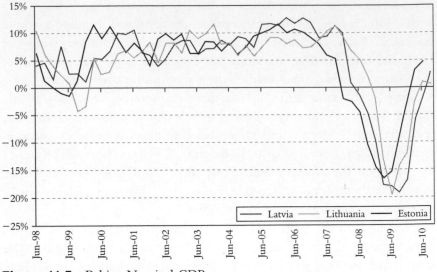

Figure 11.7   Baltics: Nominal GDP
SOURCE: Bloomberg, Variant Perception.

estimates 30,000 people left Latvia in 2009, and another 30,000 will leave in 2010, which is a worry for a country with a population of a little over 2 million.

Now if you're ahead of us, gentle reader, you're probably seeing some similarities between the Baltics and countries we looked at in Chapter 10, like Greece, Spain, and Ireland. They, too, are (effectively) on a currency peg, the euro, and like Latvia and the other Baltic countries, they are having a hard time as wages and costs, rather than the currency, are having to fall to restore competition. We called it "a modern-day gold standard." The difference with Latvia or Lithuania (but less so Estonia, which was recently approved for euro membership in 2011) is that it could quite easily drop the pegs and revert to local currencies. (The Greek drachma, the Spanish peseta, and the Irish punt are long dead, and resurrecting them would be a huge undertaking.)

Endgame for the Baltics? Estonia looks like it will be the best of a bad bunch, as its prospects should improve when it adopts the euro in 2011. Lithuania and Latvia, however, will continue to stagnate. Indeed, unemployment in Lithuania continues to increase and has fallen only marginally in the other two Baltic countries. (See Figure 11.8.)

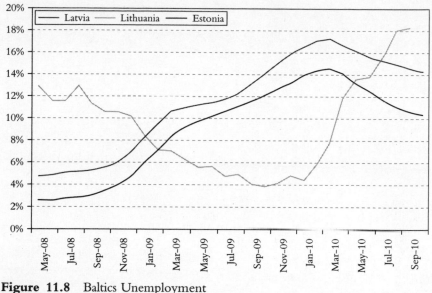

Figure 11.8 Baltics Unemployment
Source: Bloomberg, Variant Perception.

If unemployment does not fall significantly and growth fails to recover, Latvia and Lithuania may yet be forced to exit the peg. Doing so would cause a wave of defaults and a risk of contagion to other countries, including Hungary, which we talked about earlier, and the Balkan countries of Romania and Bulgaria as credit dries up.

We should pay close attention to the Baltic countries. Small as they may be, they are symbolic as to what happens when financial crisis mutates into sovereign crisis. If we want to see the outcome of excessive credit and austerity measures—key for the outlook in the United Kingdom, the United States, Spain, and many other countries—then we need look no further than Latvia and its close neighbors. The Baltics, like Greece, do matter.

CHAPTER TWELVE

Japan

A Bug in Search of a Windshield

Jitters in Europe stemming from the financial collapse of Greece are no longer somebody else's problem. If Japan fails to tackle fiscal reform, we could come under the control of bodies like the International Monetary Fund, which could tell us what to do in the sovereign matter of fiscal management.

—Prime Minister Naoto Kan, June 17, 2010

Japan is a country that has spent the past 20 years in a hangover from one of the greatest bubbles of the modern era. After the great Japanese equity and land bubble burst in 1990, a long, painful process of deflation and deleveraging started. Even today, the country is still trying to rid itself of deflation. Japan is particularly important because it is the poster boy for the deflationary disease that the Fed is trying to fight.

In this chapter, we'll look at Japan, a country that has all the conditions for a major upheaval. We'll look at how the country's public debt has exploded and how revenues have collapsed over the past two decades. We'll also look at how quickly the population is aging and what lessons that might have for the United States and Western countries with quickly aging populations. The picture is grim to say the least, but we'll plunge right in.

I (John) have often written that Japan is a bug in search of a windshield. That may sound harsh, but as you'll see in this chapter, I'm probably being too kind.

The Mother of All Bubbles

In all of world history, the Japanese bubble in the 1980s will stand out as one of the craziest bubbles ever. At one stage, the Japanese Imperial gardens were reckoned to be worth more than all of the real estate of California.

Partly, the bubble was due to extremely loose Japanese monetary policy. In 1985 at the Plaza Accord,4 finance ministers and central bank governors of the G5 decided to do something about the strong dollar, and the yen strengthened a lot after that. When the yen strengthened, the Japanese faced a currency loss in the dollar-denominated assets such as U.S. government bonds. The Japanese started bringing their money home, and the yen kept on strengthening. The Bank of Japan tried to fight the strong yen with low interest rates. The official discount rate was lowered five times by February 1987 to help Japanese exports. The official discount rate hit 2.5 percent, the lowest level since World War II. With inflation above the discount rate, money was pretty much free.

Very low rates and a strong yen led to a boom in real estate and stock prices. In a classic bubble dynamic, rapidly rising prices only encouraged people to invest more and more. Japanese companies bought as much real estate in Hawaii and California as they could, including the Pebble Beach golf course, the Hotel Bel Air in Los Angeles, and the Grand Wailea and Westin Maui hotels. Eventually, though, the air came out of the bubble.

The bubble peaked in December 29, 1989, when the Nikkei reached a historic high of 38,915. Within two years of the collapse in the Nikkei, stock prices had declined 60 percent. The only comparable example in the twentieth century was the Great Depression.

Once the bubble had already started to burst and the damage was done, the government and the Bank of Japan very belatedly applied the brakes. In 1989, the Bank of Japan changed to a tight-money policy, and in 1990, after the stock market had started to fall, it raised the official discount rate to 6 percent. Also in 1990, the Ministry of Finance made banks restrict their financing of property. The very tight monetary policy and fiscal tightening only made the downturn that much worse.

By January 1993, reality sank in when the Japanese prime minister finally recognized that the bubble economy (*baburu keizai*) had collapsed. By that time, it was far too late, and deflation had started to take hold. Prices fell by 1.1 percent in the first quarter of 1993, and by mid-1993, wholesale prices were falling at an annual rate of 4.2 percent. The collapse was extraordinary. In 1990, Japan represented 14 percent of the global economy. Today in 2010, it is only 8 percent. Before the Japanese bubble burst, 8 of the top 10 companies by value were Japanese. Today, there is not a single Japanese company in the top 10.

Japanese Government: Spending Money Like There Is No Tomorrow

It too often seems that whenever governments are confronted with a problem, they pretend it doesn't exist. The Japanese bureaucracy's first attempts to deal with the collapse involved quick fixes coping with the symptoms, rather than correcting structural problems. At first, the government ordered public-sector financial institutions to buy stocks to keep stock prices up, but this failed. The banking system suffered severe losses from loans used to buy property, but the bank tried to pretend these losses had not occurred. Employees were paid with unsold company inventory.

To cushion the blow of the downturn, the central Japanese government spent insane amounts of money building bridges to nowhere and on other public works projects with no ability to increase productivity in the real economy.

Japan started out as a healthy, dynamic economy. Today, Japan has public debt of almost 200 percent of total GDP. It is running out of its ability to use captive domestic savings to maintain or increase this level of debt. The figure is even worse if you look at Japanese debt as a percentage of private GDP. This is already at almost 240 percent.

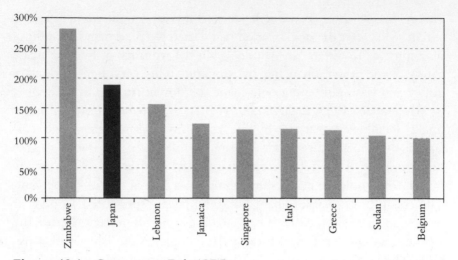

Figure 12.1   Government Debt/GDP
SOURCE: *CIA World Factbook,* Variant Perception.

Japan's debt levels are now at levels seen historically only in hyperinflationary countries. Either Japan will right itself soon through political reform, or it will be the prime candidate in the world for hyperinflation. Japan is now in the company of Zimbabwe, Lebanon, Jamaica, Sudan, and Egypt in the high government debt-to-GDP stakes, as Figure 12.1 shows.

As you can see from Figure 12.2, the level is even worse if you look at the government debt to private GDP. After all, it is the private sector that will need to generate the revenue for taxes to pay down the public debt.

Most analysts are complacent. So far, increases in Japanese government bond (JGB) issuance has not necessarily led to any rises in Japanese long-term yields, due to (a) abundant domestic savings, (b) strong home bias among Japanese investors, and (c) contained inflation expectations. Any of these could change very quickly.

Japan's debt is more than 12 years of general account tax revenues, and within a year, it will be closer to 15. It would take half a generation of Japanese taxes to pay down the debt. This ratio is twice as high as the next highest in history, Britain, following World War II. With the current recession, Japan's FY2010 budget will be the first in the postwar

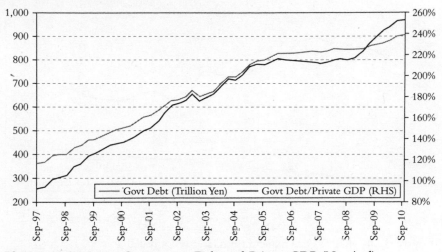

Figure 12.2 Japan: Government Debt and Private GDP (Nominal)
SOURCE: Japan Ministry of Finance, Variant Perception.

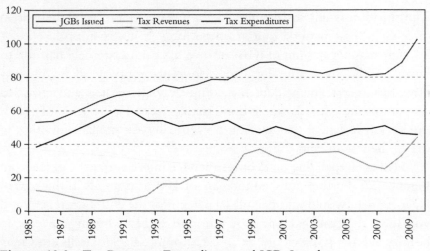

Figure 12.3 Tax Revenue, Expenditure, and JGBs Issued
SOURCE: Japan Ministry of Finance, Variant Perception.

period where revenues from debt (JGB issuance) will exceed tax revenues (Figure 12.3). This situation is unprecedented.

The most extraordinary thing about Japan, though, is that in 2009, the government had to borrow almost half of what it spent. As Figure 12.4 shows, tax revenue as a percentage of all expenditures is at all time lows, and government borrowing is about to exceed tax collections.

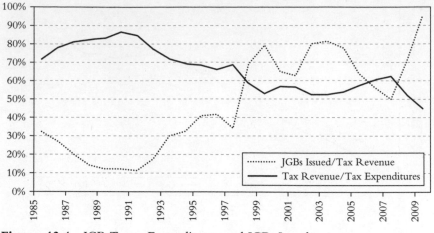

Figure 12.4   JGB Taxes, Expenditures, and JGBs Issued
SOURCE: Japan Ministry of Finance, Variant Perception.

The situation is not sustainable. As the great economist Herbert Stein once said, "If something cannot go on forever, it will stop."

The massive amount of JGB issuance has been extremely harmful to Japan. While fiscal stimulus can help replace private demand in a downturn, government debt has completely dominated and crowded out almost the entire Japanese bond market. (See Figure 12.5.) There is the very real danger that we could eventually see similar outcomes in the United States and Europe.

Half of all spending on debt is to service interest, as you can see from Figure 12.6. Furthermore, an increase of 100 basis points in the cost of Japanese debt would eat up a full 10 percent of the entire tax revenue. If you look at Japan that way, you can start to see why any increase in bond yields for JGBs would be so catastrophic. Paradoxically, this may be why the Japanese government prefers deflation. Any increase in inflation expectations would blow up the budget! This means they have an incentive to deflate to keep the game going. What an upside-down world. This means that all the smart hedge fund managers shorting the yen may have to wait a very long time to win.

Almost all the debt is of very short maturities, so rollover risk and higher interest rates are a very real danger. Of the G5 countries, only the

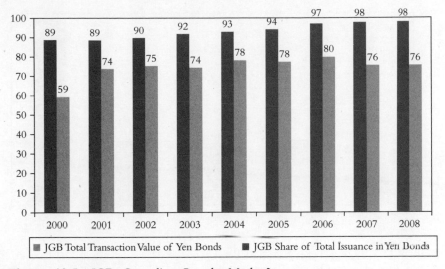

Figure 12.5 JGBs Crowding Out the Market?
Source: Japan Ministry of Finance, Variant Perception.

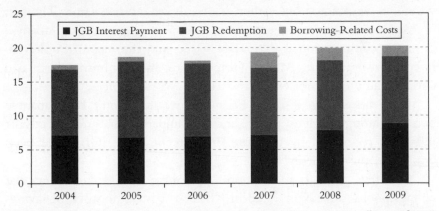

Figure 12.6 Changes in Government Debt-Related Expenses (trillions of JPY)
Source: Japan Ministry of Finance, Variant Perception.

United States has fewer long-term bonds as a total proportion of debt issued, as Figure 12.7 shows.

All bubbles burst when financing becomes an issue. The Japanese bond market will, in the not too distant future, face a fiscal crisis that will require either draconian tax increases and spending cuts that would be extremely socially divisive or the decision to monetize its own debt,

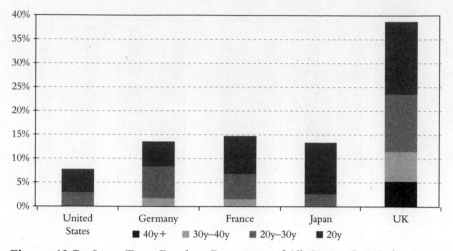

Figure 12.7 Long-Term Bonds as Percentage of All Outstanding Debt
SOURCE: Japan Ministry of Finance, Variant Perception.

which, as we pointed out earlier, is default by another name. The first option implies a massive economic contraction, given that Japanese domestic consumption is extremely weak, and the second implies an inflationary holocaust. As we wrote before, most countries have bad choices and worse choices. Japan has only worse choices.

Japan has survived so far because foreigners don't buy Japanese bonds. Through savings and insurance companies that are directly or indirectly controlled by the state, 94 percent of all JGBs have been bought by the Japanese.

Optimists point to a large pool of Japanese savings. However, that savings pool is already invested in JGBs, so it isn't the stock of savings that matters, but the flow. The flow has been steadily decreasing. Japanese savings rates are now approaching the low that we saw in U.S. savings rates just a few years ago. And this is not due to the Japanese somehow becoming profligate Americans but almost entirely due to demographic necessity.

The three largest holders of JGBs are Japan Post Bank, Japan Post Insurance, and Government Pension Investment Fund (GPIF). Prior to the 2001 Fiscal Investment and Loan Plan (FILP) reform, postal savings and pension reserves were required to be deposited at the Fiscal

Figure 12.8   Japan Savings Ratio
SOURCE: Bloomberg, Variant Perception.

Loan Fund. As part of the reform, the compulsory deposits were discontinued, and existing deposits and interest on deposits were to be sequentially returned. From 2001 to 2009, Japan Post Bank and GPIF used those returned deposits to buy JGBs, and those deposits are now almost completely liquidated. Japan Post Insurance will soon not be a likely buyer because insurance reserves have been on a steady decline, given Japan's sad demographics, and their year-over-year JGB holdings growth is almost 0 percent. Banks have been filling the void, but they don't have a ton of additional capacity, given Basel 2 interest rate risk guidelines.*

Given the lack of internal demand, Japan will be forced to finance their issuance in international markets for really the first time. It's not going to be pretty. We doubt that any of our readers will want to buy a 10-year Japanese bond for 1 percent interest. If rates went to just the OECD average, interest rates could triple. Does anyone think Japan will get rates lower than Germany, which is at 2.5 percent as we write? When rates start to rise, interest expense is going to consume a bigger and bigger portion of tax revenues. Then comes endgame. (See Figure 12.8.)

It is highly unlikely that the savings rate will increase much from here. An aging population dictates that Japanese savings rates will go

---

*Many thanks to Matt Klein of Hudson Advisers for pointing this out.

down, not up. Literally, Japan is a dying country, as their population is now shrinking each year. Economics 101 dictates that savings rates conform to the life cycle savings hypothesis. You spend when you're young, you save when you get older, and then when you get much older, you spend all the money you've saved in your lifetime. Now the Japanese are getting really old, and they're about to start drawing down their savings. The savings rate will go negative.

In fact, as Figure 12.9 shows, Japan's dependency ratio is now approaching 100. The dependency ratio is percentage of retired people supported by working people. Very soon, Japan will have more retired people than working people, and savings rates will continue to be drawn down.

The process of Japanese demographic decline has been ongoing, and as Figure 12.10 shows, Japan is really the worst of the developed countries in terms of its decline. The United States, fortunately, has much a brighter demographic profile in comparison. Through immigration and higher birth rates, the U.S. dependency ratio will deteriorate much more slowly.

The percentage of households in Japan with either one person or a couple older than 65 has shot up recently. In 2005, it was 17 percent; in 2010, it is 20 percent. Twenty percent sounds low, so let's put it

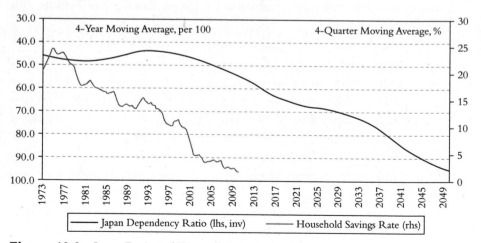

Figure 12.9 Japan Projected Dependency Ratio
SOURCE: George Magnus, "Demographics Are Destiny, Deflation Isn't (or Needn't Be)," UBS Investment Research, *Economic Insights—By George,* July 14, 2010.

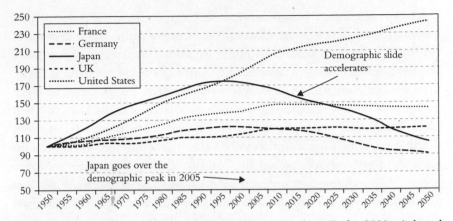

Figure 12.10 Japan's Demographic Decline Started in Early 2000s (rebased working-age population)

SOURCE: Societe Generale, "Popular Delusions: A Global Fiasco Is Brewing in Japan," January 12, 2010, UN.

another way. One in five households has an old person to look after. The demographics show that by 2015 that will rise to 23 percent and by 2020 to 25 percent. These are statistics taken from the Japanese National Institute of Population and Social Security Research, so we take the current figures and the projections as gospel. There is no country in the world with similar numbers.

Japan's Endgame

A major debt and currency crisis in Japan is a case of when, not if. Forecasting when it might happen, though, is difficult. We can't remember who said it, but the old line is true. "You can't call yourself a real macro trader until you have lost money shorting Japanese bonds." But when the crisis of confidence in Japanese bonds happens, it is likely to be swift, and the lucky traders who are short will become legends.

The realization that crises happen suddenly and unexpectedly is not lost on Japanese politicians. Recently Prime Minister Naoto Kan stated, "Our public finances have become the worst of any developed country. Like the confusion in the Eurozone triggered by Greece, there is a risk of collapse if we leave the increase of the public debt untouched and then lose the trust of the bond markets."[1]

Japan has two options. Either it engages in extremely painful contraction of government spending, or it prints money and gets rid of the deficit via monetization. There is simply no way to pay back Japanese debts. Japan's government is running one of the largest structural budget deficits in the world at more than 7.2 percent of GDP every year until at least 2015, according to IMF calculations. By that stage, Japan will be in the range of 230 percent debt-to-GDP ratio. Cutting the deficit significantly will be extremely difficult. Governments typically print money rather than doom the economy to a severe recession or a depression induced by economic contraction. When this happens, the yen is likely to fall dramatically in value, Japanese interest rates will go up, and Japanese bonds will sell off.

Such an abrupt change for Japan would be nothing new. Japan has a history of making 180-degree turns. In 1868, during the Meiji Restoration, Japan went from being an inward-looking country to a rising economic and military power. In the 1950s, under the Yoshida doctrine, Japan abandoned militarism and instead embraced pacifism. Both of these moments marked a dramatic turn in Japanese society. Even in 1990, after the bubble burst, Japan turned overnight from high consumption and ostentation to frugality and sobriety. What will happen if Japan makes a 180-degree turn, and Japanese savers decide to abandon the yen and Japanese government bonds?

Can we hear a bid for 100 yen to the dollar? 125? 150? 200? 250? 300? It seems unthinkable now, but it is quite possible unless the Japanese willingly embrace a contractionary, severely deflationary depression. Not a good set of choices.

We have said before that Japan is a bug in search of a windshield. The only question is when the bug will be crushed. But it does have consequences for the rest of the world. Japan matters. *Japan matters a lot.* Not only is it the third largest economy in the world (depending on how you measure size) but also it is a major export power.

What happens if the yen starts to lose value? What happens when you can buy a Honda, Toyota, or Lexus cheaper than you can buy a Kia or a Hyundai? Or any of a number of European cars? Now take that same analogy and apply it to scores of industries that compete with Asia, the United States, and Europe. How does Korea deal with a real loss of competitiveness? In the past, they have devalued their currency. But can they really keep up with a hyperinflating Japan? And that goes for all of their neighbors, not to mention Germany and the emerging market countries.

Yes, the cost of Japanese inputs (like steel) go up, but not their labor or engineering or the infrastructure and factories they already have. For a while, in the early stages of endgame, it is a very dicey atmosphere in world trade and currency markets.

Then, what if you are Mrs. Watanabe and the cost of everything you buy from overseas is going up rapidly? And you are on a fixed income? Your savings are not inflation indexed. First, you end up buying less. But you also figure out (because the Mrs. Watanabes of the world are very smart and currency savvy) you need to move your savings into other currencies. And since the Japanese are serious currency traders from their homes, they can do it with a click of a mouse. So there is even more pressure on the yen.

Yes, we know that the Japanese have huge hoards of foreign currencies, especially dollars. But that is not their salvation as they spend yen at home.

Once they start down the endgame path, it is difficult to get off it. It goes back to our chapter on *This Time Is Different*. It is a ***Bang!*** moment. And because it is Japan, it is a ***BIG BANG!*** moment.

CHAPTER THIRTEEN

The United Kingdom

How to Quietly Inflate Away Your Debt

Who would be prepared to lend with the fear of being repaid in depreciated currencies always before his eyes?
——Georges Bonnet, French foreign minister of the 1930s

The United Kingdom is a wonderful test case of how a central bank creates a housing bubble, props up the economy after the banking system collapses, and works hard to inflate away debt through stealthy inflation. After years of rising house prices where the average person thought a house was the safest investment in the world, the British banking system imploded in 2008. The United Kingdom is now in the process of trying to recover from a painful bust, and the central bank is doing all the heavy lifting by monetizing public debt, weakening the currency, and providing an ultraloose monetary policy.

This chapter will look at the United Kingdom. We will look at how the crisis started, how it unfolded, and what the central bank's response was. We will also explore how the central bank is using inflation to increase the nominal level of GDP and reduce the burden of debt to GDP. So far, the Bank of England is being very successful at creating inflation, and this holds clues to how the Federal Reserve could create similar levels of inflation to fight the threat of deflation in the United States.

The United Kingdom Economy: Not as Safe as Houses

If you wanted a totem for the credit crisis, you could do worse than the United Kingdom. The United States may have been the nucleus of the credit blowup, but the United Kingdom displayed an even greater verve for borrowing and spending than its ally across the Atlantic. This left the United Kingdom uniquely exposed to the credit crisis.

A booming property market, cheap credit, and a seemingly insatiable appetite for spending all reinforced one other and led to what Mervyn King, governor of the Bank of England, described as the NICE decade (noninflationary consistent expansion). Indeed, policy makers became so confident that this time really was different that in 2000 Gordon Brown, then U.K. chancellor, proclaimed there'd be no return to boom and bust, thus single-handedly consigning to the trash bin two centuries of work on business-cycle theory.

Of course, this time it wasn't different: NICE turned to nasty, and Gordon Brown was forced to eat his words. When subprime in the United States started to unravel in 2007, the U.K. household sector owed more than the country's entire GDP. British consumers were more indebted than those in the United States. The situation looked even more alarming from the standpoint of household debt as a percentage of disposable income. This figure reached a high of 160 percent in the United Kingdom, again way more than for the United States, where a high of 130 percent was recorded.

When total debt is looked at—that is, debt held by the household sector, the corporate sector, the banking sector, and the government— the United Kingdom is more in hock than any other country in the world. Total debt in the United Kingdom stands at a migraine-inducing 4.7 times GDP. And this is before we add in the unfunded liabilities taken on by the government, which could take the total debt figure to over 6.5 times GDP. If you like big numbers, that's $15 trillion of debt,

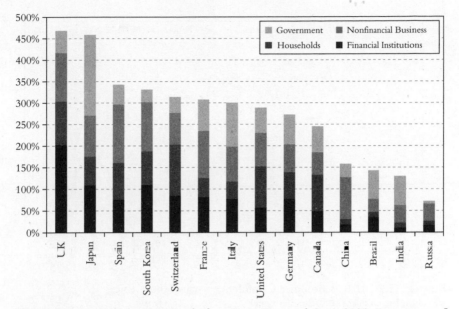

Figure 13.1 Debt by Country before Great Financial Crisis 2008, Percentage of GDP

SOURCE: Bloomberg, Variant Perception.

or $250,000 for every man, woman, and child in the United Kingdom. Truly mind-blowing. (See Figure 13.1.)

Why is it important to look at total debt? As we mentioned earlier, to be able to understand and make any sensible guesses about how endgame will play out, it is critical to look at debt across all sectors: Remember, one sector's surplus is another's deficit—always. Keep Figure 13.1 in mind, as it is key to understanding the difficulties the United Kingdom will face going forward.

Indeed, the United Kingdom will probably face greater difficulties than most developed nations in coming years. This is because many of the United Kingdom's problems are structural in nature, so they won't automatically improve when the economy returns to something even approximating normal.

The crisis in the United States began in the housing sector and rapidly infected the financial sector. This hit the United Kingdom with a double whammy. (See Figure 13.2.) Not only was the U.K. economy highly reliant on the property sector, with consumer confidence tightly

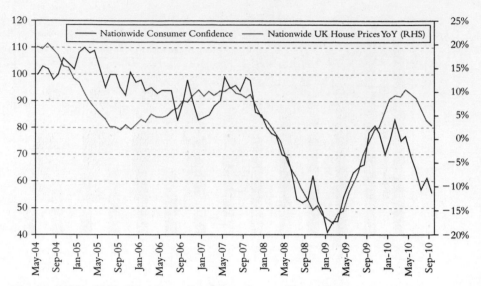

Figure 13.2 U.K. Consumer Confidence versus House Prices
SOURCE: National Statistics, Variant Perception.

linked to house prices, but also a sizable chunk of the economy's output came from the banking sector. (Finance accounted for almost 10 percent of U.K. GDP in 2007, more than in the United States.)

Unsurprisingly, tax revenues were hit hard. (See Figure 13.3.) Banking contributed more than 40 percent of all corporate tax revenue in 2007, and a third of income tax receipts come from the finance and property sectors. In the period November 2008 to November 2009, the tax take in the United Kingdom was down 12 percent, amounting to a shortfall of £37 billion ($60 billion).

As a result, the United Kingdom's public borrowing requirement swelled rapidly to reach 11.5 percent of GDP at the end of 2009 from under 5 percent a year earlier. This was among the highest budget deficits in the world and highlighted the United Kingdom's unenviable position in the eye of a perfect economic storm. To plug the gap, the U.K. government started to borrow like it had never done before in peacetime. Debt skyrocketed to more than 60 percent of GDP, more than in 1976, when the United Kingdom had to go cap in hand to the IMF for a loan of £2.3 billion (that's $3.7 billion, or more than $21 billion in today's money).

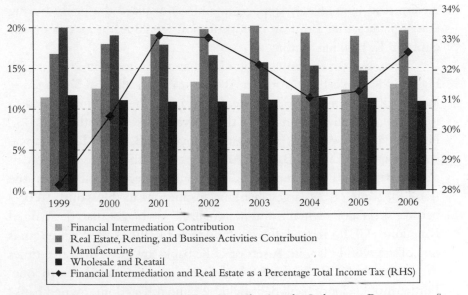

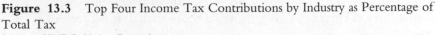

Figure 13.3 Top Four Income Tax Contributions by Industry as Percentage of Total Tax
SOURCE: HMRC, Variant Perception.

Not only were the authorities in the United Kingdom battling to make up for lost tax revenues (as well as paying out more in benefits as unemployment rose) but also they had to contend with bailing out the banking sector. As problems in the Western financial sector grew, U.K. banks, struggling with dried-up liquidity and plummeting asset prices, looked increasingly vulnerable.

Northern Rock: A Modern Bank Run

Northern Rock, a small U.K. bank, became one the first major casualties of the credit crisis. It had little in the way of customer deposits and heavily relied on borrowing from other banks to fund its lending. As banks became more and more skeptical about what assets other banks were holding on their balance sheets, and their value, they stopped lending to one another. Northern Rock watched its funding base evaporate virtually overnight as its lenders deserted it, and what followed was the first U.K. bank run in more than 100 years. The government immediately stepped in and nationalized the bank, fearing that as panic set in, a run on one institution would lead to a run on the entire U.K. banking sector.

Worse was yet to come. When Lehman went under in 2008, much bigger U.K. banks than Northern Rock—categorically too big to fail—looked like they might not survive. Once again, the government had to intervene, partially nationalizing the Royal Bank of Scotland (RBS), Halifax Bank of Scotland (HBOS), and Lloyds-TSB, emulating what was happening with Citi and Bank of America, two of the most vulnerable of the big banks in the United States. Now the United Kingdom is on the hook for some of the largest banking institutions in the world. (RBS's balance sheet alone when it was nationalized was bigger than the United Kingdom's GDP.) Indeed, the banking sector in the United Kingdom is one of the world's largest: Assets of U.K. banks are more than five times the country's GDP. In the United States, the ratio is closer to one. Furthermore, a lot of bank debt held by United Kingdom–owned banks is in a foreign currency (amounting to more than 100 percent of GDP). This raises the question that, if there was another financial crisis, would the U.K. government be able to credibly back its banking sector? We think this is a major structural issue for Britain, highlighting its over-dependence on, and overexposure to, the financial sector. (Shades of Iceland?)

Let's just pause for a second and recount where we are. The United Kingdom had enjoyed many years of expansion and low inflation. Property prices were seemingly excused from the effects of gravity, people were able to borrow more, and consumer spending went through the roof. Then the crisis came, and the United Kingdom's miracle was shown for what it was: a mirage, based on low interest rates and easy credit. The United Kingdom's heavy reliance on the property and financial sectors left it uniquely exposed to the worst ripples of the credit crisis.

As a result, the U.K. government had to ramp up its borrowing at a lightning pace, leading it to run one of the largest budget deficits in the world. With a huge debt load, banks that are too big, and taxpayers on the hook for large parts of the financial sector through nationalizations, there's no doubt that the United Kingdom's fiscal situation was—and remains—precarious.

The Bank of England, for one, agrees. To support the U.K. debt market through one of the greatest borrowing binges since the Second World War, it embarked on one of the largest quantitative easing (QE) programs ever attempted. (QE is a technical term for when a central bank or monetary authority creates money—so-called prints money—to buy assets in order to support their prices.)

As part of its QE program, the Bank of England has so far purchased £200 billion ($320 billion) of U.K. sovereign debt (known as *gilts*). It may yet buy more. The Bank of England now owns almost a third of all outstanding gilts, as Figure 13.4 shows. This dwarfs the QE programs in the United States or Japan.

The Bank of England's rationale is that QE helps the economy hit the inflation target instead of undershooting it. Furthermore, by keeping interest rates on government bonds low, it encourages investors to buy other, higher-yielding assets (corporate bonds, shares, even mortgage-backed securities). If you think that sounds like a blatant manipulation of interest rates to encourage savers to speculate with their savings in risky assets, then you probably understand QE well enough!

Nevertheless, QE undoubtedly stabilized the gilt market through one of the rockier periods in U.K. economic history. The next problem

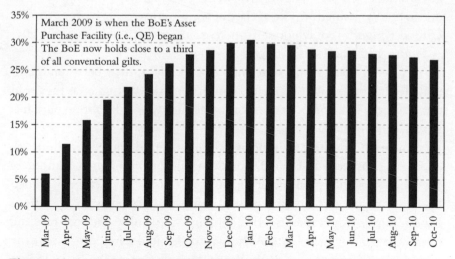

Figure 13.4 Bank of England Gilt Holdings as Percentage of Gilts Outstanding
SOURCE: Bank of England, Variant Perception.

will be how to reverse it. The bank's stated aim is to eventually sell its gilts back to the market once the economy recovers, essentially extinguishing the money it had created to buy the debt in the first place. However, given the sheer size of QE in the United Kingdom, it is anyone's guess how the Bank of England will be able to do this in a stable manner. The bank probably envisages a time in the not too distant future when growth has returned to trend, unemployment has dropped, property prices are rising healthily once more, and the financial sector has cleansed itself. It can then unload its gilts back to the market in an orderly manner.

But remember the massive 4.7 times balance sheet debt-to-GDP figure for the United Kingdom we mentioned earlier? This will continue to be a significant headwind to any long-lasting recovery. Interest payments erode income, and that's before we even consider paying back the principal. Normal levels of spending, and thus a normal recovery, will be difficult to achieve with this backdrop. Thus it is hard to see exactly when the Bank of England will be able to sell out its gilts without risking bond yields going sky high.

And if that's not enough to deal with, the United Kingdom has the additional headache of a significant number of foreign holders of its debt. In Chapter 12, we pointed out that 94 percent of all Japanese government bonds (JGBs) are held by the Japanese. This has undoubtedly helped to keep Japanese rates low. However, in the United Kingdom, only about 70 percent of gilts are held domestically, as Figure 13.5 shows.

If foreign investors become wary of U.K. debt, then between them, they hold enough gilts that yields would go markedly higher as they sold out of them. The consequences for the economy would not be pleasant. as you can imagine.

Furthermore, the mammoth QE program undertaken by the Bank of England makes the United Kingdom one of the likeliest candidates for a hyperinflation. All hyperinflations in history have been preceded by large budget deficits, the reason being that, faced with enormous expenditures, governments with big financial holes end up printing money to pay for their costs. Although the United Kingdom wasn't the only country to implement QE, it was the only country to have done it in such size, and by buying primarily government debt (as opposed to

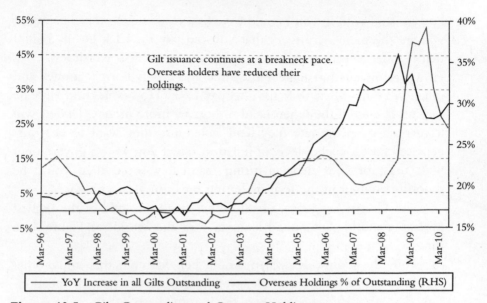

Figure 13.5   Gilts Outstanding and Overseas Holdings
SOURCE: Bloomberg, Variant Perception.

private debt, as in the United States, where the Fed purchased largely mortgage securities). In 2009, the United Kingdom de facto monetized its entire budget deficit; that is, the Bank of England essentially printed enough money to pay for the entire shortfall in government revenues. If you, like we do, respect history's tendency to rhyme, then you have to bet the United Kingdom is at risk of very high inflation in the years to come.

However, we should note that we do not think the United Kingdom will experience actual hyperinflation, even though all the a priori conditions are there. The leadership in the United Kingdom recognizes that such a path would be totally destructive and will pull back at some point.

That being said, there's a very good reason that the authorities in the United Kingdom might like a reasonable amount of inflation, certainly more so than the United States, Japan, or most European countries. Inflation, if it is high enough, helps to erode the value of debt. If I lend you $1,000 for five years, and I am generous enough not to charge you any interest, then when I come to collect my $1,000 back from you in five years, inflation will have eroded some of that $1,000 value: I can buy less stuff with it than I could have five years ago. You feel happy (if you are the mercenary type) that you can pay me back in full $1,000 that is easier to earn than it was five years ago, as it is worth less.

Governments can achieve the same end if they borrow money and inflation erodes what they have to pay back. However, they must be careful, because if they then need to borrow more money, lenders will have pushed up the rate they lend at because they want to be compensated for the higher level of inflation. So, if you were a government with most of your debt maturing reasonably soon, then you'd be shooting yourself in the foot by letting inflation get too high.

The United Kingdom, on the other hand, has one of the highest average maturities of outstanding debt in the world, as Figure 13.6 shows.

Thus the United Kingdom would benefit more than most other countries if inflation were to rise, even taking into account the inflation-linked bonds it has issued (as these rise in value with inflation, there is no benefit to the government in trying to inflate this debt away). Inflation in the United Kingdom has remained stubbornly high, even when most other developed countries are experiencing disinflation (falling inflation)

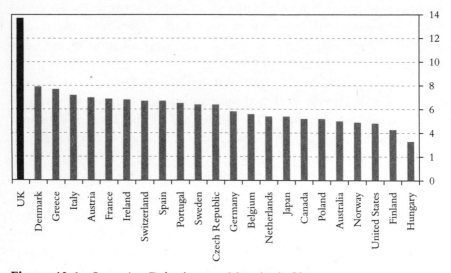

Figure 13.6 Sovereign Debt Average Maturity in Years
SOURCE: Variant Perception.

or outright deflation. The Bank of England refuses to acknowledge there's a problem. On the one hand, they are hesitant to raise rates while the U.K. government turns the screw on public spending—the combination of higher interest rates and fiscal austerity would almost certainly spell another U.K. recession with a capital *R*. On the other hand, the Bank of England maintains that it sees the rise in inflation as temporary and that it will soon return to target. Possibly it will. But the longer the Bank of England keeps rates low and monetary policy loose, the greater the risk that higher inflation will escalate. Indeed, the Bank of England's tolerance of inflation and the United Kingdom's long debt-maturity profile may not be entirely coincidental. For the investment-minded of you, the combination of loose monetary policy and tight fiscal policy should be bad for sterling but good for U.K. large-cap stocks.

The United Kingdom's Endgame: Higher Inflation Ahead

So what is endgame for the United Kingdom? Well, maybe we're seeing the very beginnings of it. A new government was elected in Britain in 2010 with a mandate to aggressively cut the budget deficit to about 1 percent in 2016, from more than 10 percent today. To achieve this, the largest spending cuts since the 1920s were announced in October 2010, with some departments seeing a third of their budget slashed. Austerity-lite this was not.

The parliamentary political system in the United Kingdom means it is likely these cuts will be pushed through. The U.S. situation is currently much more balanced, as the 2010 mid-term elections highlighted, with the Democrats losing the House and just holding on to the Senate, and thus political paralysis rather than decisive action is more likely. But will the U.K. approach of cut now rather than later work? To some extent, the United Kingdom is the canary in the coal mine for this crisis, with an austerity program more severe than any other developed nation. If the cuts bite too hard and the private sector does not return to health as quickly as expected, not only may this lead to another recession but also the retrenchment will test the resolve of public-sector workers who will face the brunt of the adjustment. Can Greek-style strikes and rioting be ruled out in the United Kingdom? Everyone has a limit, even the stiff-upper-lipped British.

The problems in the United Kingdom are too entrenched—too structural—for the longer-term picture to be rosy. As we wrote previously, the United Kingdom is one of the most heavily indebted nations on earth. The resistance to a sustainable economic recovery this provides is vast and cannot be understated. This heavy debt burden has led to a huge de facto monetization of public debt that will be extremely difficult to reverse in a stable manner. The risks of high—that is, double-digit—inflation in the United Kingdom are probably higher than anywhere else in the developed world. Whatever happens, endgame for the United Kingdom is unlikely to be pretty.

And that endgame is not good for the world. The United Kingdom has been a force for good and a staunch ally of the United States. There have already been significant military cuts, and more could be forced.

As sterling drops in value, the consumer spending that goes out to the world will also drop. Domestic purchases of industrial production are flat, but as the pound has dropped, exports have risen. And that trend will continue if the pound drops even more.

CHAPTER FOURTEEN

Australia

Could It Follow in Ireland's Footsteps?

All the countries we have looked at have had property bubbles and banking collapses. When future crises happen, most will involve housing bubbles and banking collapses as well. What housing bubbles are still out there that haven't burst? Australia was one of the few countries in the world where house prices made new highs following the Great Financial Crisis, and its housing market is in nosebleed territory.

This chapter looks at the Australian housing bubble and how it looks like other countries with housing bubbles: the United States, the United Kingdom, Ireland, and Spain. On the surface, Australia looks like an extremely well-run country with very low public debt. Ireland and Spain did as well and had very low debt-to-GDP levels. However, if you let a housing bubble get out of hand and the state has to intervene to prop up the banks, then the state's debt levels will balloon.

Let's dive in and explore Australia's endgame.

The Lucky Country

As the financial crisis progressed, hand grenades went off left, right, and center, from Latvia to Spain, from Dubai to Hungary. We have covered many of these in this book. Not only that, in 2008 and 2009, there was barely a major economy that did not experience a severe contraction in growth—outright recession in most cases. One glaring exception was Australia. Its GDP on a yearly basis never went negative, and even quarter-on-quarter growth went negative only once, before quickly rebounding into positive territory.

Most of the economies we have discussed so far have already had some sort of upset, whether it be the United States, where the housing market collapse marked the beginning of the crisis, or the United Kingdom, which had a severe housing correction all of its own, as well as having to contend with bank runs and nationalizations. We have talked about what happened, and we have put forward what we think will be the next steps for these embattled economies.

Australia is a bit different. Here, we can't really talk about what happened, as nothing really *has* happened. However, we can discuss what we think *will* happen. And that really isn't very pretty. In short, we think Australia may turn out to be one of the biggest bubble implosions yet seen. So sit down and pour yourself a Scotch, as what we will discuss should shock even those of you with the hardiest of economic constitutions.

Australia's economy was able to survive the economic crisis virtually unscathed in large part due to its trading relationship with China. Japan used to be Australia's largest trading partner, but in the last year China took this honor by importing vast amounts of commodities, mainly iron ore and coal, to fuel its own economic miracle.

The boost this gave to the economy was, and remains, significant. Business confidence has remained high, unemployment is low by G10 standards and continues to fall, and consumer confidence was buoyant through the worst months of the crisis, while it plummeted across much of the rest of the world. Bullish consumers were bullish for one major reason: the Australian property market. And it is here we find one of the biggest modern-day bubbles yet to burst.

The rise in Australian house prices is extreme no matter how you look at it: price to income, rental yields, whatever. The Economist House Price Index shows that Australian housing is 63 percent overvalued. (See Figure 14.1.) This is clearly in nosebleed territory and surpasses previous levels of overvaluation seen in other countries before they imploded.

Australia was one of only two countries that did not see house price drops over the past few years (the other is Canada). Australia has gone from being merely overvalued to bounding with verve into the housing bubble category. Australian house prices are 20 percent above their five-year average. (See Figure 14.2.)

As Figure 14.3 shows, Australia's housing market has continued its ascent even after the housing prices in the United Kingdom and the United States have turned down.

Fully half of investors have interest-only mortgages, and the number for owner-occupiers is 30 percent. The number is higher if you include low-doc and other nonconforming loans. Australia may not have the

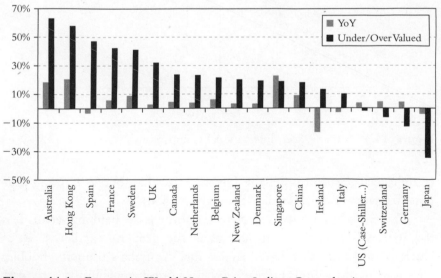

Figure 14.1 Economist World House Price Indices Overvaluation
SOURCE: *The Economist.*

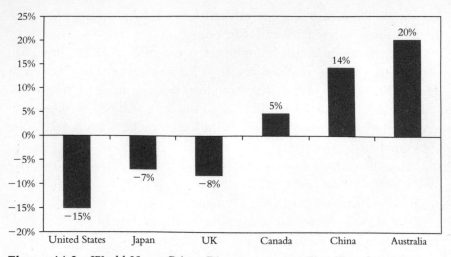

Figure 14.2 World House Prices: Divergence versus Five-Year Average
SOURCE: Bloomberg, Variant Perception.

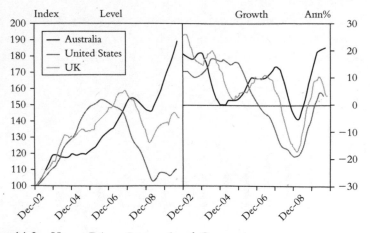

Figure 14.3 House Prices: International Comparisons
SOURCE: Westpac.

terrible securitization issues the United States has, but its housing presents far worse fundamentals. (See Figure 14.4.)

The weak link in the Australian economy is the banking sector. It is this that will exacerbate any fallout in the property market. It is, of course, the banks that have helped fuel Australia's property bubble. Credit growth for housing reached halo-jump heights in the early part of this decade—more than 20 percent year-on-year—and has never

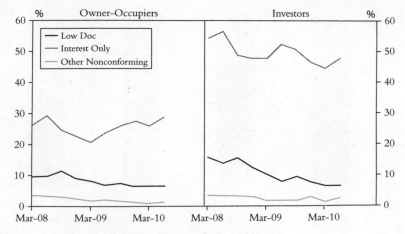

Figure 14.4 Banks' Housing Loans Characteristics
SOURCE: Westpac.

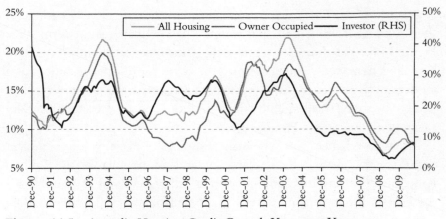

Figure 14.5 Australia Housing Credit Growth Year over Year
SOURCE: Bloomberg, Variant Perception.

gone negative in at least 20 years. It sits today at a still punchy 7 percent year-on-year rate. (See Figure 14.5.)

Australia's banking sector also has the highest loan-to-deposit ratio in the G20, with more than AU$180 of loans made for every AU$100 of deposits. For Australia's four biggest banks, the ratio is lower, at over 160 percent, but this is still higher than any country in Asia. Consequently, Australia relies heavily on wholesale funding provided by other banks or

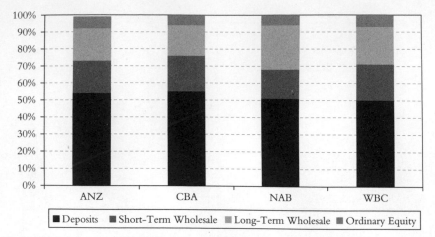

Figure 14.6 Australian Banks' Funding Mix
SOURCE: Morgan Stanley, RBA.

large institutions. The major Australian banks get more than 40 percent of their funding from abroad, and roughly half of that is short-term. (See Figure 14.6.) The shorter-term the debt is, the more frequently it needs to be rolled (renewed), and therefore, there are more opportunities for a lender not to extend credit. Longer-term loans are to be preferred as they need to be rolled less frequently (by definition) and are therefore less risky for the borrower. (See Figure 14.7.)

It was reliance on wholesale funding, especially of a shorter maturity, that caused the collapse of at least one bank, the United Kingdom's Northern Rock, mentioned earlier, and was responsible for the near-collapse of many others. The problem with wholesale funding is it can vanish very rapidly at the merest hint of trouble. Deposits tend to be much stickier and are thus a much stabler form of funding. Northern Rock had very little in the way of deposits and watched its funding vanish almost overnight as the true extent of the subprime crisis became apparent.

Furthermore, Australian banks managed to escape the worst of the financial crisis because they had little exposure to the subprime debt that the U.S., U.K., and European banks had so eagerly loaded up on. The flip side is that Australian banks remain very geared to the domestic economy. Any problems in the property market would be

Figure 14.7 Australian Banks' Offshore Debt as Percentage of Total Debt
SOURCE: Morgan Stanley, RBA.

catastrophic for them. The multiplier effects—where banks freeze their lending as they race to salvage their balance sheets, damaging the economy further and causing yet another wave of asset write-downs—would be severe.

A House of Cards

Australia is a house of cards. We are confident the bubble will burst and that it will be spectacular, but we do not know what will provide the spark. This brings us back to our fingers of instability metaphor we introduced in Chapter 2: We know it takes only one grain of sand to trigger the avalanche; we just don't know which one. With Australia, there are some obvious possibilities, although whether any one of these proves to be the one that tips the balance, we don't know for sure. Nevertheless, they are worth looking at.

The most obvious catalyst is a slowdown in China. After double-digit growth for most of the last decade, China is probably due for some sort of tempering of growth. At the time we are writing, there are signs that this is indeed happening. And we may be seeing the pass-through to Australia, whose trade surplus has shown signs of reducing as China has imported less of its coal and iron ore. (See Figure 14.8.)

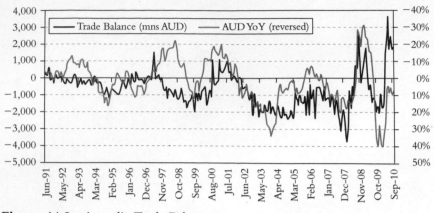

Figure 14.8 Australia Trade Balance
SOURCE: Bloomberg, Variant Perception.

A strong Australian dollar will also begin to affect Australian exports. Quantitative easing (QE) in other G10 countries is partly to blame here. As we have already discussed, QE creates what we call excess liquidity, essentially extra money that is surplus to requirements for productive purposes in the economy. Excess liquidity tends to flow along the path of least resistance, and in the economy, that generally means it flows into asset markets, such as stocks, bonds, commodities, and property. For Australia, more QE in the United States may lead to higher commodity prices and higher inflation, which in turn may lead to further interest rate rises by the Reserve Bank of Australia, Australia's central bank. More tightening will make it harder for Australian households to pay their mortgages as increasing rates feed through to higher mortgage payment costs. Approximately 90 percent of Australian mortgages are variable rate, which means that rate rises are passed straight on to the majority of mortgage holders.

Higher interest rates in Australia are also pushing the currency much higher, providing another headwind for Australia's exports. The Australian dollar reached 25-year highs on a trade-weighted basis in 2010 and shows signs of pushing yet higher.

Quantitative easing might also negatively affect China, which would crimp Australia's trade balance further. As excess liquidity pours into these commodities, QE will help push food and energy prices higher. Countries like China are very sensitive to such input prices and

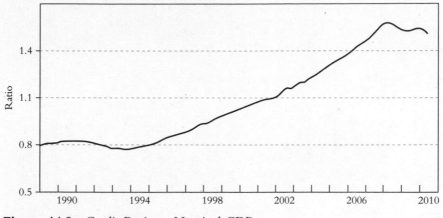

Figure 14.9   Credit Ratio to Nominal GDP
NOTE: Not adjusted for breaks.
SOURCE: ABS, RBA.

will be forced to raise interest rates. If they do too much too quickly, the economy could suffer. Australia, whose largest trade partner is China, would feel the effects sharply.

And the credit binge in Australia may be showing the first inklings of coming to an end. (See Figure 14.9.) After a breakneck expansion of credit over the last two decades, total credit as a percentage of GDP in Australia is showing the first signs of meaningfully declining since the mid–1990s.

Australia never experienced an economic slowdown to speak of in the aftermath of the financial crisis. Economies that did, and that is most of them, have had at least some chance to release some of the pressure built up by the imbalances of the previous decades (even if many are implementing policies that will help build some of these imbalances back up again, we hear you sigh). Thus Australia's endgame, when it happens, is likely to be all the more spectacular.

CHAPTER FIFTEEN

Unintended Consequences

Loose Monetary Policies and Emerging Markets

So far we have focused on the United States and other mature, developed economies that have far too much debt.

With Japan, the United States, the United Kingdom, and Switzerland at close to zero percent interest rates, it seemed like a good idea to stimulate the economy. However, emerging markets that maintain pegged currencies or that shadow the dollar are essentially reduced to importing excessively loose monetary policies.

Reserve growth across many emerging countries has been very strong over the last year. Emerging Asian countries account for almost 50 percent of global foreign exchange reserves. Huge Asian reserve growth since early last year is a result of mimicking loose monetary

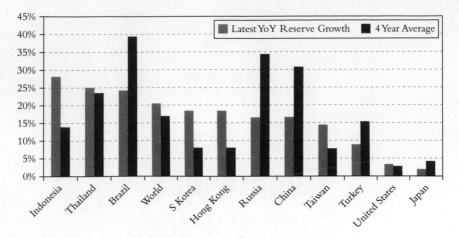

Figure 15.1   Global Foreign Exchange Reserve Growth
SOURCE: Variant Perception.

policies in the developed world to keep their currencies competitive. China has accumulated the most reserves of any emerging market country. This is directly related to its currency peg and its need to recycle the dollars it gets from its exports.

A result of Asian emerging markets' importing loose monetary policy from developed markets is that domestic inflation rates are rising quickly, as policy rates remain too accommodative. Asian emerging market countries are facing a trilemma: They can fix any two of a pegged exchange rate, free flows of capital, or independence in monetary policy, but not all three. The end result is likely to be higher policy rates and currency appreciation. (See Figure 15.1.)

Bubbles in Emerging Markets

Many emerging markets will double or triple over the next few years. Emerging markets are extremely small as a percentage of total global market capitalization. When investors diversify away from developed markets, it will be like putting a fire hose through a straw. Liquidity from developed markets will overwhelm emerging markets.

Part of this is from investors in the developed world wanting to go where the growth is, but part of it is a result of quantitative easing all

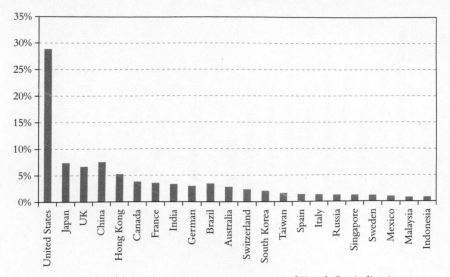

Figure 15.2 World Stock Markets as Percentage of Total Capitalization
SOURCE: Variant Perception.

over the world, especially in the United States. That is why you see emerging markets like Brazil taxing inbound capital flows in an effort to keep their own economies from developing a bubble. (See Figure 15.2.)

There are good reasons why the United States and the United Kingdom are among the highest capitalizations. In part, this is because a higher percentage of companies are publicly traded in the United States and the United Kingdom, whereas in other countries, many more are privately held, family-owned, or indeed government-run.

Individually, almost all emerging markets are less than 0.5 percent of total world capitalization, as Figure 15.3 shows.

To further emphasize the small size of some emerging equity markets and their potential to grow, in Figure 15.4 we have compared the total market caps of some of these markets alongside the market caps of some well-known blue chip stocks (in millions of $).

Consider the following examples: Microsoft has a bigger market cap than all of Indonesia, General Electric and Wells Fargo have market caps almost double that of all of the Philippines, Monsanto and Time Warner have bigger market caps than all of Vietnam and Pakistan, and GAP Inc's market cap is almost double that of Sri Lanka's.

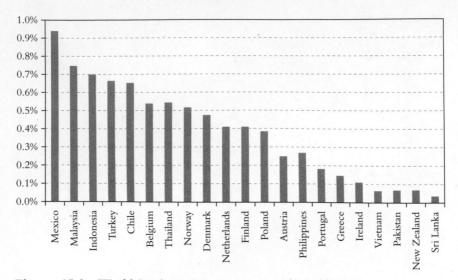

Figure 15.3   World Stock Markets Percentage of World Market Cap
SOURCE: Variant Perception.

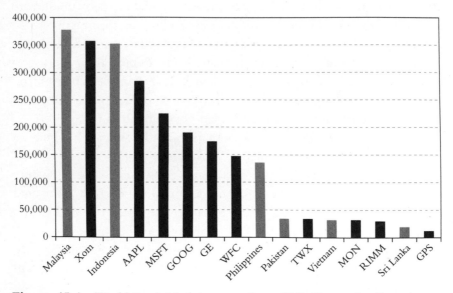

Figure 15.4   World Stock Markets versus Large U.S. Companies ($ mns)
SOURCE: Variant Perception.

In the reflation trade, a few characteristics drive outperformance in emerging markets:

- Generous liquidity, that is, rapid monetary expansion
- Positive demographics
- Declining real interest rates
- Underleveraged consumer
- Banking sector with low loans-to-GDP ratio

The main countries that satisfy these requirements are Turkey, Malaysia, India, Indonesia, and Brazil.

Local conditions in some emerging market countries will act as a fire starter to excessive liquidity from abroad. In countries like Indonesia, Brazil, and Turkey, due to solid economies, increasing productivity, and thus falling inflation, they are transitioning to lower interest-rate regimes. This often has the consequence of detracting investors from the falling returns on cash and debt products and pulling them toward higher-yielding equities.

Further, large populations and still relatively low levels of GDP per capita give some idea of the scope for expansion in countries like China, India, Indonesia, and Sri Lanka if the prosperity of more developed economies, such as Taiwan and the Czech Republic, is anything to go by.

In this scenario, liquidity is likely to remain well above the norm for some time, and China will be little different from the other emerging markets:

Small markets + Ample liquidity + Investor risk appetite

+ Historically low interest rates = Bubblelike conditions

Chinese equity, property, and other asset markets will benefit hugely.

China differs from many other emerging markets because it has tight capital controls that keep a lid on overseas speculation. If these controls were relaxed, however, and the currency allowed to freely fluctuate, then all bets are off as to the effect on Chinese markets. This would be no different from Japan in the 1980s, when the capital accounts were opened up and the yen was allowed to float. Indeed, many if not all of the bubbles that have occurred since the Dutch Tulip Mania in the seventeenth century have been precipitated by a combination of financial liberalization and innovation.

There is always a bull market somewhere. If you go back to the 1970s in terms of loose monetary policies and excessive government debt, does that mean that we'll see a repeat of a decade in the doldrums for U.S. and European stock markets? Possibly, but it should not matter to a global macro investor. Again, there are always bull markets somewhere.

Figure 15.5 shows that from 1970 to 1985, if you had invested $1 in the United States, you would have $2 by 1985. If you had invested in Japan, you would have made $6 over the same period, and if you had invested in Hong Kong, you would have made more than $8.

Emerging markets will be the big winners of the loose monetary policies around the world. Just as the Fed's loose monetary policy after the Internet bubble burst created the housing bubble, the Fed's money printing will inflate emerging markets.

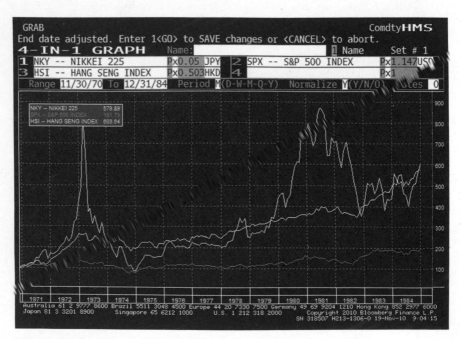

Figure 15.5 Emerging Market Stock Market Performance, 1970s
SOURCE: Bloomberg, Variant Perception.

The surplus liquidity isn't likely to ignite an inflationary boom in the U.S. economy if consumers refuse to borrow and spend. But that liquidity has to go somewhere, and emerging markets look like the most likely destination. Emerging markets and commodities took the first hits in the credit implosion because they were viewed as warrants (long-term call options) on global growth.

As history shows, the leading sector of the previous bull market typically is not the leader of a new bull market. The emerging markets look like they are the new global leaders. Emerging economies account for 43.7 percent of global output and, according to the IMF, will account for 70 percent of the world's growth going forward, yet they represent only 10.9 percent of global stock market capitalization. China by itself makes up 15 percent of the global economy but less than 2 percent of market cap, while the United States provides 21 percent of output but 43.4 percent of market cap.

Most investors weight the American and European markets too heavily. This is partly due to home bias in investing, but it is really more

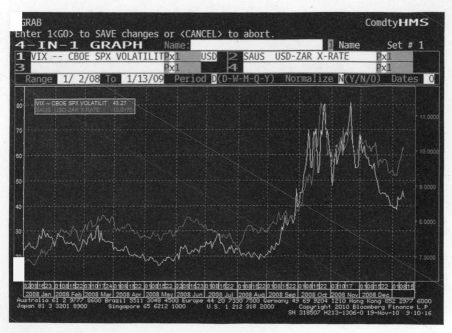

Figure 15.6   South African Rand versus VIX
SOURCE: Bloomberg, Variant Perception.

like a drunk searching for his keys under the lamppost. He searches there not because he is likely to find his keys but because there is light. In the same way, most investors in emerging markets do not look for the right data and merely decide to either take risk and invest or reduce risk and withdraw funds. Their investments into emerging markets are unsystematic.

Most investors buy or sell emerging markets indiscriminately based on their willingness to take on further risk or shed risk. Figure 15.6 shows the extremely high correlation between the VIX Index, global equity volatility, and the U.S. dollar versus South African rand exchange rate (USDZAR). You can't make up charts like this.

During the emerging markets rally in 2006 and 2007, almost all markets traded in line with the others. Figure 15.7 shows that for much of 2006, the Indian Sensex and the Mexican Bolsa Index had a 96 percent correlation, even though their economies could not have been more different. (File under the "investors are lemmings" category.)

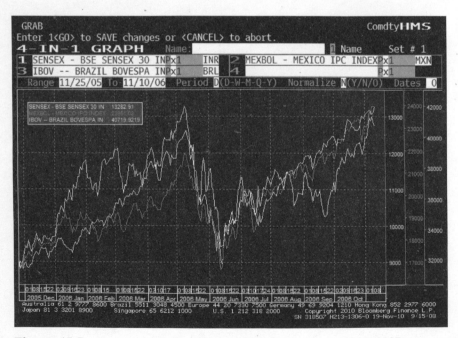

Figure 15.7   Emerging Market Stock Market Performance 2006–2007
SOURCE: Bloomberg, Variant Perception.

Emerging markets could easily be the next bubble. However, they don't even need to be the next bubble or the next big thing for investors to profit from them. As recessions ended in the United States and Europe in 1992 and 2003 and central banks kept liquidity flowing freely, almost all emerging markets rallied indiscriminately.

Loose liquidity and undervalued emerging market currencies are leading toward excess foreign exchange reserve accumulation and loose credit conditions. Underleveraged emerging markets with higher velocity will continue to benefit from the accommodative monetary policies of a developed world beset with high debt and low monetary velocity. Continued reserve accumulation can lead to inflationary pressure, over-investment, complications in the management of monetary policy, misallocation of domestic banks' lending, and asset bubbles.

Difficult Choices

We have written about the difficult choices developed countries will face as they deal with the hangover from too much debt. Emerging market countries face the flip side of the same problem. They are, for the most part, underleveraged and have higher monetary velocity, yet they are importing the loose money policies from the United States and Europe.

What can emerging markets do to try to reduce inflows of hot money and prevent bubbles? There are a number of tools available to policy makers of liquidity-receiving economies in response to excess global liquidity and large capital inflows. As the IMF has pointed out, emerging markets can allow a more flexible exchange rate policy. They can accumulate reserves (using sterilized or unsterilized intervention as appropriate). They can reduce interest rates if the inflation outlook permits, and they can tighten fiscal policy when the overall macro-economic policy stance is too loose. All of these involve difficult trade-offs where the costs and benefits are not obvious.

The bottom line is that governments around the world need to be alert and make difficult choices to deal with a world excess liquidity.

From an investor's point of view, we would enjoy the current ride in emerging markets but recognize that they are high beta to the U.S.

economy and stock markets. The next time the United States goes into recession—and there will be a next time—it is likely that emerging markets will suffer significant losses. So, emerging markets are a trade and not a long-term investment.

That being said, at the bottom of the next U.S. recession, we think emerging market countries could see their economies and stock markets finally decouple from the United States, and at that point, they could become the trade of the decade. We suggest that investors use the time to find specific stocks and not just country ETFs, or find someone who can do that work for you. Fortunes can be made if you do your homework.

CONCLUSION

Investing and Profiting from Endgame

The person that turns over the most rocks wins the game. And that's always been my philosophy.

—Peter Lynch

This book has primarily been concerned with the larger picture of what problems we are facing and what the likely endgame is, based on these scenarios. There is a vast difference between understanding the broad economic issues we face and making money with that understanding. You, dear reader, might say, "It all sounds very good, but what do I do to protect my savings and invest?"

This chapter offers practical advice for putting your money to work based on the various scenarios we have outlined in this book. Almost all books we read on the challenges we face do not offer any practical investment advice. We hope this chapter will help.

Before we start, let's get something out of the way. We could bore you with a long legal disclaimer telling you that we are not financial advisers, we do not know your personal situation, and not all investments are suited to everyone. But we hope that if you were curious and smart enough to pick up a book on macroeconomics and financial markets, you won't need any disclaimers. Obviously, you should consult your financial planner, tax adviser, and so forth and do all your own homework and due diligence before buying or selling anything. We can offer insights, but only you can invest money according to your own personal needs.

How should you then invest?

In the previous chapter, we covered emerging markets and how excess liquidity from the developed world can cause a huge bubble and rapid price increases in asset markets around the world. This will probably be one of the bigger investment themes of the coming decade. But closer to home, the picture is murkier.

The future in many parts of the world—the United States, the United Kingdom, Europe, and Japan—is fairly binary. Either the forces of deleveraging will lead to a long and crushing deflation, or the policy responses will succeed in leading to devaluations and inflation. The excessive level of debt may lead people to consume less, save more, and pay down their debts, which could lead to a deflationary dynamic like Japan has seen for the past two decades. Or governments may encounter too much success in their experiments with quantitative easing, money printing, and fiscal expansion. We are not certain which is the lesser evil.

If you believe in deflation, then you should seek investments that offer a high chance of return of capital rather than return on capital. Investors will seek a low yield with a high degree of confidence they will get their money back. If you believe in deflation, U.S. Treasuries offer great value. Unsurprisingly, the biggest proponents of deflation are David Rosenberg and Lacy Hunt. Both work at firms that manage a lot of money in bond funds.

The following list is only partial, but it highlights the best ways to invest if you believe that *deflation* will predominate.

- Buy treasury bonds.
- Buy income-producing securities.
- Buy the dollar. Cash is king in a deflationary environment.
- Sell equities.
- Sell homebuilder and selected related stocks.

- Sell selected big-ticket consumer discretionary equities. Frugality will lead people to spend less.
- Sell banks. In a deflationary environment, demand for loans falls, and interest rates fall. It is difficult for banks to make money in this environment.
- Sell consumer lenders' stocks.
- Sell junk bonds.
- Sell most commodities.

If you believe in inflation, then you should seek to buy things that the government cannot print or create at will. Gold is an obvious choice, but in the 1970s other commodities did just as well, if not better. Hard commodities and even real estate can be very good hedges against inflation.

The following list is only partial, but it highlights the best ways to invest if you believe that *inflation* will predominate.

- Precious metals: gold, silver, platinum, palladium. Historically, precious metals act as a hedge against money printing when real interest rates are negative.
- Steeper yield curve. If you are a bond investor, you want to bet that long-term rates will rise faster than short-term rates. This happens as investors price in higher long-term inflation.
- TIPS (or real return bonds). Make sure that the yield you are paid is real, not nominal. High inflation erodes returns for bonds.
- Short-duration corporate bonds (and go out the credit curve). Companies that have pricing power will be able pass on prices rather than have their margins crushed.
- Commodity currencies: Canadian loonie, New Zealand kiwi, Aussie dollar (although see our chapter on Australian housing), Brazilian real, and Norwegian krone.
- Basic material stocks and energy, as well as consumer staples.

Where do we stand on the issue of deflation versus inflation? We think we'll have both. Deflation first, and then inflation. It will probably take further downturns and a greater collapse of borrowing and lending to induce even more extreme responses from governments.

In the endgame, we see a very low likelihood that the Federal Reserve and other central banks will be able to do the right thing and get us out of the deflationary problems we face without letting inflation get out of hand or causing large collateral damage. Let's hope policy makers will do the right thing and succeed in their task.

We recognize that this list of potential investments is limited in scope, but that is the nature of such things. Given the era of volatility that we expect, timing will be more critical than usual. Whatever we might write in any greater specifics has the potential to be out of date (or worse) by the time this is read.

To counter this problem, the authors are setting up a special forum for readers of *Endgame*, which can be found by going to www .johnmauldin.com/endgame. If you want to comment or ask questions, a simple sign-up form will allow you to register. We will be visiting the site regularly to look at questions. While we obviously cannot address investment advice specific to one person, we will be looking at broader issues and aspects of the Endgame.

And you can register for John Mauldin's free weekly letter at his web site where he covers the issues in this book and a whole lot more.

EPILOGUE

Some Final Thoughts

Your authors recognize that for some countries, we are not painting a pretty picture, while for others, mostly in the emerging markets, the future holds a more exciting, if volatile, experience.

As we travel around, we are constantly asked some variation of the question, "Don't you think the lifestyle of the average person in (the United States, various countries in Europe, Japan, etc.) will suffer? Will they be happy with a lower lifestyle?" The question assumes a static world, where change does not bring about a better life for all.

Yes, on a *relative* basis, the average person in China or Brazil is going to see their lifestyle improve more than average citizens in most developed countries, but that has been true for years. There was a lot of room for improvement in many emerging market countries. And yes, the buying power of many currencies will fall.

At our core, your authors are inveterate optimists. We see the future as exciting and full of opportunities and promise for people all over the world. In 2021 or 2031, no one is going to want to go back to the "good old days" of 2011. The progress we make on so many technological fronts is getting ready to astound us.

Change is not linear. It is accelerating. And unlike waves of technological change in the past that seemed to come one at a time, like steam engines or electricity or railroads or the personal computer, we are getting ready to be hit by multiple waves of change simultaneously, all of which will feed off one another. It is what John calls the Millennium Wave. The pace of accelerating change will appear overwhelming to many, although our children seem to think of that as normal. And when our grandchildren as babies are given iPads, the world in which our parents grew up will seem quaint.

The immediate wave in front of us is in the biotechnology sector. There are prospects for nontoxic (and relatively inexpensive) cures for most cancers; viruses could be brought under control (all sorts of viruses, not just the common flu); and Alzheimer's could be brought to a halt. Mike West at Biotime will soon be in human trials to replace vascular and heart systems with new, young cells, putting a halt to dying of heart disease. Other researchers are working day and night to slow down or even reverse (!) the aging process. (If they do, the trade of the decade will be to go long insurance companies and short annuity companies!) The medicine of the next decade (and even some in this decade) is going to make our current state of the art seem positively Stone Age.

Telecommunications is in for a major transformation, as competing technologies are racing to bring you ubiquitous and ultimately very cheap wireless broadband. Developing countries will leap from slow and simple connectivity to ultrafast broadband at speeds that seem unrealistic today. Think how slow the Internet was 10 years ago and then fast-forward 10 years into the future! This will allow people to access the world in ways we can only speculate about now. Talk about changing the way we do commerce. If you think the Internet has changed business and communications today, wait until you see 2022.

A major side benefit is that children in developing countries all over the world will be able to access higher-level education that for all intents and purposes will be free. Think of the true inventions and breakthroughs we will get from finding those budding geniuses hidden in the backwaters of the world, held back today by a lack of ability to grow and learn.

In fact, that is one of the main reasons for the power and breadth of the Millennium Wave. In the mid-1700s, the number of scientists and engineers who really understood the steam engine numbered at most maybe a few dozen. Today, we throw hundreds of researchers at problems that are relatively trivial (compared to the import of the steam engine). Companies compete to bring us the latest innovation. Any company that is not trying to find the bleeding edge of research and productivity for its customers will soon fall victim to Schumpeter's force of creative destruction. As more and more scientists and engineers work to solve problems that we face, the faster we will see changes come at us.

And when we add another 3 billion people to the truly connected world (not connected just by what will be seen in the not too distant future as our primitive cell phones) with maybe 30,000 of those possessing Nobel Prize–level genius added to the mix? The change we are talking about is going to come so much faster as we all benefit from their efforts that it is almost too much to contemplate.

And just about the time we start to absorb all that, a wave of true nanotechnological inventions will begin to show up on our doorsteps, changing the way me manufacture a whole host of goods and almost requiring that manufacturing be brought even closer to the markets in which companies wish to sell.

And let's not forget new (and most likely cheaper) forms of energy, batteries that can store a lot of power, and electric cars that are not expensive toys, and a whole new industry is needed. And you can't forget robotics, coming in the future decades. We are talking real robots here, not just vacuum cleaners. The promise of artificial intelligence has been AWOL for a long time. We are not too far from seeing it come back in an all-new form. It will be fascinating to see what we actually do with all this innovation. What new products and services will spring from the minds of entrepreneurs and scientists all over the world?

So, yes, developed countries are going to have to restructure, and that will likely mean an unemployment rate higher than we would like for longer than we would like. Pension plans will be under attack. There will be difficulties. But the promise of the future is bright if you know where to look and are willing to make it work for you. New opportunities await even as old ones seem to fade. Our counsel would be to embrace the change rather than resist it.

But that is a subject for another book.*

---

*Actually, that book should be out in 2012. It will be called *The Millennium Wave* and be written by John Mauldin with a lot of help from his friends.

Notes

Introduction: Endgame

1. In addition to Zimbardo's numerous books, there is a particularly well-done illustrated 10-minute lecture at www.wimp.com/secretpowers/. Readers are encouraged to check it out.
2. "Popular Delusions," June 30, 2010, by Dylan Grice, who is based in London, www.sgresearch.com/publication/en/ 91FAF3E698AE56F0C12577520027262D.pub?puid=.

Part One: The End of the Debt Supercycle

1. Bank Credit Analyst, "The Debt Supercycle," November 19, 2007, www .beearly.com/pdfFiles/BCAsep07_05sr.pdf.

Chapter 1: The Beginning of the End

1. Gary Shilling, *Insight,* November 2010.
2. Board of Governors of the Federal Reserve, www.federalreserve.gov/pubs/ fdp/2002/729/default.html.
3. Paul A. McCulley, "After the Crisis: Planning a New Financial Structure Learning from the Bank of Dad, Based on Comments before the 19th Annual Hyman Minsky Conference on the State of the U.S. and World Economies, April 15, 2010, www.pimco.com/LeftNav/Featured+Market+Commentary/ FF/2010/Global+Central+Bank+Focus+May+2010+After+the+Crisis+ Planning+a+New+Financial+Structure.htm.

301

4. Barry Eichengreen, "Competitive Devalution to the Rescue, *The Guardian*, March 18, 2009, www.guardian.co.uk/commentisfree/2009/mar/17/g20 -globalrecession.

Chapter 2: Why Greece Matters

1. John Mauldin, "What Does Greece Mean to Me, Dad?" March 26, 2010, www.johnmauldin.com/newsletters2.html. Note: The remainder of this chapter was originally published in my newsletter.

2. Mark Buchanan, *Ubiquity: Why Catastrophes Happen* (New York: Broadway Books, 2002).

3. Mark Buchanan, *Ubiquity: Why Catastrophes Happen* (New York: Broadway Books, 2002).

4. Mark Buchanan, *Ubiquity: Why Catastrophes Happen* (New York: Broadway Books, 2002).

5. Mark Buchanan, *Ubiquity: Why Catastrophes Happen* (New York: Broadway Books, 2002).

6. Mark Buchanan. *Ubiquity: Why Catastrophes Happen* (New York: Broadway Books, 2002).

7. Didier Sornette, *Why Stock Markets Crash: Critical Events in Complex Financial Systems* (Princeton, NJ: Princeton University Press, 2002), Chapter 1.

Chapter 3: Let's Look at the Rules

1. Kauffman Foundation Research Series, July 2010, www.kauffman.org/ uploadedFiles/firm_formation_importance_of_startups.pdf. Note: Vivek Wadhwa is an entrepreneur turned academic. He is a visiting scholar at the School of Information at the University of California, Berkeley, a senior research associate at Harvard Law School, and director of research at the Center for Entrepreneurship and Research Commercialization at Duke University.

2. John C. Haltiwanger, Ron S. Jarmin, and Javier Miranda, "Who Creates Jobs? Small vs. Large vs. Young?" Working Paper 16300, www.nber.org/papers/ w16300.

3. If you have not read Woody Brock's paper, or would like to read it again, it is at www.investorsinsight.com/blogs/john_mauldins_outside_the_box/archive/ 2009/05/18/the-end-game-draws-nigh-the-future-evolution-of-the-debt-to -gdp-ratio.aspx.

4. Carmen M. Reinhart and Kenneth Rogoff, *This Time Is Different: Eight Centuries of Financial Folly* (Princeton, NJ: Princeton University Press, 2009).

5. GaveKal Research: http://gavekal.com/.

6. From a paper done by Rob Parenteau, editor of *The Richebacher Letter,* Agora Financial. You can read it in two parts at www.nakedcapitalism.com (www .nakedcapitalism.com/2010/03/parenteau-on-fiscal-correctness-and-animal -sacrifices-leading-the-piigs-to-slaughter-part-1.html?utm_source=feedburner& utm_medium=feed&utm_campaign=Feed%3A+NakedCapitalism+%28na ked+capitalism%29).

7. Martin Wolf, FT.com, "UK Economy Must Perform a Rebalancing Act," April 13, 2010.

Chapter 4: The Burden of Lower Growth and More Frequent Recessions

1. Gerard Baker, "Welcome to 'the Great Moderation': Historians Will Marvel at the Stability of Our Era," *London Times,* January 19, 2007, www .timesonline.co.uk/tol/comment/columnists/article1294376.ece.

2. ECRI Institute, www.businesscycle.com/news/press/1870/.

3. Committee on the Fiscal Future of the United States; National Research Council, and National Academy of Public Administration, *Choosing the Nation's Fiscal Future,* www.nap.edu/catalog/12808.html.

Chapter 5: This Time Is Different

1. All quoted material from this chapter, unless otherwise noted, has been taken from Carmen M. Reinhart and Kenneth Rogoff, *This Time Is Different: Eight Centuries of Financial Folly.* (Princeton, NJ: Princeton University Press, 2009).

2. You can read the whole report at the McKinsey web site. The 10-page summary is also there: www.mckinsey.com/mgi/publications/debt_and_ deleveraging/index.asp.

3. FT, Lex, "Deleveraging," January 14, 2010.

4. Andrew Smithers, *Wall Street Revalued: Imperfect Markets and Inept Central Bankers* (Hoboken, NJ: John Wiley & Sons, 2009).

Chapter 6: The Future of Public Debt: An Unsustainable Path

1. All quoted material from this chapter, unless otherwise noted, has been taken from Stephen G. Cecchetti, M. S. Mohanty, and Fabrizio Zampolli, "The Future of Public Debt: Prospects and Implications." BIS Working Papers #300, Bank for International Settlements, March 2010. The full paper is available here: www.bis.org/publ/work300.pdf?noframes=1. We highly recommend reading it.

2. Jean-Claude Trichet, President of the ECB, and Lucas Papademos, Vice President of the ECB, Lisbon, May 6, 2010.

3. Carmen M. Reinhart and Kenneth Rogoff. *This Time Is Different: Eight Centuries of Financial Folly* (Princeton, NJ: Princeton University Press, 2009).

4. John Hussman's Newletter, www.hussmanfunds.com/weeklyMarketComment .html.

5. Morgan Stanley Research, Arnaud Marès, "Sovereign Subjects: Ask Not Whether Governments Will Default, but How," August 25, 2010.

6. Morgan Stanley Research, Arnaud Marès, "Sovereign Subjects: Ask Not Whether Governments Will Default, but How," August 25, 2010.

Chapter 7: The Elements of Deflation

1. R. A. Radford, "The Economic Organisation of a P.O.W. Camp." *Economica* 12, no. 48, November 1945.

2. You can read the speech at: www.federalreserve.gov/BoardDocs/speeches/ 2002/20021121/default.htm.

Chapter 8: Inflation and Hyperinflation

1. Translation by Peter Bernholz in *Inflation and Monetary Regimes: History, Economic and Political Relationships* (Northampton, MA: Edward Elgar, 2006), 98.

2. Athanasios Orphanides and Simon van Norden, "The Reliability of Output Gap Estimates in Real Time," 1999, www.neumann.hec.ca/pages/simon .van-norden/wps/realgap.pdf.

3. Charles I. Plosser, "Output Gaps and Robust Policy Rules," 2010 European Banking & Financial Forum, Czech National Bank, Prague, March 23, 2010, www.philadelphiafed.org/publications/speeches/plosser/2010/03-23-10_european-banking-forum.cfm.

4. Ricardo Caballero, "A Helicopter Drop for the Treasury," August 30, 2010, www.voxeu.org/index.php?q=node/5449.

5. Peter Bernholz, *Monetary Regimes and Inflation: History, Economic and Political Relationships* (Northampton, MA: Edward Elgar, 2006).

6. "Values of the most important German Banknotes of the Inflation Period from 1920–1923," www.sammler.com/coins/inflation.htm.

7. Max Shapiro, *The Penniless Billionaires.* (New York: New York Times Book Co., 1980), 203.

8. Peter Bernholz, *Monetary Regimes and Inflation: History, Economic and Political Relationships* (Northampton, MA: Edward Elgar, 2006), 23.

9. Peter Bernholz, *Monetary Regimes and Inflation: History, Economic and Political Relationships* (Northampton, MA: Edward Elgar, 2006).

8. Dennis Cauchon, "Federal Workers Earning Double Their Private Counterparts," *USA Today,* August 13, 2010, www.usatoday.com/money/economy/income/2010-08-10-1Afedpay10_ST_N.htm.

9. Elizabeth McNichol, Phil Oliff, and Nicholas Johnson, "Recession Continues to Batter State Budgets; State Responses Could Slow Recovery," Center on Budget and Policy Priorities, www.cbpp.org/cms/index.cfm?fa=view&id=711.

10. David Wilson, "Soaring Federal Aid Bails Out U.S. States, Cities: Chart of Day," August 11, 2010. Quoted at www.ritholtz.com/blog/2010/08/bailout-nation-states-municipalities/.

11. Mary Williams Walsh, "State Debt Woes Grow Too Big to Camouflage," *New York Times,* March 29, 2010, www.nytimes.com/2010/03/30/business/economy/30states.html?_r=1&pagewanted=1.

12. Laurence Kotlikoff, "The US Is Bankrupt and We Don't Even Know It," *Bloomberg News,* August 11, 2010, www.bloomberg.com/news/2010-08-11/u-s-is-bankrupt-and-we-don-t-even-know-commentary-by-laurence-kotlikoff.html.

13. Martin Feldstein, "The 'Tax Expenditure' Solution for Our National Debt," *Wall Street Journal,* July 20, 2010, http://online.wsj.com/article/SB10001424052748704518904575365450087744876.html.

14. Edmund Conway, "Geithner Insists Chinese Dollar Assets Are Safe," *The Telegraph,* June 1, 2009, www.telegraph.co.uk/finance/financetopics/financialcrisis/5423650/Geithner-insists-Chinese-dollar-assets-are-safe.html.

15. David Stockman, "'Game Over' for the 30-Year Fiscal Wars," *Politico,* February 24, 2010, www.politico.com/news/stories/0210/33412.html.

16. www.dagongcredit.com/dagongweb/uf/Sovereign%20Credit%20Rating%20Report%20of%2050%20Countries%20in%202010.

Chapter 10: The European Periphery: A Modern-Day Gold Standard

1. Barry Eichengreen, "The Euro: Love It or Leave It?" May 4, 2010, http://Voxeu.Org/Index.Php?Q=Node/729.

2. Michael Lewis, "Beware of Greeks Bearing Bonds," *Vanity Fair,* October 1, 2010, www.vanityfair.com/business/features/2010/10/greeks-bearing-bonds-201010.

3. We highly recommend reading the following piece by Robert Parenteau, a research associate with the Levy Economics Institute: www.creditwritedowns.com/2010/03/leading-piigs-to-slaughter.html. The article is on the longer side, but it captures very clearly the debt deflationary dynamic in the Eurozone area.

Chapter 11: Eastern European Problems

1. Barclay Capital, *The Emerging Market Weekly,* www.scribd.com/doc/34764289/
BarCap-The-EM-Weekly.

Chapter 12: Japan: A Bug in Search of a Windshield

1. Justin McCurry, "Japan Prime Minister Naoto Kan Warns of Greek-Style
Public Debt Problems," *Guardian,* June 11, 2010, www.Guardian.co.uk/
Business/2010/Jun/11/Japan-Naoto-Kan-Debt-Warning.

About the Authors

John Mauldin is a renowned financial expert, a multiple *New York Times* best-selling author, and a pioneering online commentator. His weekly e-newsletter, *Thoughts from the Frontline*, was one of the first publications to provide investors with free, unbiased information and guidance. Today, it is one of the most widely distributed investment newsletters in the world, translated into Chinese, Spanish, and Italian. He is regularly seen on TV and in national print media. President of Millennium Wave Investments, he is the father of seven children (five adopted) and lives in Dallas, Texas.

Jonathan Tepper is a writer, entrepreneur, and investor. He is the founder and Chief Editor of Variant Perception, a macroeconomic research group that caters to asset managers, banks, hedge funds, and high-net-worth individuals. He is also the founder of Demotix, an award-winning citizen-journalism web site and photo agency, and started a long/short equity hedge fund with Hinde Capital. Jonathan is a Rhodes scholar who went to Oxford University.

Index